Attending to Work

Attending to Work

The Management of Attendance and Shopfloor Order

Paul Edwards and Colin Whitston

BLACKWELL
Business

Copyright © Basil Blackwell, 1993

The right of Paul Edwards and Colin Whitston to be identified as authors of this work has been asserted in accordance with the Copyright, Designs and Patents Act 1988.

First published 1993

Blackwell Publishers
108 Cowley Road
Oxford
OX4 1JF
UK

238 Main street,
Suite 501
Cambridge, Massachusetts 02142
USA

British Library Cataloguing in Publication Data

A CIP catalogue record for this book is available from the British Library.

Library of Congress Cataloging-in-Publication Data

A CIP catalogue record for this book is available from the library of congress.

ISBN 0-631-191151

Prepared on PageMaker in 10 on 11pt Palatino by Simone Dudley, Industrial Relations Research Unit, University of Warwick, CV4 7AL, Coventry.

Printed in Great Britain by T.J. Press Ltd, Padstow, Cornwall.

Contents

List of tables

Text Tables

Appendix Tables

List of Figures

Series Editors' Foreword

The University of Warwick is the major centre in the United Kingdom for the study of industrial relations. Teaching of the subject began in 1966 in the School of Industrial and Business Studies, which now has one of the country's largest graduate programmes. Warwick became a national centre for research in industrial relations in 1970 when the Social Science Research Council (now the Economic and Social Research Council) established its Industrial Relations Research Unit at the University. In 1984 the Unit was reconstituted as a Designated Research Centre within the School of Industrial and Business Studies. It continues to be known as the Industrial Relations Research Unit, however, and it now embraces the research activities of all members of the School's industrial relations community.

The series of Warwick Studies in Industrial Relations was launched in 1972 by Hugh Clegg and George Bain as the main vehicle for the publication of the results of the Unit's research projects, as well as the research conducted by staff teaching industrial relations in the University and the work of graduate students. The first six titles were published by Heinemann Educational Books of London, and subsequent volumes have been published by Blackwell Publishers of Oxford.

The present volume reflects continuity and development in the Unit's work: continuity in that it is based on careful analysis at the level of the workplace; and development in addressing new sets of issues. These issues concern the management of the employee as an individual. During the 1980s, there was growing interest in 'commitment' and 'participation'. Two things remained rare, however. The first was detailed assessment of what managerially-led change actually means to shopfloor workers. The second was an integrated approach: new initiatives were treated in isolation, and other leading cases of the management of the individual employment relation were neglected. This book sets out to remedy these limitations.

In order to tackle the potentially elusive issue of the management-worker relationship, the authors focus on the specific theme of the regulation of discipline and attendance. As they note, this topic has been curiously neglected by researchers in industrial relations and industrial sociology. As well as addressing shopfloor change through the lens of absence and discipline, therefore, the study also provides a close analysis of these topics, and thus helps to fill a significant gap in knowledge. A further feature of the study is the selection of case studies. White-collar workers, a group whose employment conditions have tended to be neglected, are included; the book thereby develops understanding of the day-to-day regulation of clerical work. Two public sector organisations are also studied. This enables two sorts of question to be addressed: how far models of change during the 1980s hold up to scrutiny; and, from a less time-specific perspective, how far the attitudes of workers are shaped by a distinct public sector ethos. The fourth study, of a manufacturing firm, explores the extent of change in a traditionalist organization.

The book thus contributes to debates, about the specific period of the 1980s, and also to less time-specific issues. As the authors argue in their conclusions, the analysis also allows the 1980s to be treated as a case study of a certain sort of situation, namely, one of intensified competition and a shift - but not a transformation - in managerial policies of labour control. It will thus interest all analysts of industrial relations and workplace behaviour, as well as specialists in the management of attendance.

Richard Hyman
Keith Sisson

Preface

This book presents the results of case studies conducted between 1987 and 1989. Our greatest debt is to the managers and workers who put up with our questioning. As a supervisor in one of the firms said, when one of us asked for a 'quick word', we had developed a reputation for rather lengthier and more intense questioning than a 'quick word' implied. Three of the organisations are discussed anonymously. We are particularly grateful to managers in the fourth, British Rail, for being less reticent - not least since the picture that we paint does not look very flattering. We would thus like to record our special thanks to Ivor Warburton of British Rail.

We would like to stress that we did not simply study the organizations and then leave them until this book was complete. They all received detailed reports, which went to managements and unions or staff associations. In three cases (two managements and one workers' side), participants took up our offer to discuss the results further. This book is primarily a piece of analysis, drawing out the general lessons of the studies. But we hope that the analysis has also helped to stimulate debate within the case study organizations.

The book reflects the intellectual community of the Industrial Relations Research Unit. The value of this community is hard to put into a few words, but the book - had it ever appeared at all - would have been much poorer without the advice of colleagues. We are particularly indebted to Anthony Ferner, Richard Hyman and Keith Sisson for their comments and support. Margaret Morgan processed our questionnaire data with her customary efficiency. Norma Griffiths, Simone Dudley and Claire Sadler did likewise in, respectively, preparing much of the text and steering it through the perils of desk-top publishing. Parts of Chapter 5 appeared originally in the *Industrial Relations Journal* (Winter 1990).

The book is very much a joint product. We conducted two of the case studies together, and divided the other two between us, and we have written the text together. It is our responsibility.

Paul Edwards
Colin Whitston

1

Introduction

During the 1980s much attention was given to new ways of managing work. Some analysts looked at the 'new industrial relations', considering changes in relations with trade unions and the collective aspects of the employment relationship such as payment systems. Others focused on the rise of 'human resource management': how far was HRM different from personnel management, how many organizations were embracing it, how coherent was it, and how far did it mark a break from traditional practice? It is generally acknowledged that the shopfloor is crucial in understanding these issues. After all, managing the human resource means finding ways to persuade workers to work. Yet the amount of detailed attention to the shopfloor was remarkably small.

This book is about one particular aspect of shopfloor relations. Its nature is best indicated by spelling out what we mean by neglect of the shopfloor. There are three aspects. The first is the general attention to the workplace. Much discussion about HRM has been conceptual or interested in firms' overall policies, with little concern for the practical impact. It is true that there has been some assessment of practice. But this is recent and tightly defined. A good recent example is Marchington and Parker's (1990) study, which set out to assess 'changing patterns of employee relations'. Yet the bulk of it is concerned with managerial policy and the influence of shop stewards, and there is very little information on how far workers had endorsed the changes to which they were subject. Storey (1992) notes that his work is novel precisely because it assesses how HRM worked in practice; yet even he restricts his attention to the effects on managers, and he does not pretend to consider what HRM was doing to the organization of work or workers' attitudes to their employers. In other respects the British shopfloor has, of course, been particularly well-served, as with the three Workplace Industrial Relations Surveys, which have charted changes in institutional arrangements and the overall pattern of relationships. But by their nature they have not investigated processes, and their interest has been on managers and workers' representatives.

The second aspect is the point of production. We know a good deal about the general issue of change on the shopfloor and how demands on workers have been changing. Dawson and Webb (1989: 236) for example looked at new production systems in an electronics company. Job definitions were widened and workers were given more responsibility. But 'far from simply improving the quality of working life, this widening of responsibility creates extra stress and makes the experience of work "more precarious", as employees live on the edge of perpetual stops in the line'. As noted elsewhere (Edwards, 1992), there are two gaps in this literature. The first is that it tends to draw on the views of workers in an illustrative way. It can point to the objective changes in work organization taking place. But it is weaker in considering workers' reactions. The implication is that workers were directly aware of growing work pressures and that this experience was shared. Yet workers may in fact perceive changes only dimly, and there may be little commonality of view. To understand the changing politics of the workplace requires attention to the nature of workers' responses. Second, certain traditional concerns of workplace study have slipped out of the analysis: up to the 1970s there was much interest in custom and practice, that is, the ways in which workers could subvert managerial aims and create some space for themselves. Again, the suggestion in many studies is that more active and self-confident managements have reduced the scope for informal bargaining over the timing and intensity of work effort, but this is a matter which requires direct investigation.

This brings us to the third level, the organization of consent. The available information has led Kelly (1990: 60) to conclude that

> pragmatic employers have obtained worker compliance in change but have failed to elicit the consent required for a new IR. The [employer] militants in the public sector have consolidated a traditional, low trust, adversarial, system of industrial relations.

We would broadly agree with this assessment, in particular with the importance of the distinction between mere compliance and active consent and with the differentiation between the public and the private sectors. But it is a judgement which requires further elaboration and empirical support.

Our interest, then, was in the changing relationship between the individual worker and the day-to-day organization of work, together with the consequences for attitudes to the employer and the whole question of how far willing consent has been achieved. The title *Attending to Work* in intended to underline several themes. First, it is generally accepted that management has played the main initiating role in workplace change. We were interested in the ways in which managers were attending to the details of workers' behaviour. We were not directly concerned with overall managerial policies but with the control of the details of the effort bargain. Second, this bargain has two aspects: persuading workers to work, and getting them into the workplace at all. We aimed to study *work*, looking not just at managerial practice but also at the consequences such as how far workers tried to retain some custom and practice and how relations with management at the day-to-day level shaped responses to wider attempts to generate a sense of morale or commitment. And we looked at *attendance*: how managers define acceptable standards of attendance, how these are policed, how far action here is consistent with other features of employment policy, and the effects on workers' behaviour.

The tradition of studying the effort bargain is well-established, and we need to say little about it in general terms. Some specific issues are worth highlighting. Much of the contemporary debate has turned on concepts such as involvement, commitment and consent. Yet, as studies like that of Dawson and Webb indicate, there is a tougher edge, as new work practices are introduced and new demands are made. It is no accident that several practising managers have begun to speak of 'self-discipline' (e.g. Wickens, 1987). By this is meant the generation of willing consent, as opposed to the enforcement of discipline through rules. But there is also the implication that the workplace has become more disciplined in the sense that work standards are clearer and expectations are made sharper. The necessary concomitant must be that workers are aware that failure to meet these standards will result in some kind of sanction. We wanted to consider how self-discipline might be created and, crucially, how it relates to older ways of establishing discipline.

This links with the question of change. Many accounts assume that the new employee relations (that is, the combination of the new industrial relations with HRM and the emphasis on the individual worker) is markedly different from the old. Some studies have begun to question this. Consider the historical record. From the 1960s, productivity bargaining was seen as a means to break down conflictual attitudes and to generate consent in the long run. The oil industry was a leading case. Yet Young (1986), giving an overview of the Mobil Coryton refinery, and Ahlstrand (1990), looking in great detail at the most celebrated case of Esso's Fawley refinery, question this. In both cases, managements had to tackle the same issues in the 1980s as had supposedly been resolved twenty years earlier. What looked like a qualitative shift proved to be much more mundane. Turning to the contemporary situation, Geary (1991) examined three electronics plants claiming to practise HRM and showed that the 'new' was in fact dependent on the 'old'. Traditional means were used to monitor workers' behaviour and police standards, and the willing commitment implied by the term self-discipline was little in evidence. One of our aims, too, is to look at differing ways of creating discipline and how far current practice is a break from the past. Like Geary, we conclude that ideas of a radical break with the past are false. There is a specific literature on discipline, some of which addresses change, and we locate some of our more detailed themes within it in the rest of this chapter.

The issues of the management of absence and attendance have been studied much less thoroughly than the effort bargain within the workplace. There is certainly a substantial literature on absenteeism, but this rarely makes any connections with the control of work (see Edwards and Scullion, 1984). We therefore need to spend more time in spelling out why the topic is important. The key points are simple. Managements have been giving increasing attention to the control of attendance; how they exert control is likely to say something significant about how they are regulating work more generally; and yet serious analysis is virtually non-existent. We are thus taking the control of attendance as an aspect of the wider issue of the reconstruction of workplace order. This is not, therefore, a 'book about absenteeism'. But it does, we claim, offer some new insights into the general issue of absence as well as the particular one of changing regimes.

The following section indicates what these insights are. We then turn to the question of discipline before underlining how the idea of attending to work ties them together. We next explain our choice of case studies, indicate the themes that each was intended to illuminate, and describe our research methods. Finally, we sketch the core arguments of the study.

The Management of Attendance

Historical Origins of the Problem

The problem of persuading workers to attend work regularly is as old as capitalism. Early capitalists went to great lengths to devise recording systems, and often used fines and other penalties for non-attendance (Pollard, 1965). The loss of the day's wages was plainly not a sufficient disincentive to going absent, for workers had not yet become accustomed to the regular rhythms of industrial labour (Thompson, 1967). In the early New England textile mills, workers would alternate spells of factory labour with time working on the land (Prude, 1983). In Birmingham, Saint Monday - the practice of taking Monday as a holiday - survived until the second half of the nineteenth century, and was so established that day excursions on the railways were held on Mondays (Reid, 1976). Indeed, there is now powerful evidence against the common view that a defining characteristic of capitalism was the emergence of a class of free wage labourers. They may have been formally free, but throughout the world the rise of capitalism was associated with mechanisms to coerce workers to accept the disciplines of a new form of labour (Corrigan, 1977; Cohen, 1987).

In much of the historical literature there is a strong presumption that norms of regular attendance were eventually established: it seems to be assumed that at some point workers accepted the new rules of the game and played within them (for example Hobsbawm, 1964; for a critique, see Edwards, 1986: 107-23). Yet Cunnison (1966) discovered workers in a Salford garment factory during the 1950s who saw the exact timing of their attendance as up to them: they were pieceworkers, and they would make their efforts when it suited them, a stance apparently accepted by the management. This might be written off as an oddity, but there is a wider point. Whatever workers' broad acceptance of the duty to work, this duty still has to be expressed in the concrete form of regular attendance, which can never simply be taken for granted. The fact that most large firms now have sick pay schemes that guarantee workers a basic wage when they are absent is also an obvious factor that might make attendance more, and not less, problematic for employers.

There is little detailed evidence on when attendance was identified by employers as a major issue: as noted below, the massive literature on absence has concentrated on some rather different issues. It does seem, though, that it came into focus in wartime, when a shortage of labour combined with long hours and an intense drive for production to generate worries that workers were using absence as a form of escape. In the United States, employers focused explicitly on absence during wartime (Jacoby, 1985: 135, 262), and the same was true in Britain during the First World War (Rubin, 1987) and the second (Summerfield, 1984: 124-32). The 'moral panic' about absence is worth comment. During the first war there were widespread managerial fears that munitions workers were going absent in large numbers. Yet inquiries within the firms in question showed absence rates to be very moderate (Rubin, 1987: 180-83). During the second war, attendance similarly became an obsession. On the railways, for example, the Railway Executive Committee, which had taken over much of the management of the industry from the companies, kept files on absence and investigated claims that absence was not only widespread but was tolerated by management; the claims generally proved to be groundless (see Railway Executive Committee, 1941-5). In other cases, absence was widespread. Under the demands of long hours in the factory and domestic duties women workers 'took time off consistently to make it possible to do their two jobs' (Summerfield, 1984: 132). Yet, Summerfield argues, this absence was not the result of irresponsibility or shirking but was the unsurprising consequence of the pressures of women's wartime role, compounded by managerial unwillingness to alter work schedules or provide shops on site: managers preferred to discipline absentees rather than seek out the underlying issues and manage them actively.

The Contemporary Importance of Absence

Absence thus comes to managerial attention when it appears to cost them money or, more worryingly, to be a symptom of a wider loss of the work ethic. Popular myths about the prevalence of absence and the ways in which it is promoted by group norms can then grow up. These myths often have little foundation. At many other times, however, absence seems to have receded into the background.

During the 1980s it came back towards the centre of attention. Elsewhere, we cite several factory case studies which mention the control of attendance as part of a firm's efforts to reconstruct its shopfloor regime, though details are tantalizingly thin (Edwards and Whitston, 1989a). Our own studies included a survey of 25 firms, in just over half of which managers said that absence control had become more important (Edwards and Whitston, 1989b). There are numerous references in the press and practitioner journals to a growing interest in attendance control; much of this has included groups, such as local authority clerical workers and even the police, in relation to whom absence was in the past generally a complete non-issue. One recent survey (IRS, 1991) looked at 104 organizations. It noted that 88 regularly monitored sickness absence. Moreover, the use of interviews on a worker's return to work from absence was 'prominent'. The use of bonuses to reward good attendance was, however, reported in only 14 cases, suggesting that the predominant management approach was one of stick rather than carrot. A look at the listing of individual replies suggests that the trend was towards more interviewing, more use of discipline and more 'counselling'. As we will see, counselling implies a caring approach but it also has a hard edge to it.

This renewed interest in absence can hardly be explained, by analogy with wartime, in terms of labour shortage. Nor does it seem to have been a response to rising rates of absence, for there is little general evidence of an increase, and very few of the managers whom we interviewed cited growing absence as a reason for action.

One specific reason often mentioned was the introduction of Statutory Sick Pay in 1982. This replaced the payment of state sickness benefits direct to workers with a system whereby employers paid out SSP and then reclaimed the relevant sums. It was not the costs of SSP which affected employers: though they had extra administrative costs, their SSP refunds were larger than they would have paid through their own sick schemes and they were in fact net gainers to the tune of £135 million a year (Disney, 1987: 31). Nor was the associated move to 'self-certification' - whereby workers require a medical certificate to claim state benefits only after seven days' of absence, as against three days previously - directly important. The anticipated rise in absence rates due to self-certification did not take place. What was important was the indirect effect: employers were now required to keep records, and this stimulated an interest in absence control (IRS, 1985; IDS, 1986).

But underlying such specific stimuli was a more fundamental influence, pressure on labour costs. As managements, in the public as much as in the private sector, have faced growing commercial pressures, the costs of absence have been brought into focus. This was made clear in our own survey. Managers underlined the need to regulate all aspects of labour costs and the fact that absence needed to be actively managed. As we will see, the issue was being given attention in all our case study organizations, and in the course of this study we will explore in more detail the reasons for this.

If managerial attention to absence leads to specific attempts at control, it is likely that the issue is also forced onto workers' attention: from being something that required little conscious thought, going absent may have to be considered more carefully as managers act against those engaging in it. To this direct effect must be added an indirect one of growing pressures within the workplace. A now widely-quoted measure is the Percentage Utilization of Labour (PUL) index (see Bennett and Smith-Gavine, 1989; Nolan, 1989). This is based on work study data on a large number of manufacturing jobs, and it shows that throughout the 1980s the measure of work effort rose. Elger (1990) combines this evidence with case-study material to argue that the intensity of labour increased during the 1980s. He also uses studies such as Dawson and Webb's quoted above to argue that new forms of workplace organization can increase demands on workers: instead of carrying out a set of specified tasks, they are now expected to use their initiative to make changes, and pressures for productivity also reduce the amount of time that workers can spend in formal meal breaks or in informal socializing. On a more anecdotal level, a Channel 4 television programme (Dangerous Lives, 27 September 1989) argued that stress was an important influence on absence in many occupations; about 10 per cent of the absences of bus drivers in Leeds, for example, were attributed to stress. As against much popular wisdom, moreover, stress was found not to be the preserve of the high-flying executive but was most common among blue-collar workers.

Such arguments are consistent of accounts of shopfloor practices under the 'new industrial relations'. Trevor (1988) studied Toshiba's television factory in Plymouth, which has been in the forefront of such advances as the introduction of common terms and conditions for all workers, improved communications, and 'no strike deals'. Yet the company was explicit in its demands for good attendance, and workers complained of the intensity with which absence was policed. Turnbull (1989) examined a car components firm which had introduced just-in-time production systems and argued that, by reducing buffer stocks and increasing the dependence of each section of the factory on every other section, these put increasing pressures on workers to attend and to work hard.

A related issue for workers is the ease with which managements can invoke disciplinary penalties for absence. It is of course true that an employer seeking to dismiss for absence must meet

> the statutory test of reasonableness by taking into account the nature of the illness, the likely length of absence, and the need to have the employee's work done. The question for the [industrial] tribunal [hearing any claim for unfair dismissal] is whether the employer could be expected to wait any longer, and if so how much longer (IRLIB 386: 2).

Yet what is reasonable is defined broadly. In one case (*Hutchinson v Enfield Rolling Mills*, summarized in IRLIB 386: 8) a worker covered by a medical certificate was observed taking part in a demonstration, and was dismissed. An industrial tribunal held that it was no business of the employer's what a worker did when on sick leave, but the Employment Appeals Tribunal upheld the employer's view that if the worker was fit enough to travel to the demonstration he was capable of work. Another case showed the falsity of the common view that an employer cannot dismiss for genuine illness. In *Lynock v Cereal Packaging Ltd* (IRLIB 361: 11-12) a worker with seven years' service was dismissed for poor attendance resulting from absences due to a series of unrelated illnesses. The EAT held that medical evidence was not pertinent here, because the unrelated nature of the illnesses made any prognosis impossible. Dismissal was therefore justified even though the genuineness of the illness was not disputed.

Any standard of reasonableness does not include a definition of a rate of absence which is bad enough to justify dismissal.

It seems that tribunals allow employers a wide measure of discretion in the disciplinary standards they require, and tribunals do not generally query the reasonableness or justifiability of a particular rule, provided the employer can give some general explanation of the need for it (IRLIB 369: 9).

This study went on to cite the case of *Silentnight v Pitfield and Pitfield* (discussed in more detail in IRLIB 405). The company had a policy of dismissing anyone going absent on days linked to the firm's annual holidays. Two workers sought permission to return one day after these fixed holidays because of their own travel arrangements; permission was refused; they went ahead; and they were dismissed. A tribunal felt that the rule making absence before or after a holiday a dismissable offence was unreasonable, but the EAT - in line with the long-established principle that tribunals must not use their own standards of reasonableness and must confine themselves to whether the employer's action fell within the bounds of what a reasonable employer might reasonably have done - overruled it. The rules had been clearly explained, and there may have been a commercial need to ensure that there was no absence at this time, and thus dismissal was justifiable.

If a worker's sick record does not meet criteria which the employer alone establishes, it seems that it will generally be fair to dismiss as long as the criteria are applied consistently, and the worker has been warned of the record, has where relevant been given a chance to improve, and has been able to state his or her case prior to dismissal. To the extent, then, that employers have become more concerned about attendance, and in view of their freedom to define the rules, absence is likely to be a more fateful issue for workers than it was in the past. This suggests a need to study the reasons for managerial concern, the policies that are put in place, and the impact on the shopfloor. This need is heightened by the lack of any serious attention to these topics in the voluminous literature on absenteeism.

Unresolved Issues in the Literature on Absence

There are two main literatures on absence: managerialist accounts of how to control it and academic studies of its incidence. The former offer advice of varying degrees of sophistication, but are not interested in the nature of absence; they will not be discussed further.

The conventional academic approach sees absence as a response of the individual worker to the work environment. It says virtually nothing about managerial control policies or the connections with other aspects of shopfloor behaviour. The approach is in something of a crisis. Two writers adopting a broadly conventional view note that 'the absence literature has tended to employ very weak methodology . . . the bulk of the literature seems somewhat pervaded by lazy acceptance of inappropriate methodology applied casually to a poorly conceptualized phenomenon' (Atkin and Goodman, 1984: 100). A more damning indictment of literally hundreds of studies would be hard to imagine. Numerous critiques have argued that the approach is implicitly managerialist, in seeing absence as a problem of organizational functioning and in failing to take account of the workers' point of view (Nicholson, 1977); that it fails to relate absence to its 'organizational settings' (Marcus and Smith, 1985: 253); that it neglects the social meanings of the behaviour (Johns and Nicholson, 1982); and that it sees absence as reflecting the inadequate adjustment of the individual employee, instead of understanding absence as part of a conflict-laden relationship between employer and worker (Edwards and Scullion, 1984). These critiques have suggested an alternative, based on relating absence to structures of power and authority.

One of the curious features of the academic literature is that, though it tends to see absence through managers' eyes (Nicholson, 1977), it does not directly offer solutions to managers' problems (Huczynski and Fitzpatrick, 1989: 12). One reason for this is that it has not investigated why and how managers themselves try to control absence: its assumptions are managerialist, and precisely because it does not make management itself part of the phenomenon to be investigated it offers analyses that are likely to be partial or misleading (Edwards and Scullion, 1984). A central concern of the present study was to rectify this omission by examining methods of monitoring and controlling absence and by relating them to shopfloor practice: considering, for example, whether supervisors had different perceptions from senior managers and how far they ignored formal procedures, perhaps because they saw absence control as less pressing than other demands on their time. There have been suggestions that supervisors tolerate absence if they believe that the work is particularly boring, and that absence up to some implicit standard may be viewed positively because it contributes to greater work effort (Chadwick-Jones, 1978: 15).

Allied to the neglect of management is the lack of attention to workers' uses of absence. One theme to emerge recently is the possibility that work groups establish collective norms controlling absence and attendance (Johns, 1984; Nicholson and Johns, 1985). A plausible expectation is that solidaristic work groups will be able to impose standards that conflict with those of management. Yet Keller (1983) has shown that the frequency of absences tended to be higher the lower was group cohesiveness, which implies that a powerful work group can in some circumstances assist management by helping to reduce the absence rate. Drago and Wooden (1988) argue that the effects of cohesiveness will vary: with strong horizontal loyalty to other employees, it will tend to increase absence rates, while a group which displays loyalty to the firm will have low absence rates. They claim to have found some support for this view, but their measures were far from satisfactory. For example, to test the view that cohesion when combined with militancy increases absence, they measured militancy as the number of days of sick leave entitlement enjoyed by workers, on the argument that more days of sick leave reflects union pressure. To equate militancy with sick leave entitlement is to say the least eccentric. Moreover, their dependent variable was not the frequency of absence but the number of days of absence. The association between it and their independent variables is likely to reflect nothing more surprising than a tendency for workers to go absent more when they have more days of paid sick leave. The argument in terms of cohesiveness and militancy remains unproven.

Little other work has addressed these questions. One might have expected the substantial ethnographic literature on workplace behaviour (Lupton, 1963; Harris, 1987) to offer insights here, for example by demonstrating the norms which support ideas of going absent or by exploring how individual workers decide when it is reasonable to take time off. Apart from a few observations such as Cunnison's quoted above, however, absence has not been discussed. Fitzgibbons's (1988) recent study promises much but in fact says very little.

As reported elsewhere (Edwards and Whitston, 1989a), we were able to find little evidence of group norms from two of the case studies, namely those of the firm that we have called Multiplex and of British Rail, that we analyse in more detail in this book. Other occupations might, however, provide examples of pro-attendance norms, an obvious case in point being nursing, where a sense of duty to the patient might lead to anti-absence expectations. The idea of group cohesiveness also merits more detailed inquiry, as we describe below.

A second issue of workers' approaches to absence is the balance between work-related and outside influences on the behaviour. A long-standing tradition sees absence as a form of 'withdrawal from the work situation' (Hill and Trist, 1953). More recently, researchers have begun to ask whether domestic and other demands might be more powerful factors. Morgan and Herman (1976) found that workers saying that they had transport difficulties in getting to work or that they needed leisure time tended to have a high absence rate. Factors within the workplace were relatively insignificant. As against this, Hackett's (1986) study of nurses suggested that work-related factors were more significant.

Our main concern is the connection between absence and relations of control and subordination in the workplace. We do not pretend to assess domestic influences in any detail. A full analysis would require a close study of workers' extra-work situations and how these impacted on their workplace behaviour. In particular, women workers are likely to have domestic duties which affect attendance, as Haccoun and Dupont (1988) have suggested. This is an issue that feminist studies might be expected to have addressed. There are a few intriguing observations, for example Pollert's (1981: 118) remark that, for men, absence is a real escape whereas for women it merely means confronting a pile of work at home. Yet no detailed analysis has been made of the negotiation of domestic and workplace pressures. We give some attention to these matters, for example in asking workers about the extra-work as well as the workplace pressures on absence and attendance, but do not claim to have studied them in detail.

A final issue is simply how workers respond to managerial control of attendance. Though there have been some studies of the impact of control policies (Nicholson, 1976), remarkably little is known about how workers perceive control. What effects does it have on their likelihood to go absent, and how fair do they think that it is? Indeed, an even more obvious question is how aware they are of it. Absence control policies are rarely made a major issue by employers, and many workers may be no more than dimly aware of it. This is likely to affect the extent to which any sense of grievance develops. We need to consider how salient to workers absence control is, as compared with all the other aspects of their work lives. We can then obtain some view as to how far absence is controlled through the threat of penalties, through group norms, through a sense of obligation to the employer, or through a mixture of these forces. This connects with the whole issue of workplace discipline.

Discipline and Workplace Order

A Trend towards Self-discipline?

Discipline can refer to systems of punishment or to a sense of duty and commitment, as in the idea of a disciplined army or even an academic discipline. In the latter sense, it has recently emerged in the idea of 'self-discipline', which has been advocated by numerous personnel management texts as the desirable situation (Torrington and Chapman, 1979: 245). The assumption that managerially-defined goals and work group interests have a natural harmony is plainly very questionable and, as argued elsewhere (Edwards, 1989), disciplinary standards are likely to be based on explicit or implicit negotiations between workers and managers as to what the rules are to be. Moreover, to counterpose current self-discipline with a presumed lack of trust in the past is far too simple. It is a truism that workers have always co-operated - to a degree - with management and that they often use their skills to assist production and, indeed, to overcome the rigidities and confusions of managerial rules (Kusterer, 1978; Manwaring and Wood, 1984; Roy, 1954). In assessing how far a new sense of purpose and discipline has been created, it is necessary to consider carefully the pre-existing pattern of workplace order, and the forms of disciplined conduct which it may have contained, before assuming that a qualitatively new form of co-operation has been created.

The historical and contemporary literature on the control of the workplace offers many insights into these matters. Montgomery (1979; 1987), for example, has explored the world of the nineteenth century craft worker in America. In the iron industry, these workers controlled the details of the work process and had a strongly defined sense of their occupational identity. There was considerable loyalty not only to the immediate work group but also to the trade as a whole. Craftsmen had a strong sense of discipline, which at one and the same time expressed apparently conflicting elements: it embraced commitment to production but also opposition to management's rights to define how and when work should be carried out; it reflected collective loyalty to the trade, but also large and rigid divisions between skilled and unskilled; and it involved solidarity but also exclusion (of unskilled workers and, in the case of America, blacks). We mention such studies to make two points.

First, managerial approaches to discipline seems to have difficulty in incorporating them. The standard literature (for example Ashdown and Baker, 1973) speaks of moves from punitive to corrective discipline, with its image of the nineteenth century being that of the autocratic capitalist. In fact, autocracy existed in some workplaces but, as the case of the craft worker shows, not in all. The idea of a transition from punishment to correction has also been challenged by Gersuny (1976), who shows that the forms of punishment used in an early nineteenth century textile mills were similar to those deployed in a similar mill in the late twentieth and also, more surprisingly, that rates of dismissal were likewise similar. He may be exaggerating in arguing that nothing changed, but as we indicate below our studies of the history of discipline on the railways suggest that some parallel themes existed in a very different industry. Punishment remains a more salient aspect of discipline than conventional accounts can allow.

The standard literature does not just have a lop-sided view of history. The approach also fails to grasp the ways in which discipline is constantly under definition and re-definition, together with the fact that any given workplace order is likely to contain several different elements which may co-exist uneasily. The craftsman for example simultaneously had a disciplined commitment to the trade and an antipathy towards management, and the workplace order of the craft shop reflected the tensions between such principles. To understand what discipline is requires placing it in the context of the contradictory world of the workplace.

Even the more recent literature, which sets out to address the 'dialectics of discipline' (Henry, 1985), seems to find it hard to spell out just what these dialectics are. It focuses on the connections between the private law of the employer and the public law of the state, which is an interesting enough theme but which hardly addresses the real dialectics of the workplace, namely those governing the capital-labour relation. More recent work in this tradition (Henry, 1987) has identified four different types of discipline. In addition the punitive and corrective forms of discipline, these are the accommodative-participative model, reflecting the fact that rules are the outcome of negotiation between competing groups, and the celebrative-collective model, wherein rules serve goals established by consensus. As indicated elsewhere (Edwards and Whitston, 1989a: 5-7), these are not in fact self-contained categories. Punishment and correction refer to principles of managerial action, whereas the accommodative-participative model refers to the totality of a regime in which a degree of workers' influence on discipline has been attained. Two firms following corrective principles may have very different systems of shopfloor order. The types offer some dimensions which may usefully be taken into account. We can, for example, consider how far a negotiated order has been established and where its limits are. But this is to make no more than the familiar point that workplace order is indeed a political process. Moreover, the fact that the types are not free-standing means that they cannot be used to categorize a particular workplace: they are not separate types, and they do not allow us to say that one workplace had, say, punitive discipline while another operated on an accommodative-participative model. They help to identify some strands that may be present anywhere, and we will pursue these in our case studies, but they do not help us to understand how these strands are connected to form a disciplinary regime as a whole.

This leads to the second and more important point. Our approach to industrial discipline is informed by the wider literature on workplace conflict and consent. But we also wish to address discipline in the specific sense of systems of punishment and correction. General studies of the workplace often throw light on such systems, but do not often consider them directly. The debate on discipline needs some new empirical information if it is not simply to revolve around some familiar themes.

Studying Disciplinary Practice

What kinds of evidence might be pertinent? Here we come to a significant difficulty. Consider for example the most extreme sanction of dismissal. Surveys (for example Daniel and Millward, 1983: 171) have estimated how common it is, and numerous studies (for example Dickens et al., 1985) have analysed the operation of the unfair dismissal system. Aspects of these studies have thrown light on the nature of disciplinary practice, as in the ways in which industrial tribunals have tried to understand what a 'reasonable' management might reasonably do. But unfair dismissal cases are a small minority of all dismissals. Very little is known about how managements identify workers as requiring discipline or about the processes which lead to dismissal. The difficulty lies in researching such topics. They plainly call for a case-study investigation. Yet in any one workplace dismissal will occur only rarely, and it may be hard to generalize from a particular case to any normal 'pattern'. Discipline naturally embraces more than dismissal, and most companies now have formal disciplinary procedures. But even these are used only rarely. To try to interview managers and trade unionists in detail about the procedures and how they work might well produce little more than anecdotes and special cases. Discipline in the wider sense, by contrast, may be so all-embracing that it would be foolish to try to separate it from the general flow of workplace relations. If a supervisor gives a semi-jocular warning to a worker about lateness, is this a case of discipline, and what weight should the analyst place on it?

Our approach to these problems has several dimensions. Most obviously, we included one case, British Rail, where formal discipline has been long-standing and where we might hope to find details about the conduct attracting penalties and to be able to explore the connections between discipline in this sense and the wider negotiation of order. Second, in all our cases we asked workers how often they had been subject to discipline in the sense of punishment and, if they had, what they thought of the experience. Though such basic information about the use of penalties might be expected to be central to debates about discipline, it has not, to our knowledge, been collected on a systematic basis. We also asked more generally about the perceived fairness of the disciplinary system. Taking this together with workers' replies about the system of absence control, we were able to develop a reasonable picture of the place of overt disciplinary sanctions in the shopfloor regime. Third, we pursued such cases of dismissal and serious disciplinary cases as we came across to see what light they might throw on the regime. More generally, we followed the tradition of workplace sociology represented above all by Gouldner (1954) in asking how formal rules were re-defined or ignored in practice: just what are the practical expectations of management, and how are they enforced, either by penalties, incentives, persuasion, or a mixture of all three?

There are certain issues which we feel that we have not fully investigated. It has, for example, become a standard argument that managerial definitions of a 'good worker' are shaped at least as much by a worker's willingness to accept authority as by technical accomplishments (Bowles and Gintis, 1976; Blackburn and Mann, 1979; Jenkins, 1988). We say nothing about this. Nor were we in a position to study in any detail possible bias in the operation of discipline arising out of gender or ethnic stereotypes on the part of managers. Similarly, managements may be able to deal with 'trouble makers' not by using formal procedures but by 'leaning on them', so that they knuckle under or leave. To address such issues would require a much more intensive observational technique than we chose to employ, and also the good luck that such activities were in fact observable. We are not, then, in a position to comment on whether formal disciplinary procedures are under-cut by a practice that is very different from prescribed methods.

What we can do is to explore the several dimensions of discipline mentioned above and to place them in the context of shopfloor practice. The links with the debate about custom and practice and the effort bargain should be evident. We set out to consider how the day-to-day conduct of the worker is managed, and the clearest way of doing so is to consider how standards of discipline are established. Such standards are, of course, subject to collective interpretation: they can become norms, customs, or even informal rules. But how far they do so is contingent on a wide range of factors. In many workplaces custom and practice has never flourished. The logical starting point, then, is discipline in its various senses, with the extent to which it becomes subject to customary regulation being a subsequent issue.

Attendance, Discipline and Shopfloor Order

What, then, are the connections between absence and discipline, and between these two topics and the wider issues of the control of the employment relationship? One simple point is that studies in Britain (Institute of Personnel Management, 1979: 28-31) and in America (Dalton and Perry, 1981: 425) have shown that absenteeism is the most frequent reason for the use of discipline. Even after more than 40 years of formal arbitration systems in America, moreover, arbitrators have found it impossible to set down clear rules about how to handle absence: 'probably the single most difficult area of contract administration and enforcement involves the assessment of discipline for excessive absence' (Dilts et al., 1985: 97). The reason for this is that it is very hard to establish what is reasonable behaviour, evidence of avoidable absence is unclear, standards of acceptable levels of absence are vaguely defined, and uniform policies are hard to develop (Block and Mittenthal, 1985).

Second, absence and discipline both concern the harder or the more overtly controlling aspects of the management of the employment relationship. A great deal has been written about the motivational aspects such as communication and involvement, but little is known about the demands which are placed on employees. As noted above, there are some indications that pressures on workers have been growing. Little is known, however, about how these feed through in concrete areas like discipline or how workers react. In short, we have some plausible but rather imprecise indications which need to be pinned down more exactly.

These topics are only the starting point. What is their connection with attempts to increase commitment? One of the more intriguing suggestions from our survey of 25 organizations was that absence control and new forms of commitment seemed to be connected: where tighter absence control was being implemented, there was also a tendency for management to practise new forms of communication and involvement (Edwards and Whitston, 1989b). The tensions between coercion and persuasion, or between what has become known in the labour process debate as the balance between direct control and responsible autonomy (Friedman, 1977), plainly merit investigation. The control of absence is likely to impinge far more immediately on most workers than is a policy of briefing groups. We wished to assess how far regimes of labour management had a hard face as well as a caring one.

The key linkage, then, is simply the detailed regulation of the labour of the individual employee. It is true that the management of attendance cannot be divorced from managerial policy more generally. Likewise, we need to relate disciplinary regimes to their context. Yet we have seen that many studies aim to consider the management of the labour relation without directly looking at attendance or discipline at all. It is a matter of the starting point. Ours is the individual worker and how he or she is treated. We aim to show that this complements other approaches by throwing a distinctive light on the management of the labour relation.

These, then, were the overall concerns which shaped the study. They were operationalized in some rather different ways within each of the case studies that we undertook, for each study threw light on some distinct strands of the general theme. It is for this reason that we analyse them on a case-by-case basis, a rationale that will be clearer once we have outlined what each involved.

Case Studies and Research Methods

The Case Studies

The research issues identified above do not lead directly to appropriate research sites. A study of, say, forms of involvement on greenfield sites would carry with it a clear idea of the sort of sites that would be relevant. Our concerns were broader in that we wanted to consider the general drift of changes in the shopfloor regime. This suggested taking sites from several sectors and avoiding the new or the special in favour of the average or the normal.

Within this broad concern, however, several issues stood out. One was the question of absence cultures. We therefore chose one organization, British Rail, where workers have long been felt to have a strong sense of occupational identity (Salaman, 1974). Price (1986: 120-26) speaks of the personal 'bailiwicks' of the railway employee and of the strong culture with which these were imbued. We might reasonably expect, therefore, that if we were to find developed absence cultures this would be a sensible place to look. Conversely, there is the question of cultures that promote attendance, and a hospital, with its norms of patient care and so forth, would be a useful place to seek such a culture.

A second general concern was with change in the management of labour towards more co-operative styles. We went to the financial services organization, which we have called FinCo, because it had made some particularly significant moves in this direction. But all of our organizations except the hospital had made some attempts at this, and we are able to make some general assessment of the issue. This was true even of Multiplex, which we chose largely for its unexceptional characteristics: we hoped that it would offer some kind of benchmark, or picture of the unexciting developments which do not hit the headlines, and so it did, but it had also been experimenting with briefing groups and with some other forms of labour control so that it, too, can throw some light on the question of how control and autonomy are connected.

Multiplex produced a huge range of food and related products, hence its pseudonym; many of these were household names. Its manufacturing took place on several sites. We studied one factory on the largest site and also a warehouse in a different location. In many respects it typified the 'average' British manufacturing company. It had none of the tradition of shopfloor militancy of the car industry, and neither was it at the forefront of 'human resource management'. Until the 1970s its reputation had been as a safe place to work: wages that were on the low side, but a high degree of job security, together with a none-too-demanding work pace and a paternalistic atmosphere. It was common for several generations of a family to work there. The firm was unionized, and the process of union recognition had followed the pattern of managerial sponsorship: by the 1970s it seemed convenient to recognize a union so that issues of pay and representation could be handled on an orderly basis.

By the 1980s, matters were beginning to change. There was growing competition in the product market, and the firm's image as a stodgy performer produced rumours of take-overs. The response was wide-ranging. The firm was divisionalized, it began to be an aggressor and not a target in the take-over field, and the first significant redundancies were instituted in an effort to improve efficiency. By the standards of the past, change was considerable, and managers stressed to us how far they had gone towards a more modern approach, even though there had been none of the traumatic change that affected, say, the coal or steel industries. The impact on labour management was a mixture of tradition and change. Existing institutions, both of collective bargaining and of consultation (the latter having a long history), remained in place. But there were also moves towards a more commercial approach. As discussed in Chapter 2, absence control was a major area in which tighter control was being sought. This was complemented in the warehouse by the introduction of a new work measurement system. This established standard staffing levels against work loads. In principle, it could have been used to institute group-based bonus schemes or some other incentive system. The company had never used incentive pay, except for an annual profit-related bonus, however, and a sudden move to bonus systems was seen as too radical. Instead, targets for staffing were established for each section, and these were increased annually. Each supervisor was thus assessed against rigid standards, and it was left to him or her to persuade the workers to work in the required manner. Pressures on workers were thus indirect, but they were quite clear.

As for involvement, there were tentative moves in two directions. First, as mentioned above, briefing groups were being introduced: each work group received a monthly briefing from the supervisor. Second, workers were subject to annual appraisals. The results of appraisals were not related to reward: there was no effort to bring in fashionable performance-related pay. Neither did appraisals cut very deeply into workers' attitudes. But they were indicative of some effort to promote individual workers' sense of commitment.

It was certainly that case that, at the level of day-to-day work performance, workers were very much aware of the need to produce and of managerial expectations of effort. In the warehouse these expectations were fed through from the monitoring system; in the factory, they came from standards for daily output. A growing managerial concern with the efficient use of labour indicates that change, though slow, was certainly perceptible. The firm offers a useful case for assessing how far shopfloor practice still depends on tradition and how far new and more aggressive styles of management have amended this tradition.

The relationship between tradition and commercialism is an even more striking aspect of British Rail (BR). As Ferner (1985, 1988) in particular has shown, pressures on public sector management to adopt a commercial approach had profound effects on the control of labour. These included the introduction of new working practices and the attempt to end long-established systems of national-level collective bargaining. Our concern is not to repeat the general analysis of such matters but to address the unexplored issue of how they have impacted at the shopfloor level. Just how far has commercialism gone, and has it totally overturned traditional sources of worker commitment? As it turned out, a focus on disciplinary systems was a particularly useful way of approaching these questions.

The approach of BR management was not simply one of forcing through change. The Customer Care campaign was instituted to encourage workers to be aware of and responsive to the needs of passengers, and the workers whom we studied had either been on a course or were aware of the programme. Efforts were also being made to improve communication to employees and to promote a sense of involvement, for example by publishing a statement of principles about involvement.

BR is a massive organization, embracing workshop staff, signalling technicians, permanent way workers, and clerical staff as well train crew and platform staff. We made no attempt to cover all these grades, and focused on the four specific groups described in Chapter 3. How typical they are is impossible to say, though we feel that we obtained a reasonable spread from skilled to unskilled. For what it is worth, some informal discussions with other groups such as maintenance staff pointed to broadly similar sets of attitudes.

Similar points apply to the Hospital: a highly complex public sector organization facing enormous pressures to be more 'business-like'. As with BR, the ways in which these pressures have impacted on traditional forms of commitment have been little studied. The additional reason for looking at a hospital was, as noted above, the desire to find a workplace where, other things being equal, one might expect a pro-attendance culture to flourish.

Though there is a large literature on medical occupations, much of it has addressed issues such as professionalism and general occupational identity. Comparatively little work has been done on the detailed way in which labour is controlled: issues which arise in the private sector, such as regulating attendance and dealing with the allocation of work tasks, also have to be handled in a hospital, but little is known about these matters. Our concern was to see hospital workers as employees and to consider the details of how their labour was managed. In addition, by placing our study in a comparative context, we are able to consider just how far these workers differ from other employees. Do they, for example, have distinctive attitudes towards attendance, or do they have attitudes in common with others?

As with BR, it was impossible to study all occupational groups. We looked at nurses and domestic ancillaries in a large city hospital. Our sample was rather smaller than we achieved in our other cases, which reflects the obvious difficulties of conducting a study of this type in a hospital. It was more time-consuming than the other studies, and the information was less detailed in some respects than we would have liked. The results had a consistency, and a similarity with other information, however, which leads us to believe that they are broadly accurate.

All three of these organizations had important aspects of tradition. The Multiplex and BR samples, moreover, were of manual workers, while the status of nurses in terms of the 'collar line' is somewhat uncertain. We wanted an organization which would offer contrasts with these three, and FINCO provided several. It was a financial services organization, employing around 10,000 clerical workers at a head office and a large number of branches. We focused on the head office, for two reasons: simple practicality, since many branches are very small; and because we wanted as far as possible to control for the size of the workplace. If, for example, we had studied branch employees and had found large differences from other samples, we would not know whether this was due to their white-collar status or to the peculiarities of working in small organizations with direct contact with the public and possibly dominated by personal relationships between the manager and the staff. The head office employed a large number of staff, and it offered the chance of studying a bureaucratic and routinized environment.

As with studies of hospital workers, analyses of white-collar employees have concentrated on some rather general issues such as whether they are becoming proletarianized and the overall level of skill that they enjoy (see Lane, 1988, for a review). The details of the control of work have been little studied. 'Direct and systematic study of the social organization of office work is almost non-existent', remarks Lockwood (1989: 231), 'and what there is relates to very atypical situations'. The literature says little, for example, about how easy it is for workers to take breaks, how far they practise collective output controls, or how on a day-to-day basis supervisors persuade them to work hard. In the published literature, one has to go back to Blau's (1963) study, which was carried out in 1949, to find serious treatment of these issues. Our concern was not with the de-skilling debate but with seeing white-collar work in the same way in which manual labour has traditionally been viewed. Thus we tried to be sensitized to the 'frontier of control': who decides work allocation and work speed, how far and why workers are able to develop collective challenges to management on these matters, and so on. As would be expected, being sensitized to an issue does not mean that it actually arises concretely in a workplace. The speed of work at FinCo was not the central concern that it was on the assembly line at Ford (Beynon, 1973). We did not necessarily have to spend a long time asking about such issues, but they helped to focus the research and have also informed the conclusions, in so far as we consider why it was that these issues were not matters of bargaining - particularly when, as noted below, management was in many ways rationalizing labour in ways that would be recognized in a factory.

On the particular issue of absence, a reason for looking at a white-collar workplace was simply that the dominant emphasis in absence research has been on manual employees. This reflects the fact that absence rates of non-manual workers have been relatively low. But it is important to ask why this has been so: it is not an automatic characteristic of non-manual labour and, in so far as these workers have generally enjoyed more generous sick pay arrangements than manual workers, one might expect, other things being equal, a relatively high absence rate. We therefore wanted to explore how 'good attendance' is managed. With increasing cost pressures in a sector like financial services, moreover, there might be significant changes towards a tighter control of absence, and indeed of work behaviour in general. This again was something that we wished to explore.

There was one key reason for going to FinCo in particular. The company had recently introduced a system of merit pay linked to performance appraisal, and this was used right down to the lowest clerical grade. There has been much enthusiasm for such payment systems, which are seen as promoting commitment to the firm and a high level of performance. As we will see in Chapter 5, managers in FinCo were rather more cautious in their expectations than some of the more extreme popular views of the merits of performance appraisal. None the less, a good deal of effort had been lavished on the scheme, which was seen as a useful device. We thus set out to discover what effect it had in fact had on morale and commitment. The conditions were certainly favourable. White-collar workers are generally assumed to have a more individualistic and pro-management view than manual workers. FinCo workers were represented by a staff association, which again might be expected to be more compliant than a self-proclaimed trade union. And the site that we studied had been established only four years earlier, so that there was little space for strong informal customs to develop. As against the traditionalism that ran deep in the other three cases, here was a situation in which the enthusiasts for performance appraisal would surely hope that their expectations would be fulfilled.

In short, we looked at the performance appraisal system not because we wanted to know about this type of innovation in particular but because of its potential impact on the ways in which effort was extracted. In FinCo, as in our other organizations, our interest was not the totality of relations between managers and workers or collective industrial relations as such. We did not, for example, directly investigate the substantial changes that BR was making in its negotiating arrangements with the trade unions. We focused on the problems of persuading workers to attend regularly and to work to required standards once they were within the workplace.

Do these four cases provide enough material to assess workplace change? It would have been desirable to have included a plant practising the 'new industrial relations', but we had some difficulty in gaining access and decided that for our purposes it was not essential to have such a site. We were interested in the average, not the exceptional. To have included only one 'new' plant would also have raised the question of how representative of newness it was. Several scholars have in any event focused specifically on such plants. They generally suggest that newness is much less evident than might have been expected. Many accounts of 'transformation' look, moreover, at the immediate impact of change. In the longer-run, the miraculous often seems to sink back to the mundane. Ahlstrand (1990) for example shows that in the celebrated case of the Fawley refinery efforts at change over 25 years produced only small tangible results. Along with a graduate student, we carried out a small study of a site where change had been attempted some time ago (see Marshall, 1987). Single status for manual and white-collar workers was introduced in 1979, but by 1987 little change was apparent. We discuss these cases in the concluding chapter.

The final chapter also relates our organizations to the results of earlier studies of absence. Direct comparison is difficult, and to the extent that differences exist we have to consider whether these represent trends over time or contrasts between different types of firm. It does seem clear, however, that our organizations were at the lower end of the range of absence rates. If they saw absence as an issue, it is likely that other firms will have been at least as likely to do so. Our cases may thus have been representative of a trend even though they were not 'typical'. Taken together with studies adopting a more specialized focus they lead to the generalization that any change has been limited and that it has not been characterized by a qualitative shift to a new form of shopfloor order.

Research Methods

We used three main research techniques. First, we assembled statistical information. On absence, this was relatively straightforward, though organizations differed in the quality of their records. The minimal requirement was to obtain data over a whole year. From these, we calculated three key indices: the frequency distribution of absences (how many people had no spells of absence during the year, how many had one spell and so on); the number of days of absence of each person; and the distribution of spells according to their duration (what proportion of all absences lasted only one day, and so on). These indices together reveal the overall pattern. One workplace, for example, may have a high frequency of short absences, leading to a low number of days lost, while another may have a few workers taking long spells of sickness. Plainly, the absence 'problem' is very different in these two situations. We compiled data for as large a number of workers as possible; the exact groups covered are described in each of the substantive chapters. In some cases, as we again detail at the relevant points, it was possible to assemble some time-series data to test managerial views that the 'problem' was growing worse, but in general records were not sufficient to permit detailed assessment of trends.

On discipline, we examined documents describing formal procedures, and in Multiplex and FinCo there was some limited information on cases which had entered these procedures. As mentioned above, this kind of material was much richer in the case of BR. These three organizations also offered some information on cases of dismissal for disciplinary reasons, and we obtained such detail as we could on these cases.

The second method was interviews with managers concerning systems of monitoring and controlling absence, how discipline operated in practice, and so on. We endeavoured to speak to managers on several occasions in order to obtain some understanding of the less formal aspects of control. Just how, for example, a worker is defined as a good attender, or exactly what degree of consideration is extended to someone wishing to be absent to deal with a sudden domestic crisis, cannot be established in one-off formal interviews. In many ways, our unstructured discussions with managers, together with casual observation of a workplace, were the most important ways of gaining a 'feel' for the climate of worker-manager relations.

Third, we used a standard questionnaire for interviews with shopfloor workers. We felt that we would need some fairly hard data to make comparisons between workplaces, and also that a questionnaire format would assist us in tackling issues that may not be at the forefront of workers' minds. Workers may not, for example, have developed views about the extent of group norms on absence, and to approach such matters in an unstructured way could lead to information that is patchy and impressionistic.

The questionnaire is reproduced in Appendix B, together with some details of its rationale. It covered six issues. The first was largely background: length of service with the firm, and reasons for staying with it. The second and third sections covered relations with the work group and with management. One purpose was to obtain some grip on the idea of an absence culture. The basic idea here is that the social meanings of absence will vary according to the strength of the work group and the nature of relations with management. With strong work groups, for example, absence is expected to be shaped by collective norms. If relations with management are also conflictual, absence may be a conscious bargaining tactic for workers. Our questions on the work group had some value in encouraging workers to talk about their work situation, and here and elsewhere in the questionnaire we often departed from the set format to talk in a less structured way. The questions themselves, however, proved to be of little explanatory value, as we explain in the appendix.

The questions on management were of more direct use. We began with a couple of fairly standard questions about closeness of relations with managers and respect for the technical competence of management. We then went on to ask directly about 'trust', focusing on how much trust a worker placed in management as a whole. We also asked about changes in trust and in ways of dealing with workers. These were open-ended questions, but we made a point of prompting all workers about new systems of communication, so that they were given every chance to give replies that recognized new managerial initiatives. In each case study, moreover, we picked up themes specific to it. It was here, for example, that we asked FinCo workers about the appraisal scheme, again prompting them about its motivational effects. Workers were thus given the opportunity of giving broadly 'pro-management' replies. This section of the questionnaire, then, helped us to assess working relationships and how they had been changing.

The fourth section turned to the specific issue of attendance. The concern here was three-fold: to assess each worker's reasons for wanting to go absent and how often he or she had in fact gone absent for reasons unconnected with 'genuine illness'; workers' awareness of fellow workers' absence and their views on whether there were any work group norms promoting absence or attendance; and perceptions of the managerial control system. The questioning here was reasonably straightforward, opening with a very general question about workers' duty to attend. In asking about reasons for absence, we wanted to take account of non-work as well as work-related influences. These questions plainly do not permit a close assessment of domestic pressures or of the attractions of outside interests as reasons for absence. Our purpose, however, was to consider absence in relation to the organization of work. We needed to take account of non-work influences in a broad way, in order to obtain some view of their importance compared with that of workplace-based factors. But we did not wish to explore them in their own right, and for our purposes our questioning was sufficient.

Departing from the questionnaire produced some interesting results here. For example, in Multiplex we began to find a surprising number of workers answering our question about managerial pressures or expectations to attend in terms of informal expectations to go to work when they were feeling ill. We asked further questions about this to try to elucidate the situation, and also made a point of asking other workers in this company about this. We also raised it where relevant in the other studies: it was not, for example, an issue worth pursuing in FinCo, but it had some significance in the hospital.

The fifth section asked some fairly brief questions about discipline. As noted above, discipline is a difficult topic to study at workplace level because, among other reasons, discipline merges with all kinds of taken-for-granted assumptions about workplace conduct. Our approach was to ask a general question about the fairness of rules, followed by one about whether the rules were applied equally between different groups of workers. We then used these standard questions to probe issues which, from our discussions with managers, appeared to be significant. In BR, for example, these included a range of practices associated with time-keeping and slipping away from the workplace during working hours; in FinCo they covered the ways in which the firm's flexitime system operated and whether or not there were customary understandings about the way in which work should be carried out. This, then, was, like the section on management, a point at which we explored norms about workplace behaviour and the effort bargain.

A third question asked about a worker's own experience with discipline. We had anticipated some difficulties here, since workers may define 'being disciplined' in different ways, but in practice most of the sample were able to offer a reply which seemed to have some connection with their actual experience. We then asked some more general questions about the disciplinary system.

The final section was added after we had completed about thirty interviews in Multiplex, which was the first case study. Replies about absence in the rest of the questionnaire had pointed to a strongly 'pro-management' picture. We became concerned that we were not tapping workers' wider views on the legitimacy of absence. They might cheerfully say that people should attend work whenever they could without necessarily being as managerialist as such a reply might at first suggest. The assumption underlying much managerial thinking is that work must come first and that, except for personal sickness or serious domestic problems, a worker has a duty to attend. But workers may see matters less starkly. Just how ill do you have to be for absence to be justifiable, and how in practice do you balance a duty to the firm with domestic and other demands? Such questions have rarely been addressed in the absence literature, and we felt that we needed to make at least some effort to tackle them.

We did so using the 'vignette technique' (Finch, 1987): mini-stories about fictitious characters which pose various moral dilemmas. Respondents are invited to choose between courses of action and to discuss the reasons for their choice. We asked three mini-stories, which did indeed suggest that workers' views on absence included acceptance of the legitimacy of being absent in circumstances which formal rules might well define as illegitimate. More detailed explanation of the stories, and what we think they can tell us, will be found in Chapter 2.

We did not, then, treat the questionnaire as an immutable research instrument: we dropped some lines of questioning and added others, and throughout pursued workers' replies where these seemed to throw an interesting light on their situation. None the less, it retained a large core of common material. This plainly could be presented in a thematic manner: workers' views on management, attitudes to attendance, and so on. As already intimated, however, we have not adopted this approach, as we now explain.

Organization and Argument of the Book

The main reason for rejecting a comparative approach is that we wished to characterize the operation of the regime in each workplace: to create an understanding of the significance of absence and discipline and to relate this to the conduct of work. Each workplace raised distinct questions: how were workers doing highly monotonous jobs on the packing lines in Multiplex's factory persuaded to keep working at their tasks; what has happened to the effort levels being demanded of train drivers after a decade of commercial pressures on the railways; and how far were routine clerical workers at FinCo being subject to forms of control that paralleled those characteristic of factories? To answer such questions requires attention to each workplace in its own right. Similarly, we wanted to relate the specific issue of absence to its context: this is not a study of absence, but an analysis of shopfloor relations which takes absence as one key illustration. As we will see, the extent to which it featured as an overt issue varied. In the case of Multiplex, it was central to the changing order, whereas in FinCo it was more marginal. To have a separate thematic discussion of absence would lead to an unbalanced treatment.

We have not, however, gone to the extreme of presenting each case entirely independently, with comparative discussion coming only at the end. In each of the main chapters, we use the comparative data as a foil for discussion of each case. Hence, in considering the hospital, a major theme is the similarity of absence rates and of attitudes with the situation in Multiplex, even though one might have expected health service workers to display greater 'moral commitment' than low-skilled manual workers. Similarly, in the FinCo case we consider how far white-collar workers really had significantly different attitudes from the manual employees in our other studies. We have therefore assembled the key tables presenting the comparative data at the end of the book, and we refer to these throughout the analysis.

The one exception to the case-by-case approach is the analysis of the vignettes. Though we refer to these in the case study chapters, they are discussed as a separate topic because they refer to the general and not the particular: they address how workers view the legitimacy of absence regardless of where it takes place, and not the specifics of workers' own circumstances. We have placed this chapter first because in some ways it clears the ground for the other chapters. It shows that workers from our very different organizations had remarkably similar views on the general legitimacy of going absent. Differences in their own behaviour cannot then be explained in terms of some broad view of the reasonableness of taking time off work. Their behaviour stemmed from the specifics of their experience within the workplace, in particular the system of control that was in place. We therefore have to look inside each workplace, which is what we do in the following four chapters.

The chapter on the vignettes naturally discusses little but absence, and absence features prominently in the other chapters. We make no apology for this. Having argued that the control of attendance is an important but neglected topic, we need to address it in some detail. Our interests are, of course, wider, and we endeavour to draw out the significance of absence for workplace control more generally. Hence in the final chapter we draw together some general conclusions and relate our material to the wider debate about changing regimes of control.

Since we have chosen to present our material on a case-by-case basis, it may help if we outline some of the arguments that run through our discussion and that we present at more length in the conclusion. In some ways absence was not a problem, and its neglect might seem to be justified. We found no evidence of a wholesale decline in the work ethic: absence rates were not increasing, and the norm of attendance was taken for granted. Nor were work group norms very significant. But absence was important from the managerial point of view, with managers giving its control increased emphasis. We doubt whether this can have had much of a direct effect on overall absence rates, which are heavily influenced by long-term absences. Yet it may have had a symbolic effect in that managers could say to themselves and to each other that they were now 'managing' the 'problem', and send messages to the shopfloor that workers' behaviour was under closer scrutiny. Such messages connect with the issue of discipline: far from there being a shift towards self-discipline, in our organizations the mechanisms of control remained as they had been in the past, and what had changed was a greater managerial willingness to use them. There was little evidence of a change of attitude among shopfloor workers. To the extent that managements were reducing the scope for workers to define workplace rules on their own terms, custom and practice was being eroded. Yet questions remained about the viability of a new managerialism: managers continued to rely on workers' co-operation and, though they were able to shift the balance of power in their own favour in the short term without destroying the bases of this co-operation, in the longer term they might find that they were undermining their own efforts, as workers withdrew the day-to-day commitment to the enterprise on which they had hitherto been able to rely. In short, it was management which was changing its definition of the problems of absence and of shopfloor order more generally. The absence problem itself was largely unchanged. It is for this reason that we have called this study *Attending to Work: the Management of Attendance and Shopfloor Order*.

2

The Legitimacy of Absence

One commonsense model of absence runs as follows. Workers develop views as to what constitutes an adequate reason to be absent from work. These views are formed in the home and at school, rather than in the workplace. The views are important in shaping their own behaviour. The implication is that the explanation for absence lies in individual proclivities, not managerial control policies. The model would find support in, for example, the literature on orientations to work, which stresses the attitudes that workers bring with them to the workplace, as distinct from norms which are learnt within work.

In this chapter we consider this model by examining what we have termed the legitimacy of absence: the extent to which workers think that it is reasonable to take time off for reasons which are, strictly speaking, avoidable. What kinds of assumptions underlie the ways in which workers think about going absent, and how far do these assumptions affect their own behaviour? As noted in Chapter 1, the principal reason for this analysis was to clear the way for what follows: we show that standards of legitimacy did not determine workers' own behaviour and that expectations from family and friends played little role in workers' decisions on attendance. The implication is that it is necessary to look at the workplace norms governing behaviour. But there are also reasons why legitimacy is interesting in its own right.

In the voluminous literature on absence, the issue has received scant attention. It is common to find references to 'voluntary' and 'involuntary' absences, the former being subject to some kind of free choice while the latter are unavoidable. Behrend (1984: 58) for example quotes approvingly a 1947 definition of voluntary absence as 'the practice of workers failing to report for work on some slight excuse or other or none at all'. The main difficulty in analysing such voluntary absence is said to be finding firms which keep records in such a way as to permit sickness to be distinguished from voluntary absences. Yet the problems go much deeper than this. How is the analyst to decide what is and what is not a genuine reason for absence? How ill does a worker have to be before an absence moves from the voluntary to the involuntary category? As Nicholson (1977) argues, a back strain might make it impossible for a miner to work, while having no effect on a clerical worker's ability to work. And just how bad does a back strain have to be before it 'really' affects a miner's capacity to work? There are plainly many factors which will shape a worker's interpretation of physical illness. And parallel forces are likely to affect other possible reasons for absence such as domestic duties.

Rather than pursue the imprecise distinction between genuine and voluntary absence, we approached the question of choice from a different angle. We asked workers what they thought of various hypothetical instances in which people went absent for reasons which might be considered illegitimate in that they were plainly not connected with 'genuine sickness'. The extant literature on absence has given very little attention to this topic. Most studies have concentrated on the determinants of absence behaviour, paying little attention to what workers think is an acceptable reason to go absent. In the course of their attempt to provide a new paradigm for absence research, Johns and Nicholson (1982) touch on this point when they discuss attribution theory: they argue that the reasons which workers give for going absent warrant investigation. But even they speak only of the reasons which workers give for their own actions, and they do not address the wider context which shapes workers' views of absence. They do not consider the moral universe in which going absent is embedded.

As explained in Chapter 1, we looked at it because of a concern that to ask only about workers' own behaviour might be to exaggerate the extent to which managerial logics prevail. In Multiplex we found that what might be termed conventionally moral replies were predominating. By managerial logics we do not mean that workers were simply managerialist in the sense of thinking that there were no conflicts between managers and workers, or that managers were always right in acting to control absence. We mean something broader: a frame of reference which shared with managers an understanding of what was and what was not a proper ground for absence. Our evidence indicated a much greater acceptance of the legitimacy of absence than might have been expected from other questions. We subsequently found very similar patterns in the other three organizations.

In arguing that workers had views which were non-managerialist in that they accepted the legitimacy of certain forms of absence, we need some benchmark of what is managerialist. It might be, for example, that individual managers have very similar views. As far as we know, this has never been tested. We show in our cases studies that managers did indeed use some discretion in considering whether someone should be allowed out of the workplace while still being paid, for example to deal with some domestic crisis. But such discretion could be exercised within narrow bounds. The sorts of behaviour that we examined to address legitimacy would fall outside any standard managerial definition of reasonableness. It may be that individual managers think that taking time off would be reasonable. But the rules which they administer are always clear that paid absence is for the personal illness of the worker concerned, except in a few special circumstances. In short, we asked workers about behaviour which would be illegitimate under usual conditions, and could in principle attract a penalty. In saying that the evidence shows that they were non-managerialist, we do not suggest that all managers would deny the legitimacy of certain absences, only that company rules define the behaviour as unacceptable.

The results have two implications beyond the narrow area of workers' beliefs about legitimacy. First, they link with the generation of shopfloor order. As we saw in Chapter 1, several managements have been trying to sharpen the distinction between acceptable and unacceptable reasons for absence, and to get over to workers the idea that work is their primary responsibility. Indeed, some have aimed not merely to have workers accept this but also to internalize it is as a desirable state of affairs. Asking workers about the legitimacy of various forms of absence is one way to see whether they have endorsed these managerial ideas. To the extent that they did not, the implication is that tighter control was based on a re-assertion of managerial powers and not on self-discipline.

Second, several studies (eg Kelly and Kelly, 1991) have suggested that new forms of labour management have not eroded a 'them and us' attitude on the shopfloor. Our results cannot address trends over time. But they show that managerialism still seemed to be weak at the end of the 1980s. This is one illustration of the general point that fundamental changes of attitude have been rare.

We employed the 'vignette technique' of asking about hypothetical situations. Finch (1987) outlines its general merits. Since it has not been used very widely, we begin by explaining how we used it, indicating what lessons can be derived from other uses of it, and describing what we hoped it would show. We then suggest some possible correlations between replies to the vignettes and other parts of the questionnaire. These expectations are tested against the data. Finally, we draw out the implications of the results, in the course of which we also use some of our other open-ended questions about why workers attend work.

The Vignette Technique

General Considerations

According to Finch (1987: 105-6), the standard way of tapping beliefs, namely, asking survey respondents to agree or disagree with a set of attitude statements, has several weaknesses. These include the assumption that attitudes are fixed and that they can be measured in a vacuum, and the forcing of replies into categories already defined by the researcher. The vignette technique, by contrast, 'acknowledges that meanings are social and that morality may well be situationally specific'. Some uses of the technique, for example by Alves and Rossi (1978), are static, in that the respondent is asked to make a single judgement on each of a series of vignettes. Finch, following the work of West (1984; also West et al., 1984), prefers a more complex method of building certain changes into a story and asking the respondent what should be done at each point. Finch uses the example from her own research on beliefs about giving material assistance to one's kin: the vignettes helped to focus attention in a concrete way on issues that might otherwise seem vague or unimportant.

We were not in a position to make our vignettes particularly long or detailed. But we tried to make them more than one-off questions. We used three. The first had an open-ended follow-up, the second had a closed-ended subsidiary question, and the third took a story through in some detail. We found that this balance of questions worked reasonably well and that workers were willing to treat the stories as indicative of real-life problems.

Two main problems are noted by Finch. The first is technical. If a vignette develops a story, a respondent may be asked to make an initial judgement only to be told that the person in the story in fact did something different, which may imply that the respondent made the 'wrong' choice. We had this problem in the third vignette. As shown in Appendix B, we dealt with it by using two different wordings for following up the initial reply. This seemed to resolve any major problems though, as Finch found, there were cases where workers commented that the person in the story was not acting in the ways which they would have recommended. It was possible to handle this line of discussion without serious difficulty.

The second problem is that vignettes may be misused to make inferences about actual behaviour: a vignette is not 'a means of predicting what a respondent actually would do in a similar situation' (Finch, 1987: 113). Our research provided us with some means to test out directly the relationship between replies to vignettes and behaviour. For example, we could measure the overall pro- or anti-absence sentiment expressed in a person's replies and relate this to their own absence rates. And there were some more detailed tests that we describe below. We were thus in a position to make some contribution to the study of the technique by considering empirically what connections existed between general attitudes as revealed by the vignettes and workers' behaviour. Moreover, the leading uses of the technique have been on general population surveys, which makes it difficult for the analyst to relate replies to their context. Since our respondents came from organizations about which we knew a good deal, we are able to try to explain the pattern of replies that we obtained.

So what pattern might we expect? An obvious assumption is that workers will differ in their responses. Most obviously, women might be more sympathetic than men in a case of a single parent wanting to take time off work to deal with a child's illness. The available material on vignettes suggests that this may not be the case. West (1984) reports on six vignettes, used on three samples totalling 727 people, asking about the ways in which people suffering from various forms of disability should be cared for. There were no differences between the samples, and neither was there any association with respondents' age, social class, religion, or voting preferences. There was an association with sex on only three of the six, and there was also some link with education and with beliefs in traditional family values. These links were far from strong. 'The overall picture in regard to community care', concludes West (1984: 441), 'is one of considerable homogeneity within the sample'. We tested for several correlations in our data, but West's work suggests that general social attitudes may be widely shared. In our case, the question is whether there is a broad, common, view of the legitimacy of absence, shared by workers in different situations, or whether, say, nurses or white-collar workers adopt a much more moralistic or managerialist view than manual workers.

The Vignettes

We used three vignettes, which are reproduced in full in Appendix B. They were designed to tap attitudes to different types of absence which are, from a managerial perspective, illegitimate. In each case, we tried to present a moral dilemma, using named characters to try to add an air of verisimilitude. The first concerned 'Bill Thompson' who was rarely absent but who went down with the 'flu at the week-end and had to stay away from work until the next Wednesday. He felt better on Thursday but thought that, since he did not normally take much time off and had lost his week-end, he might as well take the rest of the week off. Was this reasonable? Workers' replies were recorded in a variable which we will call EXTEND. The second, SINGLE, was about a single parent, 'Janet Roberts', with a young son who needed a couple of days off when he was ill. If she asked for time off unpaid she would be short of money and the absence might be counted against her, but if she reported sick she could claim sick pay and the absence might not be questioned. Which option should she take? Third, 'Sally Harris' was feeling under pressure at work and had had rows with her work mates and the supervisor. Should she take a day off the get away from the pressure? We call this STRAIN. On the second question we also asked how serious it would be to report sick, and on the third we asked a series of follow-ups concerning whether the woman should report sick or ask for leave, what she should do when she comes back to work if she decides simply to take a day off, and what the supervisor's action should be in terms of allowing or withholding payment if the woman explained the situation.

Can pro-absence replies be treated as non-managerialist? We think that they can, in the sense of managerialist as meaning the normal rules of organizations. In the first case, the worker felt fit but decided to stay away. In the second, if 'Janet Roberts' claimed that she was sick, she would be claiming sick pay under false pretences. In the third, 'Sally Harris' was not physically incapable of work. Any worker going absent in the cases described would be in breach of formal rules.

These replies plainly cannot tap the whole moral universe in which workers locate absence. There are many reasons why workers may feel the need to go absent. But we feel that we had identified some reasonably common situations in which, to repeat, most managements will see going absent as illegitimate. In Behrend's terms, these are cases of 'voluntary absence'. We wanted to know how far workers felt that going absent was reasonable, why they said this, and what they felt of possible managerial reactions. We think that the vignettes give us a reasonable insight into the legitimacy of absence. We will offer no formal tests of this claim. What we can say is that the questions seemed to work well. No-one refused to answer them, and most workers took them seriously and thought about the issues involved. As will be seen, many offered comments on the situations which suggested that they related to them in terms of their own experience.

Theory and Data

Expected Linkages with the Vignettes

The most obvious source of variation in these views is the organization for which someone worked. The white-collar workers of FinCo might be expected to adopt a more moralistic tone than blue-collar employees. In addition to any general 'social class effect', FinCo workers did not do physically demanding jobs (thus reducing any rationalization of the need to be fit in order to work adequately). Nor did they work shifts, so that ideas of strain and clashes between work and non-work duties would not be pertinent; indeed, they worked flexi-time, which should further reduce any tendency to see absence as necessary for domestic duties. Workers in the hospital might similarly be expected to have a moralistic view of duty, though possibly tempered by the pressures of shift working. Pro-absence replies may be more common in the blue-collar environment of Multiplex. Finally, they may be most pronounced in BR, for two reasons: as we will see in Chapter 4, workers complained of the tensions of shift work; and they expressed high levels of discontent about their work. They did not see obligations to the employer as of overwhelming importance.

A second obvious set of relationships to explore are those with the sex and marital status of respondents. Women might be expected to be more sympathetic to absence in the two vignettes about women, and married women might display particular understanding of the case of the single parent.

We were also able to relate the vignettes to workers' attitudes concerning their own behaviour. The first vignette, about extending a spell of absence, can be linked to our question, 'some people say that workers use sick pay benefits to stay off longer than they really should. Have you ever extended a spell off work longer than was needed to get fit?' Replies have been dichotomized in a variable called EXTRA-ABS. The second and third vignettes can be correlated with replies to a question asking what reasons prompted a worker to think about taking time off. We created a measure called DOMEST, which records whether family illness or domestic duties were mentioned as a reason for thinking of going absent. One might expect workers citing these reasons to be sympathetic to absence in the second vignette. The third vignette, which is essentially about strain, did not have an exact counterpart. But it would be covered by a category of 'general boredom': for many manual workers, boredom in the sense of not being able to face the monotony of work is broadly equivalent to the situation described in the vignette. In addition, workers were free to specify other reasons. In the hospital in particular they cited strain specifically, and these replies have been combined with those mentioning boredom into a dichotomous measure called OWNSTRAIN.

We can also consider the association between the vignettes and wider measures of workers' attitudes. Some of these relate to absence specifically, for example the question asking, 'have you ever taken a day off work when you have been able to get in?' This measure, which we will label here as VOLABS, would be expected to be associated with pro-absence replies on the vignettes. It might also be expected that perceptions of the managerial control of absence would be related to the vignettes, with those most aware of pressures to attend being most likely to be sympathetic to taking time off.

Finally, we could correlate the replies with the data that we were able to collect on individual absence rates. In most cases, we knew the names of workers, and were able to relate questionnaire replies to organizational data on absence. But in some cases, notably BR, workers agreed to be interviewed only if no names were used; in some cases we did in fact know a worker's name, but did not use absence data if anonymity had been agreed. We computed the number of short absences (that is, separate spells of one or two days' duration), the total number of absence spells, and the number of days absent. These measures are called SHORTABS, FREQABS, and DAYSABS respectively. To allow for non-linearities, we also coded the absence frequency measures into three groups: no spell of absence, one or two spells, and three or more spells. The obvious expectation is that high absence rates will be associated with tolerance of absence. In particular, to the extent that a large number of short absences indicates frequent 'voluntary absence', or at least a frequent perceived need to take time off even if the worker in question sees the reasons for absence as legitimate and to an extent non-voluntary, SHORTABS would be expected to be correlated with the vignettes.

The Questionnaire Samples

We interviewed a total of 300 workers. Details of the occupational groups covered and the reason for their selection would be found in each of the following chapters. In brief, we studied 89 Multiplex workers from semi-skilled grades from two sites; there were no differences between sites. In BR, we interviewed 82 workers from four manual grades. Access was, as noted in Chapter 1, more difficult in the hospital; 57 workers, from nursing and ancillary grades, were eventually interviewed. Finally, 72 FinCo workers from routine clerical grades were included. In the cases of Multiplex and FinCo the samples were drawn randomly from lists of names; there were no refusals in FinCo and four in Multiplex. In the other two organizations, no such lists were sought, since shift patterns made it difficult to find times to interview named individuals. Moreover, it turned out in BR in particular that some workers would participate only on an anonymous basis. We therefore approached workers and sought interviews, making an effort to obtain a balance of age and length of service. Sampling here was in effect a form of quota sampling. It may have introduced some bias, but we doubt whether this was severe.

Extent and Pattern of Legitimacy

Extent of Considerateness

We may call a response which accepts the legitimacy of going absent a considerate reply. The distributions are shown in Table 2.1 and in Figure 1. Three facts stand out. First, the great majority of respondents (84 per cent) gave a considerate reply to at least one vignette, and there were only small differences between the four organizations. Second, there was more sympathy for extending a spell of genuine sickness than for the other two cases. Third, on two of the vignettes there were organizational differences. Multiplex workers were most likely to be considerate in the cases of extending a spell of absence and the single parent; BR workers shared this tendency on the first but not the second.

The reasons given for a considerate reply illustrate the thinking that informed it. On the first vignette, the most common justification was that an illness like 'flu did not disappear over night, and that it was important to regain one's full health before returning to work. As one FinCo worker put it, 'Bill Thompson' should ensure that he was fully over his illness. Other workers underlined the importance of his generally good attend-

TABLE 2.1   Considerate Replies to Vignettes

Per Cent	Multiplex (N = 65)	BR (N = 82)	Hosp. (N = 57)	FinCo (N = 72)	All (N = 276)
EXTEND	65	45	68	47	54
SINGLE	63	35	43	36	44
STRAIN	35	31	45	46	39
CONSID[a]	85	76	93	85	84

Note: [a]CONSID indexes whether a considerate reply was given on any of the three vignettes.

ance: one Multiplex worker noted that with a good record it was reasonable to stay away. Such replies indicate that workers were taking the vignettes seriously and were trying to reach a judgement on the basis of all the available facts.

The second vignette, being closed-ended, attracted relatively few comments (and for that reason the closed-ended format may not be the most helpful). Workers tended to argue that one's family must come first. One Multiplex worker made the interesting comment that 'Janet Roberts' should discuss the problem with managers and that if she met with an unsympathetic response she should consider going absent. One or two other replies picked up similar themes: if managers played by the book, workers had more of a right to take time off. This implies that the duty to the firm was not seen as absolute, and that how far one chose to attend work should depend on how management treated the bargain.

On the third vignette, several workers argued that 'Sally Harris' was suffering from stress, which was a form of illness and which hence justified taking time off. As one respondent put it, even without a specific physical illness she must have felt unwell and was, in the circumstances, justified in staying away from work.

Even the non-considerate replies rarely contained overtly moral arguments about the duty to work. Some workers certainly argued that it would be 'dishonest' for Bill Thompson to stay away longer than necessary, but others simply said that, as long as he really felt fit then he should return to work, but how far he was fit was a matter for him, and him alone. One FinCo worker even said that staying away in these circumstances might not be right, but she herself would do so; interestingly, in reply to the question on her own behaviour, she said that she had extended a spell of absence longer than was really necessary because 'you might as well

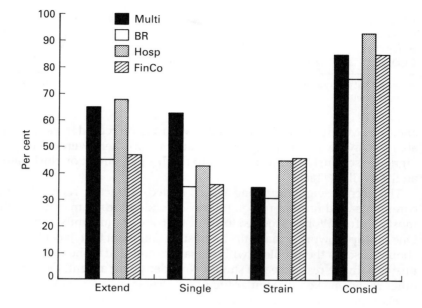

Figure 1   Considerate replies to vignettes

have an extra day'. On the second vignette, arguments for not going sick were as much pragmatic as moral. Some workers, for example, said that reporting sick carried the danger that Janet Roberts might really be ill, so that questions would be asked. On the third, it was often said that going sick would solve nothing and might make Sally Harris feel even further isolated. Other workers argued that anyone feeling this pressurized should look for another job. In this particular case, it was very rare for workers to dismiss the problem out of hand.

TABLE 2.2   Detailed Responses to Vignettes

	Multiplex	*BR*	*Hosp.*	*FinCo*	*All*
Single parent: reporting sick to cover son's illness would be:					
Understandable	60	79	69	78	71
Quite serious	34	20	29	21	26
Very serious	5	0	2	0	2
Other reply	2	2	0	2	1
Worker under strain who needs to stay away					
a. She should:					
Report sick	44	26	58	37	40
Ask for unpaid leave	15	10	24	31	20
Stay away and say nothing	0	2	0	1	1
Come in to work	41	63	18	25	37
Other reply	0	0	0	6	2
b. If she stayed away, on return should she:					
Admit what happened	54	52	83	82	67
Say she had been ill	46	39	17	12	29
Other reply	0	9	0	6	4
c. If she explained, should supervisor stop her pay?					
Yes	48	32	37	15	33
No	50	53	63	79	61
Other reply	2	15	0	7	6

Considerateness was also apparent in replies to the follow-up questions to the second and third vignettes. On the second, respondents were asked to contemplate Janet Roberts's staying away, and to say how serious this would be: understandable and not very serious, serious enough to need a warning, or a very serious offence. As Table 2.2 shows, very few chose the last option, and nearly three-quarters opted for the first. On the Sally Harris question, after making their original choice workers were asked further what she should do. If they said she should stay away, they were asked whether she should report sick, ask for unpaid leave, just stay away and say nothing, or even come in to work regardless; if they said she should report for work, they were told that she felt really worn out the next day, and were then offered the same four choices. As the table shows, workers took a 'proceduralist' view in that they felt that simply staying away was wrong. But in every case except BR there were clear majorities favouring reporting sick or asking for leave. Not surprisingly in view of the disapproval of staying away, workers generally felt that if she did take this option she should try to explain the situation on her return. Most explained this on the grounds that it was best to be honest and that hiding the problem would solve nothing. The one-third who favoured claiming illness said that there were times when openness to management was not always the best policy and that what she should do would depend on circumstances, with a case of a tough management requiring a degree of dissimulation.

The final part of the third vignette asked about managerial responses: if Sally Harris did stay away and then come back explaining the situation, should the supervisor stop her pay? The majority (61 per cent) said that, in general, pay should not be stopped, suggesting that management should respect the worker's honesty and should try to get to the bottom of the problem. Some argued that for a 'first offence' stopping pay would be unreasonable but that subsequent absence might be treated differently. Those justifying stopping pay rarely did so on 'moral' grounds, arguing instead that Sally should have called in to notify her supervisor of her absence and that her failure to follow this procedure made it difficult for a manager to justify payment. But the fact that the majority of the sample supported payment even in a clear-cut case of 'voluntary' absence and not adhering to procedures indicates the extent to which the legitimacy of absence was accepted.

A couple of actual cases will illustrate the point. One male Multiplex worker had, in replies to the earlier parts of the questionnaire, said that he himself never thought of taking time off work and had cited the interest of his job as the main reason for attending. Yet he gave considerate replies to two of the three vignettes, and an 'understanding' non-considerate reply to the third. On the first, he felt that taking an extra couple of days off in order to 'clear out' the illness was acceptable, and on the second he saw taking off the odd couple of days to care for the child as reasonable. On the third, he argued that Sally should attend work because staying away would only heighten her sense of rejection. In short, despite having a strong pro-attendance view of his own behaviour, he took a sympathetic view on all three vignettes. A woman working for the same firm gave three non-considerate replies but still displayed sympathy for the problems faced by the three hypothetical individuals. In Janet Roberts's case, she felt that going absent could become never-ending, and that it was not really a solution to the problem. Similarly, absence would not tackle the underlying problems facing Sally Harris, who should consult her doctor.

The replies to the vignettes thus reflect a widespread acceptance of the need for workers to go absent in situations which managements might see as voluntary or illegitimate absence. The moral lens through which workers understood absence was very different from what managers might wish.

TABLE 2.3   Associations between Measures of Considerateness

		SINGLE		*STRAIN*	
		Yes	*No*	*Yes*	*No*
EXTEND					
	Yes	53	58	58	54
	No	47	42	42	46
		100	100	100	100
SINGLE					
	Yes			38	50
	No			62	50
				100	100

Dimensions of Considerateness

The three vignettes were designed to tap attitudes to different situations, but it is possible that they have one underlying dimension. It appeared that in fact they were measuring some rather different attitudes. As Table 2.3 shows, replies on one were not strongly correlated with replies on the other two. For some purposes, it may be useful to distinguish respondents with a consistently 'moral' view from the remainder, and we will use the variable CONSID to indicate whether a considerate reply was offered to any of the vignettes. But there does not appear to be one basic dimension that was being tapped. This suggests that the vignettes were usefully addressing different aspects of workers' views, an argument which is strengthened by the fact that, as shown below, various explanatory variables correlated with replies on one vignette but not with those on the other two.

Differences between Organizations

Some organizational differences stand out from Tables 2.1 and 2.2, but they were not as large as might have been expected, and neither were they always in the expected direction. At least three-quarters of each sample gave a considerate reply to one or more of the vignettes. On the strain question, replies were similar across all four organizations. The question about the single parent produced the widest range of replies: 35 per cent of the BR sample supported the idea of going absent whereas 63 per cent of Multiplex workers gave this reply.

It was, indeed, the BR employees who were the least, and not the most, considerate of absence. And FinCo workers, far from being moralistic about attendance, came close to the average on the summary measure CONSID. They were more likely to be non-considerate in the case of extending a spell of absence, but were particularly sympathetic in the case of strain. The hospital workers had the highest level of considerateness.

The case of BR is apparently anomalous because absence rates were relatively high here and because, as shown in Chapter 4, there was more of an absence 'culture' than existed in the other organizations. This culture was not directly pro-absence in the sense of encouraging workers to take time off. But there was a strong sense of work group solidarity which meant that a worker taking time off would feel free to talk about this. Moreover, levels of trust in management were low. Why, then, were workers so 'moral' about the duty to work, and why did this morality not lead to low rates of absenteeism?

The answer to the first question probably lies in the nature of workers' attachment to their jobs. They were committed to the idea of railway work, and found the actual job itself rewarding. What they disliked were the disciplinary regime and what they saw as a concerted managerial attack on long-cherished working practices. The norm of doing one's 'turn of duty', itself a phrase full of meaning, has been long-established among railwaymen. As argued in Chapter 4, the point about this general commitment to attend is that it did not necessarily translate into high levels of attendance because of other pressures on workers. Absence rates were no more than moderately high, and reflected such things as the extremely varied and constantly changing shift patterns worked and the high levels of overtime which have been long-established: absence could often reflect literal tiredness. The replies to the vignettes captured something of workers' general thinking, but their behaviour was shaped by other forces too.

As Table 2.2 shows, BR workers did not adopt a particularly moralistic stance about attendance. They were in fact the most likely to argue that if the single parent Janet Roberts reported sick this would not be very serious. And in the case of Sally Harris they were more likely than average to suggest that her best course, if she had decided to stay away, was simply to say that she had been ill. Both tendencies plainly reflect the workplace culture in BR, with the strong belief that managers were unreliable inclining workers to believe that the best course was not to trust them.

There were also differences between occupational groups. In BR, we studied four groups: train drivers, guards, station staff, and carriage cleaners. Of the 15 guards who replied to all the vignettes 8 took an anti-absence line on all three. Excluding the guards would give a score for CONSID for the other three groups of BR employees similar to the overall mean. Looking at each vignette separately showed that it was the second on which there were the greatest differences: all but one of the guards gave a pro-attendance reply, compared with only 24 per cent of other occupational groups. The guards' replies may have been connected with their ethnic origins. Ten of the 17 guard interviewed were Asians, and throughout the questionnaire this group gave quite distinctive replies. The tone of the interviews with many of the guards was one of the responsibility of the individual, combined with little sense of collective worker solidarity which contrasted strongly with the attitudes of train drivers. For example, all the Asians chose the pro-attendance option on the general question offering the choice between 'duty to attend' and 'it's a free society'. And 62 per cent, as against under one-third of other BR workers, said that they themselves had never felt like taking a day off work. Looking at the vignettes by ethnic origin showed statistically significant differences on the first two, with the Asians giving the most pro-attendance replies, but not on the third.

The particular group of Asians working as BR guards thus seemed to have distinctive attitudes to attendance. Turning to the other extreme, the hospital sample was most sympathetic to absence. The reasons are not hard to find. As shown in Chapter 5, hospital workers gave great weight to the pressures of work and not surprisingly found it easy to sympathize with a person experiencing strain. The particularly pro-absence replies on the first vignette may have reflected the nature of work in the health service, with workers being very conscious of the risks of carrying infection and thus justifying taking an extra day or two off.

This factor may also have been at work in Multiplex. Several workers here argued that they were handling food and that it was important to ensure that they were not carrying infections. The factory had several regulations covering attendance after certain illnesses, so that these arguments had some basis in fact. Multiplex workers were also, however, particularly likely to sympathize with the single parent. With the lack of any detailed follow-up question, it is hard to offer concrete reasons for this. As shown below, potential explanatory factors such as the sex distribution of the sample in fact played little role. It may have been that Multiplex workers were particularly sensitive to the problems of childcare, but the reasons for this would need further study.

Finally, the FinCo figures are notable for their similarity to those from the other samples. As we found with other measures of attitudes, these white-collar workers were no more likely than manual employees to adopt a managerialist view of attendance. On the strain question, they were actually the most pro-absence group, and several of them underlined the stress that Sally Harris would be feeling. As we will see in Chapter 6, FinCo workers were well aware of the pressures of their own work.

It is, then, possible to relate replies to the vignettes to the wider climate of opinion in an organization. What really stands out, however, is the similarity of replies. These replies were, moreover, often independent of other indices of attitude and behaviour. The BR guards, for example, did not have particularly low rates of absence despite their general opinions. It is to this issue of association with the vignettes that we now turn.

Correlates of Considerateness

Vignettes and Other Attitudes

As shown in previous chapters, the climates and understandings of our four organizations differed widely, and it would plainly be desirable to control for organization in assessing correlates of considerateness. The difficulty is that the pattern of replies on several explanatory variables was highly skewed. Very few workers, for example, said that they themselves had extended a spell of absence beyond the time necessary to regain physical fitness. For some formal tests of significance we are forced to rely on results for the whole sample. We report illustrative results in Table 2.4. The first column lists the vignette under consideration, and the second the variable with which it was correlated. The third column summarizes the pattern of association across the whole sample and the final column shows, where numbers permitted, how far this association held within each organization.

TABLE 2.4   Associations between Considerateness Measures and Demographic Criteria and Attitudes

Dependent	Independent	Association	Control by Org.
EXTEND, SINGLE, STRAIN, CONSID	SEX	None	No assoc.
EXTEND	EXTRA – ABS	None	No assoc.
SINGLE	DOMESTIC	None	No assoc.
STRAIN	OWNSTRAIN	None	No assoc.
CONSID	REGATT	Sig. at 0.01	Sig. in M and B
EXTEND	REGATT	Sig. at 0.01	Sig. in B
CONSID	VOLABS	Sig. at 0.05	Sig. in B
EXTEND	ABSNORM	Sig. at 0.001	Sig. in M
SINGLE	ABSNORM	None	–
CONSID	ABSNORM	Sig. at 0.001	Sig. in M
EXTEND, CONSID	MGTPRESS	None	–
EXTEND, CONSID	STRICTER	None	–

Note: M and B refer to Multiplex and BR '–' means no control was made.

Most notably, demographic variables had very little effect. On the second and third vignettes, women might be expected to display more considerate views, but there was no tendency in this direction. It might be argued that it is specifically married women who are most likely to be considerate in the case of the single parent, but this did not prove to be the case. Other variables, such as length of service with the organization, similarly failed to show any link with considerateness.

Neither were there any strong links with reports of one's own behaviour. There was a small, but non-significant, tendency for replies on EXTEND to be related to those on EXTRA-ABS, which summarizes replies on whether a worker had extended a spell of absence longer than was necessary to regain physical fitness. But there was no association at all on the other two possible links, namely, between SINGLE and seeing domestic needs as a reason for one's own absence and between STRAIN and the variable OWNSTRAIN indicating whether a worker cited boredom or strain as a reason for thinking about taking time off work. Slightly clearer connections appeared with wider opinions about absence. Before asking about reasons for not wanting to attend, we asked how often a worker had consciously thought about not going in to work. Some denied that they had ever thought of doing so. Contrasting them with the remainder on the variable REGATT produced a significant association with the vignettes, with those who had never thought of taking time off being the less considerate. The effect was consistently present, however, in only one organization, namely BR. The same was true of the link with workers' reported 'voluntary absence', as measured by VOLABS, where the overall association reflected the situation in BR, with there being no clear association in the other three organizations.

A wider feature of attitudes to absence is the climate of the work group. As noted in Chapter 1, some studies have begun to consider group cohesiveness as an influence on behaviour and perhaps also on attitudes. We will see in later chapters that strong work group norms were rare, but we thought it worthwhile to explore whether considerateness was related to work group support for the idea of going absent. We took the question as to whether workers discussed with others 'the idea of taking the odd day off work'. For the statistical analysis, this was dichotomized in ABSNORM, indicating whether or not any discussion took place. There was some tendency for discussion of absence to be linked to considerateness: two-thirds of those saying that they sometimes talked with work mates about taking time off were considerate on EXTEND, as against half of those who never did so. But it was only within Multiplex that this association held. The same was true for CONSID, but there was no link with SINGLE. Given the lack of strong cultural norms, this association does not support a causal link from cultures to considerateness. It suggests, rather, a more diffuse situation wherein individuals who feel comfortable talking about going absent are also the most considerate of others' absence but clear-cut norms are lacking.

Finally, considerateness could be connected with managerial policy, with strict attendance control perhaps making people see taking time off as legitimate. Additionally, the general state of worker-management relations might be expected to have an effect. Neither expectation was met. Table 2.4 reports two sets of result. MGTPRESS indicates whether workers perceived any general pressure from management over attendance, while STRICTER indicates a belief that in recent years the control policy had become tighter. Neither variable was associated with measures of considerateness. In addition, we examined links with measures of general satisfaction such as the perceived amount of trust between workers and management. Again, no significant associations were evident.

In view of these largely negative results, more complex multivariate techniques would not be warranted. We did conduct a few experiments with loglinear analysis to check, for example, whether the link between REGATT and EXTEND was dependent on organization, but the associations were so weak that a clear answer could not be offered. The formal test is whether a 'saturated' model of a three-way interaction between the variables is significantly better than a model of only two-way relationships. But the two-way model fitted so poorly that the interaction model had so little to compete against that nothing could properly be inferred. The chief conclusion is that considerateness was not related to other attitudinal measures.

Considerateness and Absence Behaviour

But what of behaviour: were the considerate most likely to go absent themselves? The most telling test is with the number of short (one or two days each) spells of absence, SHORTABS. The total number of days absent, for example, will be heavily influenced by long spells of 'genuine' sickness and would not be expected to correlate with views the legitimacy of taking off short amounts of time. But SHORTABS is widely seen in the literature as the most appropriate index of 'voluntary' absences. The sample can be divided into three roughly equal groups: those with no short absences in the course of a year, those with one or two, and those with three or more. The results are shown in Table 2.5.

TABLE 2.5　Considerateness by Frequency of Short Spells of Absence

| | *Multiplex* | | | *BR* | | | *Hosp.* | | | *FinCo* | | | *All* | |
	0	1/2	3+	0	1/2	3+	0	1/2	3+	0	1/2	3+	0	1/2
EXTEND (Per Cent):														
Yes	71	61	57	20	60	64	50	67	86	29	57	54	51	61
No	29	39	43	80	40	36	50	33	14	71	44	46	49	39
SINGLE (Per Cent):														
Yes	52	57	100	71	60	42	50	59	21	50	33	38	54	50
No	48	43	0	29	40	58	50	41	79	50	67	63	46	50
STRAIN (Per Cent):														
Yes	37	30	57	40	33	15	25	47	36	50	67	36	39	47
No	63	70	43	60	67	85	75	53	64	50	33	63	61	53

Note: Short spells of absence are those lasting 1 or 2 days. They are categorized into 3 groups: no such spell during a year; 1 o
spells; and 3 or more spells.

There was no tendency for the high-absence groups to be the most considerate. Indeed, in some cases the level of considerateness declined as the absence rate rose, as for example across the whole sample, and in the BR, hospital, and FinCo sub-samples, on the single parent question. A similar pattern was observed with the measure of total absence frequency, FREQABS.

This lack of association might be written off as the result of the failure of the vignettes to tap attitudes. Yet absence researchers would need to be careful of advancing such an argument. The correlates of absence rates have received enormous attention, yet it is only recently that multi-variate models have been deployed. And the results have been disappointing. Thus Price and Mueller (1986), despite employing an impressive battery of measures, were able to explain only a tiny proportion of the variance of absence rates in a sample of hospital employees. The lack of association between the vignettes and absence rates does not show that the vignettes are bad measures. It suggests that workers' broad views on the legitimacy of absence did not depend on their own behaviour.

Non-work Pressures on Attendance

We have so far considered general views on the legitimacy of absence, the implication being that workers' broad moral judgements do not directly shape their own behaviour and hence that relations within the workplace require attention. But it may be that other extra-workplace influences are more important than workplace ones. It is convenient to consider this point here, for it is a general one relating to all the samples. It also helps us to introduce some overall themes about absence.

We began by asking workers about their own behaviour by raising the general issue of how often they thought about staying away from work. We asked, 'how often would you say that you *consciously* thought about not going to work when there was nothing actually preventing you from working, for example you were not ill?' They were offered options of daily, weekly, occasionally, or never. Replies are shown in Table A.1 in Appendix A; this Appendix contains all the comparative tables which will be referred to in the course of the following four chapters.

One might expect all workers to say that they thought about going absent at least sometimes. In fact, as Table A.1 shows, almost a quarter claimed never to do so. Moreover, very few workers thought about doing so more than occasionally. Those who had ever thought of going absent were then asked what reasons prompted this. As Table A.2 shows, family and domestic duties were at least as important as frustrations with the job itself, each being mentioned by about 40 per cent of the entire sample. In addition, about 20 per cent cited the positive aspects of non-work matters, that is time with the family and leisure interests, as distinct from non-work duties. It is clear, then, that going absent was not a purely work-related phenomenon.

It was not, however, driven by direct pressures from outside the workplace. We asked whether family and friends were important in workers' thinking about taking time off. As Table A.3 shows, three-quarters said that they were of no importance at all, and only 1 per cent felt that they were very important. As several workers put it, they decided what they wanted to do, and they were not led by the pressures of others.

Two conclusions follow. First, extra-workplace influences were important in leading workers to think about going absent, but these were mediated through workers' own judgements. It was not the case that there were direct pressures from outside shaping how workers behaved. Second, therefore, just how workers made sense of pressures from outside, and also inside, the workplace is likely to have depended on their views about the encouragements and discouragements of going absent. For example, they will have had to decide how far they could afford to attend to domestic needs, when these needs were set against loss of earnings, fear of being punished, a sense of duty to the firm, and so on. This therefore turns attention again to the regime of absence control, for this regime will help shape the balance of costs and benefits. The nature of the calculus involved is considered in the following section.

Discussion and Conclusion

We saw the vignettes as a means to explore aspects of workers' thinking which were not accessible by other means. The fact that replies did not correlate strongly with other attitudes or with demographic characteristics suggests that distinctive attitudes were, indeed, uncovered. As noted above, other uses of the vignette technique have found that replies do not correlate with respondents' background characteristics, which suggests that our results are not idiosyncratic. The general conclusion is that vignettes at least begin to address people's broad frames of reference in thinking about moral dilemmas. In the present case, there was considerable sympathy for workers who feel the need to take time off, or at least there was understanding of the reasons for such action even if workers were not actively sympathetic.

The vignette technique remains unusual, though it has a considerable ancestry. It was, for example, used to good effect by Jones (1941) in his study of workers' attitude to property rights and industrial militancy. It may be useful to set down a few conclusions about the method. First, like Finch, we incline against the deployment of a large number of vignettes each requiring a closed-ended response: such a use is not very different from any other kind of attitude scale. Vignettes need to be used to explore how people think. Our own were too few to do this fully, and the second one in particular would have benefited from more careful follow-up questioning, but we hope that they have at least been indicative. Second, it might help to contextualize the vignettes by spelling out in more detail the sort of firm for which a worker worked. For example, some workers offered the view that the justifiability of absence depends on how reasonable and understanding managers are; this could be examined more thoroughly. Third, the results bear out Finch's warning that replies should not be used as surrogates for measures of people's own behaviour: answers to the vignettes were largely independent of workers' other views and also of their own absence records.

This points to the main lesson. There seem to be aspects of absenteeism which are not captured by direct questions about workers' own behaviour. Workers appear to be surprisingly tolerant of absence and to recognize the personal and domestic pressures which may require others to take time off work. They would plainly put limits on the reasonableness of absence, as in the case of the first vignette when workers justified a couple of days' absence because the worker had a good record. But they are aware of the many demands on fellow workers' time other than the needs of work, and they widely recognize the reasonableness of placing these demands high on the list of priorities.

This theme may be pursued by reference to some of our other questions. Having explored features of workers' specific views, we asked a general question as to why 'most people attend work as regularly as they do'. We did not expect very coherent or detailed replies. Indeed, one reason for asking it was to assess the salience of absence: the more vague and general the replies are, the more it appears that absence is not a major issue for most workers. And many of the answers were empty of substance. Others focused on general reasons to work such as job satisfaction and the need to earn a living, and did not therefore specifically address the issue of why workers attended regularly, as distinct from having a job at all. Most replies that considered regularity were variants on the theme of habit: some workers said that they had been brought up to attend regularly, while others noted that turning up for work was just a routine that they came to take for granted. As one Multiplex worker put it, going to work was just an 'everyday thing'. Other workers spoke of 'self-respect' or a duty to themselves.

This suggests a picture of the ways in which workers thought about absence. Chadwick-Jones (1978) has usefully spoken of absence being governed by an implicit contract between employer and employee. The employer, through formal rules and informal expectations, establishes many of the important terms of the contract. Our findings in this chapter relate to the ways in which workers perceive the contract. They do not seem to make sharp distinctions between legitimate and illegitimate absence: some types of absence would be acceptable depending on the circumstances. But plainly there is some kind of boundary between the two cases. We have found that among all our samples the boundary was not where managers might have liked, with a range of types of absence receiving endorsement. Workers are indeed engaged in an implicit bargain with employers. One key point is that the features of the bargain pertaining to needs for absence are defined widely. A second is that the bargain is very implicit. As in their replies as to why workers attend regularly, few workers thought explicitly in terms of a trade-off between the employer's needs and their own non-work commitments. Going to work was simply a habit, and a range of contingencies might arise which required the habit to be broken. Any calculus of the costs and benefits of absence was inexact and implicit.

Workers appeared, then, to be remarkably tolerant of the personal and domestic pressures which might require others to take time off work. Yet this did not affect their own behaviour, which was not associated with their general opinions. Two conclusions therefore emerge. First, workers' overall views on the legitimacy of absence are unlikely to be of direct importance to management: managers are concerned with what workers do, and only with how they think to the extent that it affects behaviour. It is thus unlikely that workers' general views will promote or support antagonism to, say, absence control programmes. Second, and by the same token, it may be hard for managements to draw on general morality when they are looking to control absence. As noted in Chapter 1, it is very common at present for companies to talk about self-discipline and responsibility to the group, and it is a short step from this to claims that a sense of moral obligation can reduce absence. It may be that some specific loyalties can be generated, but it would be a mistake to assume that these rest on a basic belief that absence is wrong. Workers in our sample accepted that there were times when absence was justifiable, and they saw absence not as a failure of duty to the employer but as a reflection of a balancing of different obligations, with responsibilities to one's family and to oneself being at least as important as duty to the firm. Workers' views on the legitimacy of absence neither help nor hinder managerial action in the workplace. This points to the need to consider such action, which we do in the following chapters.

3

Multiplex: From Paternalism to Managerialism

Multiplex was a large and long-established company, manufacturing food, pharmaceuticals, and other 'drug store' products. In many ways it can be seen as a mainstream British enterprise, in neither a declining sector, nor at the forefront in technology or product development. It produced largely for the final consumer market, and had a well established reputation and brand image. Nevertheless, competition in the sector had been increasing and diversifying, and these factors exerted a steady pressure on company structure and performance. For all these reasons the company seemed to provide a promising starting point in characterizing the changing face of shop floor control as it might affect the large majority of manufacturing employees.

The site of our research complemented these characteristics of the company. We studied one factory on a large manufacturing site, and a warehouse located nearby, in an area with slightly below average unemployment and a history of union organization, but not union militancy. In the factory direct production was the preserve of about 60 men, while some 170 women and a few men worked on the packing lines. There were also stores and despatch departments, but these did not form part of our study. The warehouse employed about 200 manual workers and, unlike the factory, was located near a city centre. In any organization of such size the typicality of the specific research sites must arise. Managers saw the factory as broadly typical of the company's operations, while the warehouse was felt to have working relationships which were perhaps better than most without being special or unusual. We certainly did not have the chance to investigate what the company saw as its problem cases, but our sites were not seen as exceptionally good. An examination of aggregate absence statistics for the whole of the company suggests that our sites were broadly representative. Our questionnaire also revealed no significant differences between workers on the two sites, despite considerable differences of work organization. Neither seemed to be distinctive.

The warehouse was an old, rambling building, using mostly old technology whereby orders were picked by hand. This hand picking system meant that workers had to move around to make up orders, which gave them a degree of freedom. The wide range of products, departments, storage areas, and final destinations gave rise to workgroups of varying sizes, and a relatively high ratio of supervisors to warehouse staff. Previously subject to large seasonal fluctuations, the workload in the warehouse had been increased and stabilized by the introduction of new product lines. Nevertheless, the nature of warehouse work evidently provided more scope for informality in the management of attendance than that associated with production line discipline, and this was reinforced in part by the site's city location. At both sites the use of holidays to cover domestic emergencies was encouraged, although it was a general rule that such absences should be limited to a minimum of half a shift. In the warehouse, however, it was not uncommon to allow even a couple of hours' absence to be booked against holiday entitlements. In addition short periods of absence at the start or conclusion of shifts, or at lunch breaks, could be negotiated with supervisors.

By contrast the factory site was dominated more by the needs of production flows. Work was organized into four departments based on different product groups, and workers were not usually transferred between lines. Unlike the warehouse, workers generally worked at fixed stations on packing lines; they had little freedom to move around, and work was routine and monotonous. The main exception comprised the men who ran the machines which made up the basic ingredients; they had the relative freedom of the machine minder. Each department had a manager and deputy, a male foreman, and one or more female supervisors, none of whom worked directly on the lines. On the packing lines there were also 'team leaders' who had primary responsibility for maintaining the flow of work, but who had no formal supervisory powers. As in the warehouse all workers received a standard weekly wage according to grade, with no incentives apart from an annual profit-related bonus. Work standards for different product lines did exist, but were not used in any formal way to control effort. Partly because of the exigencies of production work, and partly as a response to the distance of the site from residential areas, work was organized on a four-and-a-half-day basis, and workers were encouraged to use Friday afternoons as far as possible to cover domestic and medical absences.

At both sites work was largely semi-skilled and routine, with little internal differentiation among the work force. Until the recent past the company had also changed little. The result had been a secure and somewhat cosy shopfloor atmosphere. Steady, though far from dramatic, change was altering this picture. Absence was a growing issue, even though its actual extent was relatively modest. We therefore begin by considering broad changes in management style and growing commercial pressures before drawing out the implications for the management of attendance in particular. We then analyse the effects on shopfloor practice. But there were also some related changes in the conduct of relations within the workplace. These are considered in the third part of the chapter.

Management Styles and the Control of Labour

Management Style

Management style is a slippery concept. Purcell and Sisson (1983) developed a typology of management styles, building on Fox's distinction between 'Unitarists' and 'Pluralists', and his subsequent elaboration of this model to take account of overlaps and differentiations between the industrial relations approaches of companies. A long-standing problem with ideal-typical analyses is that the ideal is a lot easier to define than the typical. Multiplex is a case in point since its management of industrial relations involves elements from different categories of management styles. Nevertheless, it is useful to explore these elements, as a way both to characterize the company and to explore how changing circumstances were affecting management approaches to the control of labour.

Fox (1974:302) characterizes as 'sophisticated moderns' managements which

> legitimize ... the union role in certain areas of joint decision making because it sees this role as conducive to its own interests as measured by stability, promotion of consent, bureaucratic regulation, effective communication, or the handling of change.

In many ways this description fits Multiplex quite well. The company was active in the 1970s in adapting to union organization, and integrating the unions into its long standing Staff Councils. However, the company fits less well with two other aspects of the style noted by Purcell and Sisson (1983:115-6), which involve either a tightly limited, 'constitutionalist', framework of agreements, or an extensive consultative framework, with a high degree of uniformity in managerial approach and outlook throughout the organization.

In the first place, management at Multiplex, despite its recognition of trade unions, retained many features of paternalism in its relations with its workers, along with many of the unitarist assumptions that so often accompany this style. This was evident not only in the extensive (though essentially modest) provision of on-site facilities for staff, but also in the active steps the company took to encourage identification with company goals. These extended from team briefings and other communications exercises for all workers to the provision for younger workers of places on a sort of company 'outward bound' course aimed at identifying potential team leaders and future supervisory staff. Managers often emphasized this paternalist tradition as being an essential part of the company's relations with its employees, and some feared that commercial pressures could loosen these ties. It had been the norm for workers to stay with the firm for many years, and often for members of the same family to work there. In our sample, as Table A.12 shows, 65 per cent of employees had been with the firm at least five years. The table also highlights 'traditional' reasons for staying with the firm: though 'money' was the most popular reason, 'security' and 'good work mates' also featured quite highly. A recent redundancy had, however, begun to challenge this tradition. Managers spoke of a gradual shift away from a cosy atmosphere of moderate wages and an undemanding regime to a more demanding approach. The change was still limited, and widespread effects on workers' attitudes would be unlikely. None the less, 39 per cent of the sample had thought of leaving, mainly because of the monotony of the work (Table A.9). We cannot say whether this was a higher proportion than would have been found in the past, and too direct a link with changing managerial policy should not be made. But it indicates that paternalism was not all-embracing and may be a straw in the wind as to trends.

Secondly, this element of paternalism had an obvious effect on the nature of the consultative process within the company. Team briefings especially, but other communications also, were designed to emphasize and reinforce the individual relationship between managers and workers. The Staff Councils, on the other hand, were viewed with some suspicion by union representatives, primarily because they lacked any decision making function, and because they were not seen as a proper forum for the collective representation of workers' interests. Collective representation thus lacked the framework of comprehensive rules and agreements which is assumed in models of industrial relations style. Moreover, in the past it had been limited by paternalist traditions and was now being , by the partial use of consultative methods, associated with 'human resource management'.

This leads to a deeper problem in analysing management style. Typologies of styles were developed to categorize approaches to the control of labour as a collectivity. In the case of Multiplex, however, we were more concerned with the management of the individual employment relationship, especially in respect of attendance and discipline. This disjunction between collective style and the management of individuals cannot be overcome simply by concentrating on managers' own perceptions of what the individual employment relationship entails. This is not simply because this relationship only exists within certain collectively negotiated constraints, important though this is, but also because of divergent perceptions and practices between different levels of management itself. These differences mean that a dominant management style identified at corporate level may metamorphose as observation moves down the management hierarchy, and this certainly seemed to be the case at Multiplex.

These divergences in management practice are, to some extent, unsurprising, not least because workers are not simply the objects of management policy, but actors in their own right. There are also differences of technical and organizational settings and related problems of organizational consistency. More interestingly, however, they may provide a clue to the linkages between the management of collective labour relations and the individual labourer in which an element of pluralism in the former may not contradict, but rather complement, more overtly unitarist practice in the latter. This problem also underlies more general arguments over the implications of HRM. Both Legge and Guest (Storey, 1989) have argued in different ways that the development of HRM involves an essentially unitarist approach to labour at odds with the pluralistic assumptions of British industrial relations. While Multiplex is not a company in the forefront of extensive HRM innovation, its particular mix of management styles had elements in common with more fashionable initiatives. It was, in short, one of the large number of British firms which had neither developed the characteristic features of shopfloor relationships of the car industry of the 1970s, nor made a massive shift in its whole labour strategy. It was thus illustrative of developments in the mainstream of large firms at the end of the 1980s.

Who's Afraid of Absence?

In the next section we deal with management systems for the control of absence. However, how and why absence was seen as a problem by managers at different levels in the organization can help put the question of management style in better perspective. All managers saw absence as a problem, and they shared many perceptions of why this was the case, most especially in terms of costs, but there were differing assessments of the nature and scale of the problem, as well as of causes and cures. In these differences lay sources both of competing policies and practices.

It was generally felt that more attention was being given to absence policy, and the central personnel departments were in the course of reassessing the usefulness of their absence data-base. Nevertheless there were differences in the main sources of pressure for this increased attention. It was clear that central personnel had long thought that absence could not be controlled satisfactorily without a strategic approach, and this view was held despite a common acceptance that absence levels were, in the main, modest. The factor that had encouraged a fresh look at the problem was the increased level of competition, especially in the manufacturing business, and the increased attention given to costs following an 'economy drive' which included the company's first redundancies.

From the viewpoint of the board of the industrial division the issue was one of numbers. The chair of the board estimated that an extra 3 per cent productivity was available by the control of an overall absence level of 7 or 8 per cent. These figures were viewed with widespread scepticism by both personnel and line managers. Quite simply, it was said, the statistics available could not justify such a calculation. In fact, a survey of its manufacturing sites subsequently conducted by the company showed only one group, namely, production workers at an 'absence blackspot' in Scotland, to have absence levels of this degree (at 9.76 per cent in 1984). Overall absence levels in 1984 varied from 7.8 per cent in Scotland to 5.6 percent at our case study plant, while in 1987 our own estimate for both production and warehouse staff in our case study areas was some 6 per cent.

Nevertheless, the impetus given to considerations of attendance control was considerable. From the board point of view it was a macro issue which required the elaboration of control mechanisms to involve line managers directly. For line managers (according to personnel, at any rate) it was a question of budget constraints. As one senior personnel manager put it, 'if the board is concerned to reduce absence levels, then we have an absenteeism problem'. This comment is revealing because it goes to the heart of how the question of attendance is seen by managers. Multiplex had long prided itself on being a good, almost paternalist, employer. This was beginning to change. 'Absenteeism', especially where relatively short periods of absence are concerned, is easily identified as a kind of deviant behaviour, and, as such, attracts solutions resting on the disciplinary process. However, the use of the term absenteeism can disguise the fact that what is at issue is in fact simply absence, which has a multiplicity of causes. As central personnel managers recognized, this meant that criteria for absence control could not, in the end, reconcile the tensions between 'caring' employment practices and coercion. Absence control, we were told, must adopt a blanket approach, without fine distinctions between persistent, justified absence, and absenteeism. The price of attacking relatively low absence levels, in other words, was to accept a new strain on the company's paternalist regime.

It would be wrong to imply from this that differences between management levels were clear cut, or indeed, that the increased attention being given to absence led to any dramatic changes in policy and practice. What was evident was a slow, incremental shift in attitudes and procedures. Nevertheless, at central personnel, new attention was being given to causes of absence, as well as recording and control measures. To do this the company monitored the causes of absence at its Scottish establishment, and studied the control practices of other firms in the locality.

The company began with a survey of 3 months' absence notes, paying special attention to short absences whose causes would not normally be addressed by the occupational health department. This revealed that over 58 per cent of absences were attributed to depression, nervous debility and back pains. A study of a longer period, from 1980 to 1984, showed that pregnancy was a major contributor to absence figures. Throughout this longer period diagnoses fell into three major categories: first, causing the majority of absences, were colds and 'flu; second, joint pains, urinary and kidney complaints, and pregnancy; third, nervous debility, depression and anxiety. The study concluded that the main villains were in fact climate and general health levels. With no obvious occupational links to absence the only concrete proposal arising from the study was to avoid hiring women of child-bearing age. This was rejected.

Of more interest here were the discussions which followed over the potential of enhanced control measures, sanctions and incentives. Pay incentives for good attendance, or other forms of reward promoted by management in parts of the manufacturing sites, were rejected on the grounds that the company should not 'pay people for doing their duty'. Similarly, 'docking' profit related bonuses, either for entire sites, or for individuals, was also rejected, partly on the grounds of difficulties in consistent application, and partly because the level of sanction would be disproportionate to the problem. More importantly, the most senior personnel managers feared that all such schemes were simply another way of relieving managers of the need to take hard decisions. Systems of control should therefore concentrate on providing line managers with suitable sanctions, and the role of senior managers should be to ensure that sanctions were used, and used consistently.

This point became clearest in respect of the sick pay scheme, and the uses of discipline. The existence of the sick pay scheme, and its 'generosity', were universally seen as a contributor to absence, combining opportunities for abuse with a more general incentive to choose absence over attendance. Some line managers claimed that a minority of workers would 'work the system', treating sickness entitlement as 'extra holidays', although in our interviews few workers in fact showed any clear idea of how the system worked. Senior personnel managers felt that line managers were unaware of the procedures for refusing to accept short term sick notes, or were simply unwilling to challenge them. At the same time, personnel felt that very few workers knew the system well enough consciously to manipulate it, although this was not the view of many line managers and supervisors. These differences in emphasis were again seen as reflecting line management's reluctance to 'grasp the nettle' of absence control, and a preference for blaming both deviant individuals and permissive rules and payment provisions.

These differences tended to cascade down the management structure. Site managers in both the distribution and manufacturing case studies regarded absence as a limited but important problem which was assuming a higher salience as staffing and financial pressures increased. In the warehouse the senior manager rejected the idea that the introduction of self-certification had led to a lowering of standards. He had also amended his previous view that casual absence was at the heart of attendance problems after a review of sickness records convinced him that the biggest problem was with relatively serious sicknesses of medium or longer term duration. While competitive pressures underlay his commitment to tight procedural controls on attendance, he thought it difficult to quarrel with workers' own reasons for sick absence. In the factory likewise the manager thought that line managers and supervisors exaggerated the effects of self-certification and the sick scheme, but still emphasized the importance of discipline in attendance control, citing availability to work, rather than the genuineness of sickness, as the deciding factor in control. Both felt that central personnel could view the question of control rather mechanically, but they also accepted the financial and competitive imperatives of close control.

Perhaps unsurprisingly, line managers and supervisors tended towards a more jaundiced view, in that the realities of control meant dealing with a complex of financial, production and personal pressures. Suspicion of 'lead swinging' and manipulation were widespread, as was a distinction between the 'sheep' and 'goats' on the shopfloor; or, as one manager put it, 'we all know who the toe-rags are'. At this level the coercive face of paternalism was much more apparent, and was complemented by a somewhat moralistic tone which closely reflected a unitarist perception of the control of labour and the maintenance of discipline. This framework of attitudes varied somewhat according to type of labour employed, as it was generally believed that the propensity to absence increased where work was at its most monotonous or least demanding in terms of responsibility or autonomy.

This was particularly so in our manufacturing case study, where distinctions were drawn between direct manufacture and the assembly and packing operations. In this case, however, such attitudes were held against the background of a marked sexual division of labour, direct manufacturing being a wholly male preserve, and seemed to be embedded in the general culture of the organization. In assembly and distribution the overwhelmingly female workforce (who also were on the lower pay grades) had an entirely male management, and the senior supervisors were also mostly male. In this factory rest rooms and toilet facilities were labelled respectively 'men' and 'girls'. As will be described later this division had a persistent, if low key, effect on the general operation of control and discipline which tended to reinforce the unitarist bias of paternalism on the shop floor. It could also lead on occasion to surprising insensitivities. The manager who knew his 'toe rags', was equally insistent that the majority did not abuse the system: after all, 'we're all entitled to a hysterectomy.'

Multiplex was in many ways a very traditional employer with highly stable labour relations, but one facing a fairly serious tightening of competitive pressures. Within this context the control of attendance had received increasing attention at all levels of management. Without making dramatic departures from established practice there was a general tightening of attendance control and associated labour discipline. The problem that the company faced was how to achieve this pattern of development without unduly disturbing its reputation as a 'good' employer, and the main focus adopted was to increase the responsibility placed on line management and supervision, under direction from personnel. In the next section we will describe both the formal control systems relating to attendance and the day to day practice, and how these were reflected in worker attitudes to attendance, effort, and management.

The Control of Attendance and the Management of Commitment

As we have seen, increased attention to attendance questions was largely fuelled by competitive pressures. It is useful, therefore, to consider control mechanisms alongside the broader issue of worker effort. At Multiplex, which had generally eschewed incentive payments schemes and detailed work measurement, the securing of effort levels was associated with attempts to secure worker commitment to company goals. While this did not extend very far, and did not involve much that was innovative, such as the introduction of autonomous work groups, it did include increased attempts at direct communication with the workforce. Thus attendance control is discussed here in the context of the management of labour as a whole.

Controlling Attendance at the Workplace

Attendance control is concerned with more than just sickness absence. It includes all aspects of securing labour at the point of production, including timekeeping and short medical and domestic absences. Multiplex had developed comprehensive procedures in all areas in which the primary concern was with outcomes that could accommodate flexibility with reasonable certainty of labour availability.

Clocking in for shop floor workers had been recently abolished at both our case study sites. This measure was widely welcomed by workers, and managers generally thought that the resultant reliance on trust in this respect had paid off well. The old system had not applied to staff, and, at the warehouse, we were told that workers of many years' service had resented a control which did not apply, say, to a newly employed sixteen-year-old in the offices. In accordance with management concern for outcomes there were no fixed penalty systems for lateness. Workers would normally be paid for a full shift even if a couple of hours late. The aim was to encourage the effort to attend, for example in bad weather, or even the results of oversleeping, rather than to encourage impromptu holidays or sick claims.

This policy did not imply any laxity in control however. In the factory supervision played a major role in enforcing presence on the line. Cloak-rooms were locked at the start of each shift, so that latecomers could not avoid advertising the fact. The day was also divided into half hour segments, and supervisors were expected to report any significant absence from work stations in these periods. In the production areas, with three-shift working and a variable work pattern, some leeway was granted to operatives. On the packing lines, where a full team was necessary to start operations, start and finish times were strictly enforced, a regime reinforced by the 'pruning' of work teams to a minimum. It was not unusual to see supervisors from various departments patrolling exits from the shopfloor at break times and the ends of shifts. While financial penalties were used on occasion, absence from a workstation, or poor timekeeping, were in the main closely tied to the disciplinary mechanism, and while supervision played a key role, action on discipline was very much the preserve of departmental managers.

The situation in the warehouse was more varied, and this seemed to reflect the more complex work organization and the diversity of workstations. As in the factory, supervisors were very active as the first line in control, but they were also more closely involved in initiating discipline, and were more likely to use pay docking as a penalty. At the same time the standards enforced were, according to supervisors' accounts, more variable between departments. Supervision on the loading dock complained that while they enforced finish times quite strictly their position was undermined by operatives from other departments 'filtering through early'. There was also diversity in the matter of breaks. No official tea break existed in the afternoons, but some managers and supervisors would allow staff to 'brew up on the job', and on the loading bay management would encourage brief breaks when work was slack. By contrast one supervisor had persuaded her manager to end this custom after timing breaks 'from brewing to getting back to work' and advised her staff to 'drink cold water', while another would simply pour away the hot water if she found a boiled kettle. Despite these differences supervisors clearly felt that they had satisfactory control, and that, in general, this was based to a large degree on workforce cooperation bolstered by their own vigilance and visible presence on the shop floor.

Formally, this pattern of structured control supplemented by flexibility also characterized the handling of minor absences for domestic reasons and medical appointments. Staff were encouraged as far as possible to make medical appointments in their own time, as well as to deal with domestic matters. In the factory, where the majority worked a four-and-a-half-day week, the expectation was for this time to be used. Medical appointments were not counted as absence, and were officially paid for the first two hours, after which staff would either use holiday entitlement, or take unpaid leave. Similarly, domestic emergencies would be covered by holiday entitlements or unpaid leave. The initial request for time off would go through supervision, but the final decision was for the departmental manager.

In practice a fair amount of informality entered into management behaviour. Less experienced managers tended to stick closely to the rules, but, as even central personnel recognized, others would adjust the regime. Some thought restrictions on paid leave for hospital appointments 'rather silly' given the realities of waiting times. Others would simply 'massage' the hours lost out of the system. For short span absences for personal reasons some supervisors would let someone go with 'a nod and a wink' if the period was about half an hour. The trade off between unpaid leave and holidays was also variable; in the warehouse supervisors would sometimes ignore the rule making a half shift the minimum holiday time 'even though wages don't like it.' By contrast another supervisor told us of stopping a quarter hour pay where a worker had insufficient holidays left to cover a four-and-three-quarter-hour absence.

Such practices raise the issue, discussed in Chapter 1, of the extent to which supervisors develop their own norms as to reasonable standards of behaviour: how is absence actually managed at the day-to-day level? Three points stand out. First, managers used their perceptions of workers' general qualities in deciding whether to grant some informal paid leave. Informality was dependent on the perception of supervisors and managers of the individual's record and commitment, and, as such, tended to emphasize judgments of personality based on loyalty to the needs of the department. We were frequently told that, where discretion was exercised, it was in favour of 'our good workers'. Second, the degree to which managers felt free to act in this way seemed to differ from the situation in our other organizations. It is hard to measure these things but we were told by supervisors in BR that it was hard to favour 'better' workers: if a worker asked for some time off, the question was whether the case was genuine, not what kind of worker was involved. Even in Multiplex, some supervisors took this view. The fact that others felt able to favour the 'better' workers indicates that there was no established custom in the area: supervisors made their own decisions. Third, however, these decisions occurred at the margins of the control system. As we will see, there was a strict system for monitoring recorded absence which supervisors were required to follow. They had a little discretion in handling issues on the border of 'absence', but it was relatively minor in scale.

One example of tight standards was procedure when workers became ill during the working day. Any decision to allow them to go home was left in the hands of the site nurse. In the factory there was a widespread belief that it was very difficult to get sent home, and that the issue was decided quite arbitrarily by whether or not the ill person had a temperature. There was no way in which we could check the truth of these claims, but it seemed significant that they held such wide currency on the shop floor. It seemed clear to us that, even with the informalities that undoubtedly existed in respect of timekeeping and brief absences, controls were generally very tight, and standards of attendance at the work station were high. The conviction among many that getting sent home was difficult may well have arisen from a pervasive awareness of this regime, even though it gave rise to relatively few disciplinary cases. It may be significant that the only explicit admission of a breach of this procedure was a site personnel officer who had been sent home sick by her manager in central personnel, without being referred to the site nurse.

Absence Control

The procedures for the control of sickness absence, which causes the majority of lost time, were far more closely defined than for other forms of attendance control, but even in this case there were notable variations between both sites and, to a lesser extent, departments. Given the growing concern with absence it is unsurprising that some senior managers felt that the company's past record on monitoring and control had been somewhat lax. At central personnel procedures for collecting data, and the usefulness of doing so in encouraging line managers to act, were viewed sceptically. It appeared that the introduction of SSP and self-certification had been seen as an opportunity to increase control measures, even thought the levels of abuse expected by many managers did not seem justified.

Sick pay was granted from the first day of absence on the condition that workers telephoned immediately. Failure to do so meant losing pay. Before self-certification, line managers had merely to record absence, and, although procedures existed for challenging reasons for absence, and imposing penalties, personnel felt that they were largely reluctant to use them. Self certification provided an opportunity to tighten these controls. Managers were expected to insist on more detailed reasons for absence than simply 'felt unwell', and, while being expected to show concern for workers' welfare, were also expected to question workers about recurrent claims of ill health. This was done through the institution of return-to-work interviews for all absentees, a procedure considered in more detail below.

In the case of longer absences, workers were expected to report after six weeks with an indication of a return date, and could be visited by the welfare department, and invited to discuss their case with the company doctor. Refusal could lead the company to ask permission to speak to the GP, and if this was refused in turn disciplinary procedures could be started on return to work. There had been cases where the company doctor's assessment differed from a worker's GP, and this had sometimes caused difficulties for personnel. In principle they reserved the right to implement disciplinary action in such cases, and doubted that GPs pay much attention to how much time they are willing to 'sign off'.

Long term absences over six months were covered by a procedure going back over thirty years. Such cases were placed on a special register and put in the hands of the welfare department. While long term absentees did not receive payment, and were taken off departmental strength, they were encouraged to maintain links with the company, and not to resign. The limit for the long-absence register was three years, after which early retirement on a pension or dismissal would follow. This policy, a part of the company's 'caring image', was coming under stress as competitive and cost pressures increased. In the early post-war years long term absentees could be accommodated with light jobs, but this was becoming virtually impossible, and created some problems with the DSS whose criterion for fitness was seen by one manager as 'sitting in a car park'. Even where a full recovery took place the company could not guarantee workers' jobs back, and disappointed expectations were felt to be injuring the company's reputation. However, proposals from welfare and personnel to limit the long-absence register to one year, in line with ACAS recommendations and local industrial practice, were rejected.

The role of welfare departments in absence control can be ambiguous. Welfare visits can be seen as 'snooping', for example. At Multiplex welfare took pains to emphasize its impartiality and role as a 'listening' department. Nevertheless, they did not see themselves as 'dumb welfare', or as a shield against discipline. They were willing to speak to people informally about the dangers of 'swinging the lead', and had, on at least one occasion, pressured management to discipline a member of staff 'with an appalling record' where they thought management had let the case drift. One supervisor in the warehouse had to reassure a worker that her friend was not being harassed after a visit from the department. The department had also been given a new role in monitoring short absences following a lost industrial tribunal case where there had been no welfare involvement in a continuous string of related short sicknesses. In short, the department could act as another source of pressure on line managers to monitor and act on absence.

Monitoring and control methods in Multiplex conform to widespread managerial usage, but they do not, in themselves, tell much about the shop floor order they promote. As with all control systems a real assessment can only be made in detail; that is, in the practice of management and the day to day experience of the system. What matters here are the kinds of behaviour likely to attract sanctions, and how they are defined.

Multiplex had no formula for triggering discipline in absence cases; each case was to be assessed on its merits, and different patterns of absence, frequent short spells or longer absences, were thought to require different approaches. Nevertheless, it soon became clear that line managers and supervisors often did operate unofficial guide-lines when considering absence. As in many of our studies the starting point would be a perceived 'pattern' of absence, although the definition and consistency of patterns was problematical. Discipline rarely progressed beyond a first written warning, and many managers and supervisors claimed that verbal warnings would usually 'do the trick'. Higher management in the warehouse relied on training and enforcement of procedures to ensure inter-departmental consistency, but denied that there was anything like a 'tariff system' for warnings. Yet interviews with supervisors threw up a consistent picture of thresholds. Commonly, three absences in one year would earn 'a word' of an informal nature, and the fourth absence would bring an official warning.

Even within this pattern however, there were two main variations which indicated both a 'negotiated' order and developing pressures for a stricter regime. Firstly, while the first stage of absence discipline remained in the hands of the supervisors in the warehouse, actual practice was more complex. Some supervisors were happy to initiate both non-procedural and procedural unwritten warnings in consultation with line managers. Others, however, clearly had matters taken out of their hands. In some cases supervisors and managers would review absence figures and the manager decide on warnings, although, as one supervisor told us 'its our job to deliver them'. In either case the decision on the use of warnings would be heavily influenced by perceptions of 'genuineness'. In one sense of course this squares with a readiness to take each case on its merits. In one instance, for example, a woman who accumulated more absences after a first warning was excused on the grounds of pregnancy, because 'she needs the time off'. In another case, however, we asked supervision how a man had escaped warning when he clearly had a record as bad or worse than others who had been warned. In this case we were told it was surprising he should stand out, and that his absences 'absolutely had to be genuine... he'd have to be desperate to take time off'. In this case there was clearly a trade between perceptions of commitment and absence.

The second variant, increased pressure for attendance controls based on the needs of the job, tended to cut across 'negotiated' interpretations of the rules, written and unwritten. While many supervisors felt it improper to question 'genuine' and certified absence, many would put the emphasis simply on the attendance record. Even where flexibility did exist, as with the pregnant woman, the final decision would be made on simple attendance grounds 'if things got unreasonable'. But what is unreasonable? For one supervisor the issue was quite simple:

> Some people say they have a doctor's note. That's not the point. We are not saying we don't believe them, but the firm is asking are they fit for work? If they continue to be ill, the company can't employ them... I ask them to put themselves in management's position.

This strict interpretation of the purposes of control was not universal, but was widespread. Others tried to temper the demands of policy by 'not making the warning too harsh', although this could confuse the issue; was the worker in danger of further action, or not? In one case a man threatened with dismissal was let off when the union showed that he hadn't realized he had been given three initial warnings, so gently had it been done.

These variations show a control system in flux, but not yet one undergoing a perceptible revolution. The general ethos of the company, grounded in paternalistic values, often was acted out by line managers and supervisors in ways which shaded into more explicitly unitarist forms. Indeed, it could hardly be otherwise, as the natural limit to concern for individual circumstance is not the mutual interest of company and employee, but profitability, and 'welfareism' at work is primarily an aspect of the subordination of labour. Both these aspects of attendance control were becoming more explicit in a harsher commercial environment, and can be viewed most clearly through the operation of the only substantial procedural innovation, the return to work interview.

Under this system any absence would lead to an interview, irrespective of the cause of absence, or a worker's previous record. The formal purpose of the interview was not disciplinary, although it would be part of the procedure where appropriate, but to reinforce the idea that regular attendance was both required and appreciated. According to the collective agreement with the union, supervisors are responsible for issuing initial verbal warnings. Under these revised procedures this first step effectively lay with line managers, since it was they who conducted the interviews. This was certainly the case in the factory where supervision played virtually no part in sick absence control. In the warehouse matters were less clearly defined. Approaches to the return to work interview seemed less consistent, and these might be conducted by supervisors, who also retained their role as the first stage in the disciplinary procedure.

These changes in agreed procedures did not seem to raise any problems with the union. Indeed, one line manager in the warehouse reported pressure from stewards for managers to supersede supervisors in regulating absence on the grounds that this would produce more consistent standards of treatment. The leading steward, on the other hand, claimed that the system was never really negotiated, but that it had developed from a union idea to encourage assistance to individuals in order to lessen reliance on disciplinary action. Central personnel claimed the change was personnel driven, but after suggestions from management in the warehouse and the pharmaceutical division. This surprising lack of clarity on the origins of the initiative was complemented by differing perceptions of the uses of the interview.

Workers' attitudes to attendance control and discipline are considered below. Here it is worth mentioning that many workers spontaneously expressed the view that they were under substantial pressure to attend, and that they had done so when feeling ill. We extended this question of attendance while unwell to 58 workers, of whom 38 per cent mentioned these pressures which they attributed in large part to nervousness over the return to work interview. Even workers of long service, and with good attendance records, found the prospect daunting. In one sense this could have been simply the result of the interview's relative formality. In the factory in particular it took place in the departmental manager's office, a place seldom entered by shop floor workers except in the event of discipline. Indeed being 'took in the office' is a widespread industrial euphemism for discipline. More importantly it seemed a more specific response to either the experience of such an interview, or a general shopfloor understanding of its nature.

As a result we returned to line and personnel management to test their views. Some managers expressed surprise that it had emerged as an issue, and denied that the interview was stressful, or meant to be in any way coercive in the majority of instances. Others felt that complaints would only have been registered by individuals who had good cause to be concerned over their attendance records, although this contradicted our findings. Others, especially at central personnel, expressed satisfaction. On being told of our findings on the interviews one responded that this was just 'tough', and said '... we hope people do find it stressful - and challenging. It has to have a warm side, but it should have a sting in the tail too.'

How far then did changes in the attendance regime at Multiplex involve a tightening of the screws? Opinions amongst managers were mixed. Some perceived renewed interest in controls arising from possible abuses of self-certification and the sick pay scheme. Others saw only an incremental formalization of existing practice. In either event two developments were widely acknowledged; firstly that competitive pressures made systematic controls more necessary, and secondly, that the increased salience of absence, amongst other pressures, was shifting attitudes away from the more easygoing patterns of the past, with a greater emphasis being placed on motivation.

Conclusion

Changes in the absence regime suggested a tightening of the screws, induced by greater managerial attention to absence, which was in turn the product of growing competitive pressures. In particular, the return-to-work interview had become established as a standard device. In the warehouse managers regularly checked that supervisors were issuing warnings if an absence record had gone over acceptable limits, while in the factory managers had effectively taken this function over from the supervisors altogether. We have also mentioned that some shopfloor dissatisfaction was evident. We now turn to the shopfloor reaction in more detail.

Workers and Absence

The Pattern of Absence

What was the outcome of this intense management interest in absence control? We begin by considering the pattern of absence before turning to workers' views on attendance and the state of shopfloor relations more generally.

As explained in Chapter 1, we collected absence data in a standard way in each of our organizations. In most cases, it was possible to study only the recent past, and it is thus not possible to assess how far control policies had altered absence levels. But we can compare the organizations, to see whether there were differences which were associated with different managerial approaches, and we could also compare our data with other information. The data are in essence straightforward, though assembling them was often a time-consuming task. They cover a period of a year. In most cases they represent a census of all workers in the departments that we studied. In the case of Multiplex, for example, we have data on 358 workers. We counted the number of separate spells of absence, the total number of days absent, and the duration of absences. Patterns of absence are summarized in Figure 2 and Table A.4 in the Appendix. The figure highlights the pattern of absence frequency by showing the proportions of each sample having no spell of absence ('cleans') and having six or more spells in the course of a year.

Multiplex came out moderately well on the usual summary measure quoted by managements, namely, the percentage of time lost to absence. The figure of 12.5 days per worker per year is equivalent to a rate of about 5.7 per cent, which is at the lower end of the usually quoted range for manual workers. The really distinctive thing about the absence pattern was the frequency of absences. Multiplex did not score particularly well on the proportion of workers going through a year with no spells of absence; BR, for example, was 'better' here. But there was a very tight control of large numbers of absence spells. Four fifths of workers had no more than three spells of absence during a year. Of the other organizations, FinCo came closest to this, with a figure of 70 per cent. The extent of the contrast is worth stressing. FinCo employees performed moderately varied clerical tasks in a clean environment; the packing lines at Multiplex represented the epitome of routine, monotonous manual labour. One would thus expect lower absence in FinCo. Other data underline the distinctiveness of the Multiplex case. An earlier study included a

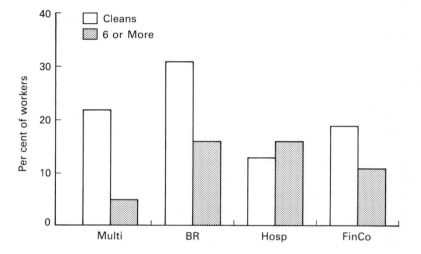

Figure 2   Summary absence frequency patterns

similar group: female workers doing routine semi-skilled tasks in a factory with no tradition of workplace militancy (Edwards and Scullion, 1982:100). Yet only 39 per cent of these workers had three or fewer spells of absence during a year. Ten years separate the two studies, and it is likely that many managements have acted to regulate absence. Nonetheless, the Multiplex pattern looks distinctive.

A second feature is the duration of absences: Multiplex had fewer short spells of absence than workers in the other three organizations. In the other three cases, it was relatively easy to take several spells of absence lasting a day or two. We cannot be certain that the managerial control policy was the key factor in explaining the Multiplex case, but there is certainly circumstantial evidence pointing in this direction. We argue in relation to FinCo in Chapter 6 that the large number of short absence spells there reflects a managerial abstention from control: workers did not feel the need to go absent particularly often, but where they decided to do so there was no direct constraint. Multiplex managers had developed clear constraints which are likely to have led workers to limit their absence. As noted above, moreover, one-third of those whom we asked about direct pressures said that they did feel pressure to attend work when they were ill, that is when they otherwise would have gone absent.

This is not, however, to argue that absence control is simply a matter of workers who would otherwise go absent being prevented from doing so by managerial action. Workers also have their own ideas as to what constitutes an adequate reason for going absent. It is to these matters that we now turn.

The Shopfloor View of Attendance at Work

Thus far we have explored the conjuncture of external pressures, policy, and managerial practice as it relates to absence. Workers' own views on the matter are equally important, both in their own right, and insofar as they relate to management attempts to define and promote a sense of commitment. In considering workers' views a distinction can be made between attitudes arising from a moral order determined by relationships between the world of work and domestic life in general, and the impact of management actions in terms of coercion and the generation of commitment. This distinction is not, of course, absolute, but is important in understanding the development of practice.

Multiplex workers' views reflected the tension between paternalism and commercialism. In line with the former, the view that workers should attend regularly was strongly present. As explained in Chapter 1, we began the section on absence by asking workers to respond to two general statements, which have been used in previous research. As shown in Table A.5, there were no statistically significant differences, but Multiplex workers were if anything the most likely to argue that workers should attend whenever possible, rather than be free to take time off if they chose. They were also less likely than BR or hospital workers to say that they themselves had actually taken a day off when they had been able to get into work. Indeed, it was this pattern of replies which led us to use the vignettes. These certainly show that Multiplex workers were no more likely than the others to take a 'moral' view of the duty to attend when the matter is considered in the abstract. But the general toleration of absence did not mean that workers saw absence as simply justifiable: they also stressed the need to attend when possible.

It is useful to compare these results with others. Workers in all our organizations gave more pro-attendance replies than those in other studies. In the study discussed above manual workers in five factories produced a range from 31 per cent to 78 per cent saying that workers should attend when they could, against an average in our organizations of 86 per cent. Asked about their own absence, generally between one-third and two-thirds had taken a day off when able to attend, compared to a range of 13 to 37 per cent in our organizations (Edwards and Scullion, 1982: 109, 112). Since this study was undertaken in the late 1970s, we need to consider whether these differences reflect trends over time or deeper differences between organizations. On self-reports, it is hard to judge: it is certainly plausible that changed managerial regimes may have reduced the freedom to go absent, and this is certainly likely to have been true of Multiplex. On wider attitudes, however, there is less reason to expect change. It may be that all our organizations were characterized by pro-attendance attitudes. If this is so, the point about Mulitplex is strengthened: routine manual workers here were likely to adopt a more pro-attendance attitude than other manual workers.

The effect of paternalism should not be exaggerated. As argued above, it was one strand of the management style, not a characterization of the basis of the labour regime. In some respects, workers took a calculative and not a moral view of their obligations. Asked about their reasons for attending work, workers were shown a card with various options. Only 12 per cent chose 'duty to the firm', a proportion similar to those recorded in our other organizations (Table A.6). The routineness of attendance was also prominent. As one worker put it, 'if I started to take time off, I'd never be here'. Pro-work responses may reflect a simple recognition of the disciplines of waged work and an adaptation to the need for regular attendance; the regularity of attendance may create a kind of 'traction', to borrow a concept used by Baldamus (1961) to characterize how workers are 'pulled along' by the routines of labour once they are in the workplace.

Nor was there the kind of pro-attendance culture that some of the writers cited in Chapter 1 might expect: here was a firm with no tradition of confrontation on the shopfloor; with, as we will see, quite favourable attitudes towards management; and with workers who individually expressed pro-attendance views. We looked at the question of cultures by asking workers whether they discussed with others the idea of taking time off, and whether there was generally any discussion of the time off taken by other people. Table A.8 suggests that the conditions for cultures to exist were lacking: three-quarters of Multiplex workers (significantly more than in the other three cases) never discussed how much time off other workers were taking. The general comment was that what people did was their own affair, or up to management to sort out. It is true that larger numbers than elsewhere said that they discussed with their work mates the idea of taking time off. When asked to elaborate, most said that they might say to a close friend that they needed a break. There was no more general discussion than this. There may, then, have been some limited social support for workers wanting time off, but no strong culture promoting absence and certainly no developed norms, still less sanctions, encouraging attendance.

The more coercive aspects of the control of attendance were also evident. As Table A.6 shows, Multiplex workers were more likely than others to cite the fear of discipline as a reason to attend. It is true that only one worker in six gave this as the main reason to attend (it was mentioned at all by 21 per cent). But one would hardly expect a regime to be so strict that large numbers of workers expect to be disciplined for an occasional absence. Seen in this light the figure is fairly high. Moreover, two-thirds of the sample were aware of pressures from management over attendance, a relatively high proportion compared with other samples (Table A.7).

Asked about changes, two-thirds could again identify a tighter managerial approach. This proportion was perhaps lower than might be expected, given that managers were openly taking an increased interest in absence. It was lower than the proportion recorded in BR, even though, as will be seen in Chapter 4, the Multiplex regime was the stricter. One reason may be that there was little mechanism for perceptions to be generalized: in BR workers had a more collective tradition, and changes made by managers were discussed far more widely. Multiplex workers were more individualized, and those without personal experience of the system may have remained largely unaware of it.

It was, none the less, quite widely known. Perhaps its most significant outcome, however, lay in the spontaneous comments on attending when ill which we discussed above. When we began asking workers systematically about this, a third said that they had felt under pressure to attend when they felt ill enough to stay away, and most of these said that the reason was that they could be disciplined if enough spells of absence occurred within a year. Several workers were aware of the specific rule of thumb used by managers; this was particularly true in the warehouse, where the rules were more formalized than they were in the factory.

Conclusion

There was thus clear evidence that workers were aware of a tightening regime, and that it was having effects on their own behaviour. Though we cannot be sure, there is a strong suggestion that these responses helped to cause the distinctive pattern of absence here, namely, the low proportion of workers having more than three spells of absence in a year. This number was the threshold for managerial action, and the proportion having more spells tailed off sharply, whereas in the other cases the distribution was much more extended. We have seen that some workers were consciously restricting their absence. This tighter control was one significant part of the workplace regime, but it was connected with other developments, as we now proceed to show.

Securing Effort Levels and the Uses of Discipline

The close controls over attendance and timekeeping at Multiplex, and the growing emphasis placed on their success, were clearly related to a changing commercial context. These commercial pressures were also reflected in the regime of work itself. As with attendance control, working practices, effort levels and discipline had not been subject to any major reorganization, but were nonetheless responding in ways which placed some strains on old established patterns and relationships. Multiplex had never relied on direct incentive schemes to maintain effort, nor was it (in our case study sites at least) involved in major technical innovation. The securing of satisfactory effort levels had long reflected the company's tradition of paternalist labour relations and steady, even tolerant, demands on its workers. Increasing competition, and the redundancies mentioned above, were, however, beginning to challenge this somewhat staid picture, and there did seem to be a general rise in the levels of effort required by the company from its workforce. We assess these issues by looking at workers' overall views of management before examining the details of workplace change. Developments under the latter head were different on our two sites, and we consider them separately.

Workers, Managers and Trust

In line with the tradition of job security and a relaxed management style, workers had a relatively favourable view of their managers. Table A.10 sets out replies to some of our key questions. On whether managers were felt to be friendly or distant, 77 per cent found them 'very' or 'quite' friendly, a proportion well above that of BR workers for example. Quite high proportions were also willing to acknowledge the useful functions performed by managers.

These two questions have been used by other researchers, but they have limitations. The question about friendliness, for example, asks about managers' personal attitudes; it would be quite possible for a worker to say that individual managers whom he or she actually met were friendly while also believing that management in general was devious or not trustworthy. We felt it desirable to ask workers directly about their confidence in management. The concept of trust has an established place in academic debates, notably in Fox's (1974) identification of high and low trust syndromes. In this usage, trust is part of the observer's overall characterization of a regime, and not necessarily something that can be measured directly. But we found that workers could think in terms of trust, by which we meant the extent of mutual confidence and the degree to which workers felt that they could depend on managers' integrity; where necessary, we added such an explanation to our questions. They revealed, we believe, a valuable dimension of workers' perceptions.

Table A.10 contains the basic data on our questions about management. Figure 3 summarizes the picture on trust, by combining the two highest and the two lowest categories. Figure 4 presents summary scores on the trust and two other measures. We assigned scores of 4 to replies most favourable to management and zero for those least favourable, and computed averages for each organization. In the Multiplex sample, 45 per cent felt that trust was complete or was present most of the time. When asked about changes, most perceived little change, and slightly more

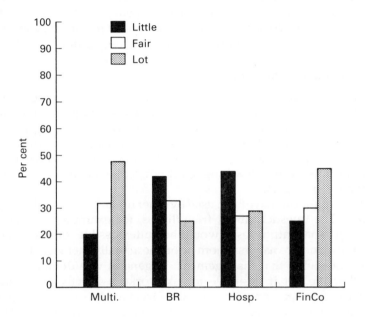

Figure 3   Extent of trust

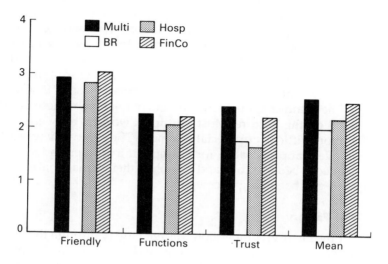

Figure 4   Summary attitude scores

noted an improvement than a worsening; Multiplex was the only organization where such a positive net balance was recorded. The key feature of these replies was, as Figure 3 shows, the extent of similarity with the white-collar FinCo sample, together with the sharp differences from both of the public sector organizations. As we will see in the following two chapters, there were specific reasons why relations with management were so poor there: it was not so much a question of Multiplex scoring especially high but of BR and the hospital scoring low. None the less, the quality of relations with management was notable. As Figure 4 shows, overall pro-management scores were even higher than those in FinCo.

The comments made by workers in relation to these questions elaborated on this picture. Most Multiplex workers answered the questions without difficulty or special comment. The general view was that managers were approachable, for example if a worker had a problem which needed to be sorted out, and capable in their managerial role. Change was, however, beginning to creep in.

The Factory

For the factory, competition was felt largely through the development of independent retailing operations, and competition to supply them. This affected not only sales outlets, but also product range and design. The company had responded by introducing new products and entering the 'own brands' market as a supplier. At the same time continuous effort was applied to raise productivity and to reduce costs. How far these changes directly effected effort levels is not easy to determine. The relationship between productivity growth and effort is a complex one which cannot be pursued in detail here. For the moment it is enough to note that managers at least felt that staff were being asked to work harder. These demands were moderated to the extent that Multiplex had decided not to take extensive advantage of the changed industrial relations context of the 1980s. Managers felt that they had never lost control to the union on the shop floor, and that major productivity programmes were initiated without resistance. Shopfloor acceptance of change was assisted by the confidence staff felt in the company's ability to secure growing demand for its products, which kept redundancies to a minimum.

Within the factory the pace of work had been increased through developing a degree of semi-automation which meant that reactions had to be faster. At the same time there was a new emphasis on quality which involved closer supervision of work. Departmental managers and supervisors all cited the impact of external competition as the driving force in this process. One result was the development of greater flexibility and stricter stock controls. While Multiplex had not experimented with 'just in time' forms of organization, the ethos had begun to permeate management practice which one described as 'sell now, make later.' These changes had, for the most part, been accommodated within the company's traditional methods of effort regulation which consisted of recognized work standards, fostering commitment, and the use of discipline.

Work standards were mainly established at departmental level. Managers use marketing information and trial runs to establish a standard time for a production run. Formal work study could come later, but this was felt by some managers to be 'a court of last resort.' At the manufacturing end of the operation 100 per cent of the standard time was the target, on the packing lines it was 70 per cent. There was no union involvement in target setting, but team leaders were consulted during the trials. Workers knew the targets, which were issued to them, and, on some lines, a constant check on performance was displayed by digital read out.

Having set the targets management then aimed to reduce the standard times progressively. According to some this was done by setting conservative, or 'soft' targets initially, but other managers were clearly more opportunist. If targets were continually met, or exceeded, then the standard times would simply be altered. This would commonly occur with new product lines which were seen as inviting 'fatty standards.' Clearly there is a limit to the tightening of standards without reorganized work methods, or increasing labour intensity beyond the point of acceptance. The aim was, however, to keep the point of pressure on the work line, and the management of effort was designed to do this.

This practice took two forms, motivation and coercion. Managers 'liked to think' that workers' general desire to do a good job would be a prime motivator, and saw good communications as a major factor in encouraging this. Monthly briefings were held for supervisors on the company's competitive and production performance, and these were cascaded down to the shop floor in work time meetings lasting twenty minutes or half an hour. There were also weekly small seminar groups on product security and quality, and work teams could be involved in meetings with outside customers to boost their sense of involvement. Managers were convinced that the isolation of small work groups, which could not see the broader picture, had to be overcome, and that communications were therefore the secret to motivation. In general, workers at Multiplex seemed only marginally affected by these procedures. Table

A.11 summarizes replies about recent changes in the management of labour. As explained in Chapter 1, we asked a general question and offered prompts relevant to each case. In Multiplex we reminded workers of team briefings, and efforts at communication. As the table shows, awareness of these changes was far from widespread: only 35 per cent of workers cited 'more communication' even when prompted, and 20 per cent explicitly denied that there was more, with the remaining 45 per cent being uncertain or having no strong view. It is true that awareness of communication was greater than elsewhere, but there was little evidence of a major shift in workers' thinking.

One element in the process was aimed at fostering competitive relations between work teams and product lines. In one case a department which had low (60 per cent) target efficiency was split into two parts. For one part performance continued to be poor. According to the manager it took three months to pinpoint the reason - a lack of morale. At the time of the split the original manager had hived off all the best equipment, and all the 'best' workers to his new section. It was management recognition in the 'backward' department of the workers' sense of grievance that enabled them to use 'target chasing' as a means of recovering self-respect, and justifying new equipment. There did exist some element of such competitiveness on the shop floor, but nothing in our interviews with workers showed it as being deeply embedded, or taken very seriously. In practice, the maintenance and development of targets and performance relied much more directly on close supervision.

Supervision monitored speeds on the packing lines hourly, and great pressure was placed on the team leader to explain reasons for targets not being met. If explanations were satisfactory nothing more was done. If not, that team received far closer supervision, and team leaders and workers could, in theory, be subject to disciplinary action. In practice many managers claimed that things did not go this far, and that where there were 'slow types' on a line 'we learn to live with it.' Nevertheless, some managers and supervisors said that they had used the disciplinary procedure for lack of effort. Even without the use of formal procedures there were variations in supervisory style or 'tightness'. Section and team leaders were responsible for break rotas, and 'toilet rules' (once between 8 and 10, and once between break and dinner) could be more or less strictly enforced. Both workers and supervisors felt that some differences did occur between departments, and that this was affected by 'team working', or the success of targets.

As with attendance the disciplinary regime was tight without being oppressive to the extent that it engendered discontent. Table A.7 shows perceptions of managerial control and discipline. At Multiplex 77 per cent thought works rules were 'about right', with 12 per cent thinking they were either 'too loose' or 'too tight'. Occasional purges on housekeeping, dress standards, and so on, did occur, and it was these peripheral issues that occasioned most adverse comment from the staff. About a third of workers said that they themselves had been disciplined. This proportion was higher than in the hospital or FinCo, as would be expected given the character of the two organizations. The similarity with BR was more notable given that, as we will see, discipline there was being significantly tightened. The similar level suggests that there may have been some change in Multiplex too. However, growing action on absence has to be taken into account; excluding this would lower the experience of sanctions. Certainly the shop floor regime was far from harsh. As far as we could discover from records dismissal from the factory was rare.

One reason for reluctance to use formal discipline in respect of effort levels may be the negative effects of such coercion on quality of output. In production areas especially it was felt that pressure can lead to mistakes in operating procedures. In fact, for these workers, errors in following SOPs (standard operating procedures) were far more commonly a reason for discipline than absence or effort levels. In part this is simply explained by the strict requirements of food and pharmaceutical production, but supervisors knew that some errors or evasions of procedure were directly related to work pressure.

Nevertheless, the men on direct production seemed to have more autonomy and room for informalities than the women on the packing lines. Supervisors acknowledged that there was room in the production targets for people to 'bank' small amounts of time for cigarette breaks, and the workers had separate canteen facilities for breaks. Despite claims that no major informalities existed, inspection of disciplinary records uncovered that one team had been banking sufficient work to organize Saturday morning overtime when there was in fact no work to do. This seemed to be an exceptional occurrence, but it does mark off this group from the general experience of workers in the factory, and especially of the women, for whom the term paternalism has an additional resonance.

As with absence control the effects of increased competition in the product market, and the push to raise productivity, had taken an incremental form which did not pose any serious problems of labour management. What changed was the balance in management practice, with more explicit demands being made on effort performance within an already tight, but generally accepted, level of labour discipline.

Table A.11 shows workers' reactions. We made a point of asking, in our general questioning about changes, whether workers felt that they were working harder than they had done in the past. As discussed in more detail elsewhere (Edwards and Whitston, 1991), asking workers directly about effort levels is an unusual but effective way of considering the intensity of labour. Multiplex workers as a whole were among the groups who were most likely to feel that they were working harder as a result of changes in work organization: 43 per cent said that work was harder, against 13 per cent who specifically denied that work had grown harder. This was the one issue, however, where there was a significant difference between the two sites: only 24 per cent of the factory workers found work harder, compared with 54 per cent in the warehouse. This difference of perception was consistent with a greater change of workplace control in the warehouse, as we now show.

The Warehouse

One aspect has already been mentioned. Seasonal shifts in workloads at the warehouse had been tackled by management by the introduction of new lines and products to even out the workflow. This did not seem to account entirely for workers' feelings however. Rather there seemed to have been a general tightening of standards overall. As one woman said, 'In the past people used to say that here you did so much, and when you were finished that was it. People would bring in their knitting and everything'.

Such patterns of work (although perhaps less extreme) can be quite typical of warehouse work. In systems based on highly variegated order picking (as at Multiplex) it is not uncommon for workers to pace production in ways which generate relatively slack periods when staff can chat, or just take things a little easier. Piecework or batch production can allow a similar element of autonomy in effort management, or at least effort distribution, and this had been the case in the production end of the factory site. Many workers in the warehouse, however, were quite explicit in saying that this no longer applied to them.

This was generally attributed to tightly formulated 'line averages' for performance within departments which were strictly monitored by supervision. One complaint was that these averages made no concessions to natural variations in workspeeds, and, in particular, to the needs of older workers. It was also clear that discipline, or the fear of it, played a prominent part in enforcing standards; as one worker said 'You have to work hard or you'd be in the office - management are quite clear on this.' This pressure did not lead to any collective restraint on output, or any attempt by people to discourage faster workers. Fear of losing employment seemed slightly more pronounced in the warehouse than at the factory, and this may have worked to keep discontent within bounds, but it was also clear that, despite growing demands on workers, they felt that the work atmosphere was generally good. It should also be noted that this perception of continuous pressure was not universal. Certainly in the dispatch areas supervision claimed that there were natural slack periods on the job, and that they made no attempt to fill these by 'making work', although this too was a male area of employment.

These increased demands on worker effort were closely linked to a computerized system of output monitoring called MANPAX which had been introduced two years earlier. The system allowed for standard times to be generated for operations in each department, and for actual performance against these targets to be closely monitored. Its introduction was described by one manager as punitive, being designed to highlight areas of poor efficiency, and to cut staffing levels. Targets, he claimed, were being incrementally increased on an annual basis, but not yet to such an extent as to create resistance. At first supervisors were suspicious, and there were feelings that people were being spied on, but the system only operated at the level of the workgroup or department, and there was currently no facility for judging the output of individuals. Target requirements for departments varied around the 75 per cent level. Most managers felt that no higher efficiency could be generated without the introduction of some form of payments by results system, which would involve a significant shift in company policy.

These limitations in the MANPAX system meant that the enforcement of individual effort levels remained firmly in the hands of supervisors and departmental managers. A cautious approach was evident. Supervisors did not translate their own target figures into a standard performance level for each worker. Instead, they allowed for variation according to age and physical fitness of each worker. Similarly, when reviewing the performance of any one worker they did not expect a constant output level but allowed for variation according to 'good' or 'bad' days. There was thus a degree of 'give and take'. None the less, this variation operated only within limits. Each supervisor knew her own targets, and hence how much work the average worker had to produce. As several said, raising targets had to be translated into higher work levels. They explained their methods for determining each worker's target in terms of their own knowledge of the group: it was possible to judge whether each person was working to a reasonable level in relation to her own normal standards. Supervisors kept records of each worker's output, and it was reasonably simple to check whether it was on the desired track. They said that it was necessary from time to time to have a word with someone about her effort level, but that this was usually sufficient and that more formal discipline was rare.

As part of this scrutiny of individual workers' performance, management in the warehouse had also instituted an annual appraisal for all staff. Unlike the FinCo system discussed in Chapter 6, no pay bonuses were attached to it. Given also that workers were assessed on a day-to-day basis, the annual appraisal was little more than a taking stock of past performance. There were no ways in which workers could significantly improve their knowledge of the job or be set targets for personal development, and appraisal had little salience, other than as a symbol of a desire by management to modernize the workplace regime.

Discipline and Informality

How far did this desire impinge on customs or understandings about the effort bargain, for example in the extent to which supervisors tolerated a little lateness, extended meal breaks or early leaving? The answer is simple: there had always been precious little of this kind of activity, and there was no evidence of any substantial change. We have described in detail how attendance was managed so that, for example, anyone arriving late at the factory would have to make this fact known to management. Similarly, supervisors in the warehouse said that they could handle lateness informally. They had no rigid rules as to how often someone could be late before a warning was issued, and it was sufficient to maintain a rough check on those who might be abusing the system.

There was one area of potential informality which is worth noting. It is widely acknowledged that pilfering is a common practice, particularly in the retail and distribution sector. As Mars (1982) shows, it is embedded in the operation of the sector, and everyone knows that it takes place. The warehouse, which handled a range of highly marketable goods, was potentially a site for the development of pilfering. Managers accordingly adopted a very strict approach. We have described examples elsewhere (Edwards and Whitston, 1989a). In perhaps the most indicative case a long-serving worker was found with some relatively cheap goods in his possession, namely, wedding stationery . He admitted taking them, and said that this was the only time that he had stolen anything, for he wanted them for a relative's wedding. None the less, he was dismissed. Managers argued that they could not be lenient in such cases, for it would then become increasingly difficult to decide where to draw the line. By making it absolutely clear that any theft would lead to dismissal, they prevented even the weakest of informal understandings from growing up around the behaviour. Though disciplinary records showed, not surprisingly, that there were instances of theft, these were very much individual actions, and the possibility of pilfering had no place in the workplace culture.

This pattern of control was rooted in the firm's long-established traditions. There had never been the space for effort bargaining or fiddles to grow up. The key implication for the analysis of change is, of course, that the new workplace regime was not a response to problems of shopfloor control. The shopfloor was very clearly, however, part of the solution: demands on workers were increasing in terms of attendance and their behaviour once at work.

Conclusions

Multiplex was, in many ways, a traditional manufacturing employer. It can scarcely be put forward as a study in industrial disorder, nor is it an obvious paradigm of future trends in labour management. Why then is it of interest to a study of attendance and worker commitment? The answer has to be that the conditions of labour at the company, the nature of the whole employment relationship, and the individual employment relationship in particular, may give a better picture of the circumstances under which hundreds of firms and thousands of workers operate than can be gained from firms in the forefront or rearguard of employment practice. This is not a plea for the comforts of the average, but a recognition that changes in employment are complex, and develop unevenly, and that this unevenness is especially important in understanding periods of rapid change.

The study of the firm illustrates the value of making absence a central focus. Changing expectations about attendance were one of the main ways in which workers were made aware of demands on them. Had we looked at shopfloor change in general, we might have found a few references to this matter, but we would not have been able to look at it in any detail. The specific interest in the management of absence is also highlighted. We were concerned, not with absenteeism in its own right, but with the rules governing the behaviour, their impact on workers, and what they say about the control of labour more generally. We found that stricter control was being instituted, that workers were aware of this even to the extent of feeling under pressure to attend when ill, and that these developments were part of a broader effort to manage the shopfloor more actively and rationally in the face of competitive pressures.

Without detailed time-series data, it is impossible to demonstrate how the pattern of absence had changed. It is likely that there had been some effect: we have stressed how few Multiplex workers, when compared with our other organizations, had more than three spells of absence in a year, and have demonstrated their awareness of managerial controls. But in may ways such direct effects are not the key issue. By acting on absence, managers were giving workers a more general signal that they were concerned with how each individual behaved: by contrast with, say, a new payment system, which relates to workers as a group, acting on absence deals directly with every worker. The signal may have been influential in workers' responses to change on the shopfloor itself. This is not an issue where direct linkages are likely to be evident: workers will not consciously note an interest in attendance, think out how managers expect them to behave, and be accordingly willing to embrace new working practices. But less direct effects are likely to have been present, as the focus on absence placed in workers' minds the weight being placed by management on the needs for efficiency and as parallel developments took place within the workplace. This theme of the symbolic importance of absence control recurs in the study of BR, and we take up its wider implications in the concluding chapter.

The extent of change should not be exaggerated. At Multiplex there was no sudden crisis such as gripped many manufacturing firms at the start of the 1980s. There was, rather, a slow but steady move towards being more cost-conscious. Eclectic, and essentially pragmatic, Multiplex incorporated some new elements, notably team briefing, in its own traditional approach, but not without producing significant strains, and not without casting doubt on the ability of the company to maintain those traditions intact.

It is worth considering some of the elements involved in this evolution. In its management style Multiplex had already combined elements of paternalism and what has been called 'sophisticated modernism'. The resulting mix evaded some of the more unitarist features of paternalism by acknowledging autonomous employee interests, and by incorporating a role for trade union representation. At the collective level Multiplex had a reputation as a 'caring' employer with formalized industrial relations structures. This research has shown, however, that the character of collective relations between the company and employees is not exactly replicated in the individual employment relationship.

For whom was Multiplex a 'good' employer? The collectively agreed structures at the company, as well as its own policies, had produced the framework for the individual employment relationship. Typically, a Multiplex worker would enjoy what was, by the 1980s, a not uncommon package of working benefits; sick pay, pension, canteen, some product discounts, and an occupational health and welfare system. In addition the company's market position and paternalist approach led to relatively high levels of job security. As well as consultation through employee councils and team briefings, Multiplex encouraged employee identification with company goals through a profit related annual bonus. Workers certainly were never at the top of the industrial earnings league, but systematic low pay was not a feature either. The implicit effort bargain was not overly demanding. That this had not been radically undermined can be seen from the results in Table A.9. Most workers interviewed had not thought of leaving the company, and pay levels and security were the most frequently cited reasons for staying on. Of those who had thought of leaving 74 per cent cited the nature of the work, and primarily boredom.

Within the paternalist tradition, however, were some less attractive elements. The sexual division of labour was quite marked, and led to variations not only in pay but in terms of work autonomy. Within the terms of the total employment relationship discipline was tightly controlled, and management had set strict effective limits to worker control over production methods and targets. For the individual employees, therefore, participation had little reality outside their place in a highly structured system.

Even before commercial pressures and competition introduced change, the elements of this system had generated their own internal contradictions. What does paternalism mean at the level of first-line management and supervision? Multiplex had avoided the centralized and rule-centered bureaucratic style of management, partly because its management style rested on encouraging personal as well as corporate identification with workplace order. Managers and supervisors were encouraged to see themselves, and often did see themselves, as having personal responsibilities to workers, and personal responsibilities in pursuit of company goals. This was displayed in various ways. Especially in the case of absence control, and the handling of domestic absences, supervisory discretion was accompanied by rather personalized assessments of what was or was not acceptable.

This had two aspects. On the one hand paternalistic relationships could blunt managerial insistence on explicit standards of behaviour, and this doubtless contributed to the belief by personnel and other senior managers that line managers and supervisors were reluctant to impose discipline. On the other hand many interviews with department managers and supervisors revealed the more authoritarian face of paternalism, a unitarist assumption of the primacy of the firm's interests combined with a degree of moral insistence on the industrial equivalent of good family behaviour. There seemed to be, in fact, a cascade effect whereby the complex intentions of management policy degraded the closer they came to the point of production. In itself this is hardly surprising. The ambivalent position of, particularly, line supervision is well known, caught as they so often are between the demands of the company and their daily relationships with the shop floor. At Multiplex these contradictions took a particular form resulting from the mixture of management styles, and, more importantly, came under yet more pressure as changes developed in the 1980s.

Similar problems arose in respect of employee commitment. There seemed little evidence that either the welfare facet of the employment relationship or measures to engage commitment had any marked effect on the outlook of the workforce. Certainly the sites researched in this study, like the company as a whole, showed no signs of militancy, or formal or informal challenges to managerial authority, but acquiescence is not the same thing as commitment. This would scarcely matter, except to those with a sentimental attachment to worker commitment, if it did not so plainly contradict the aims of management policy.

In fact, these aspects of the employment relationship at Multiplex were becoming more salient in a period of competitive pressure. The increasing stress being laid on good attendance by management is one example. The attendance control policy pursued by the company attempted to combine both disciplinary measures with those designed to appeal to worker commitment to the firm. The 'face' of workplace order, therefore, can be seen in how the 'flesh' of welfare employment policies is built onto the disciplinary 'skeleton'. It is in this sense that the meanings of self-discipline and commitment must be judged. The collective-celebratory discipline cited by Henry (1987), 'the normal human tendency to do ones share' (Strauss and Sayles 1980:218), was seen by many managers as the natural basis for company policy. However, this fails to acknowledge that this is expressed not autonomously, but within a control structure defined by management, for management.

At Multiplex the tendency was, albeit not in any dramatic fashion, to extend reliance on the explicitly disciplinary approach to attendance, but in the name of self-discipline and commitment. To the extent that these changes were gradual, and only affected small numbers at any time, they had not engendered any challenge to established relationships on the shop floor. Nevertheless, many senior managers recognized that the implications of stricter standards and stricter enforcement could not proceed very far without putting the company's traditional reputation under stress. For supervision these contradictions exacerbated their already ambiguous position, and, in the factory at least, had in fact led to more centralization of control, rather than the devolution required by both the company and its collective agreements with the union.

Similar forces were acting in respect of the management of effort. While rejecting payments by results, or other incentive schemes, management was engaged in altering the implicit effort bargain contained in the total employment package. In the warehouse in particular, effort was being more tightly controlled, more directed, and its intensity increased. Here again motivation, payment systems, and the demands laid on workers were increasingly in an uncomfortable relationship.

None of the changes being experienced at Multiplex was particularly traumatic in the way that rapid restructuring so often is. None the less, managers were sure that adaption to new market circumstances was proceeding, and that, on the whole, the workforce was being taken along. In particular both attendance and effort levels were seen as responding to managed change, and indicative of the companies success in dealing with a new environment. If success is measured by management's ability to impose change without costly challenges from labour this claim would seem justified. However, it is far less clear that management had, in any decisive way, established control over hearts and minds. The workers' relationship to the firm, and to the demands that it placed on them, remained essentially instrumental, pragmatic, and detached. In the case of discipline, attendance, and effort, in fact, changes had worked largely in a direction opposite to commitment, and more in the direction of discipline and coercion. As we will see, this tendency was evident even more starkly in the cases of BR and the hospital.

4

British Rail: Between Tradition and Managerialism

There is now a substantial literature on industrial relations in the public sector during the 1980s. This has focused on the extent of change from the 1970s, in particular how far an ethos of competition and market forces altered the behaviour of management. The inference is often that shopfloor regimes became more autocratic. Yet the nature of these regimes has rarely been considered in detail. In this and the following chapter we explore this issue in the cases of British Rail and the health service.

BR has received considerable attention. Ferner (1988) has examined the growth of commercialism and its effects on management practice. Managers had an agenda for change, including efforts to alter relations with unions and to press through a series of wide-ranging changes in working practices. As Ferner stresses, however, it cannot be assumed that there were direct effects at shopfloor level: managers had to handle conflicting pressures, with the need to maintain a service calling for a more moderate and conciliatory approach than a stress on commercial logics alone might imply. There remained considerable space for managers to interpret the financial systems in which they were operating.

To pursue this theme further, study at shopfloor level is required. Two studies by Pendleton point to the limited extent of change. The first (1991a) looked at one of the most heavily debated issues on BR, 'flexible rostering'. Managerial efforts to introduce new systems for rostering train crew provoked a major strike in 1982. Yet, Pendleton found, by the mid-1980s no significant increases in flexibility had been recorded; indeed, in some respects the new system introduced new rigidities. The second study

(1991b) surveyed representatives of the train drivers' union, ASLEF, and suggested that workplace collective bargaining remained largely unchanged.

Our study complements these accounts. In line with our overall approach, we did not analyse change on BR as a whole. We did not, for example, examine the institutions of workplace representation. We focused on the effort bargain: how far had the massive changes in the rhetoric of the organization impacted on how hard workers were working and on their scope to bargain informally over the pace and timing of their labour? Our findings parallel those of Ferner and Pendleton: there was significant change in the conduct of shopfloor relations and in the state of management-worker relations, but elements of traditional practice remained important. Indeed, managers continued to rely on these elements for the generation of day-to-day consent. It is for this reason that we describe BR as lying, somewhat uneasily, between a traditional and a fully commercialized approach. There certainly had been no qualitative shift, towards either unchallenged managerial control or a 'new shopfloor order' based on self-discipline.

We also hoped to throw light on two sub-themes of our overall approach. First, many BR workers are felt to have strong occupational communities, and these communities could be expected to sustain strong cultural norms about attendance. If we were to find absence norms, we should find them here. Second, the railways have been noted, from their very earliest days, for a bureaucratic approach to industrial discipline. We hoped that we would be able to explore the nature of disciplinary practice in some detail. This chapter, unlike others, therefore makes discipline a distinct topic in its own right.

We studied an operating area of BR, that is groups responsible for the movement of trains and the operation of stations; workers such as signalmen and maintenance and clerical staff were excluded. A total of 82 workers was interviewed, from four grades: train drivers (20) guards (17), station staff (22) and carriage cleaners (23). The train crew were all based at one depot. The station staff were from one large station and one smaller one; they all worked on platforms handling train arrivals and departures. The carriage cleaners worked in a cleaning depot some way apart from the other parts of the area; the depot had the air of being a world of its own.

Train crew differed from the other two groups in several respects. Platform staff and cleaners worked at fixed locations, on standard eight-hour shifts, and were subject to direct surveillance of their work by supervisors. Train crew were highly mobile, their hours of work varied widely from day to day, and when operating a train were away from any direct supervision. Train crew have also been the subject of the most significant changes in working practices introduced during the 1980s. In 1982 management and unions agreed to focus discussion on six items (for details and background, see Ferner, 1988: 96-100). In addition to flexible rostering, the key ones were driver-only operation of some trains, involving the removal of guards; an 'easement of manning', which provided for a reduction in the number of occasions when two drivers are required in a cab and for more flexibility in the taking of meal breaks; the 'train(wo)man' concept, which would break down the distinction between guards' and drivers' lines of promotion; and open stations, which replaced ticket barriers with ticket inspection on trains. The first three of these affected drivers directly. The fourth, while having no direct effect on existing drivers, promised to break down drivers' long-cherished craft-like exclusivity. And all five changes affected guards. (Under the trainman concept as it has been introduced, the term 'guard' has been replaced with 'conductor', but 'guard' was current when we carried out our study, and we retain the term below).

These four groups of employees thus permit some analysis of differences within BR, in two respects. First, there have been traditional contrasts in work practices. Train crew, particularly drivers, have long been noted for organized means of the control of effort and for a strong sense of solidarity. Perhaps less is known about more informal behaviour such as 'fiddles' of time-keeping. We tried to assess the pattern of controls of effort, and to compare this pattern with that characterizing platform staff and cleaners. These two groups have not enjoyed the bargaining power of train crew, and we asked how they were induced to continue to labour at monotonous jobs, often in unpleasant conditions, for low wages. We were, again, interested in the covert ways in which workers might gain some influence over effort, and in the ways in which these were constrained by management. Second, we explored how far the traditional system had changed as a result of the new commercialism of management. Were traditional forms of job control being swept away, and what was the nature of the emerging régime?

A brief characterization of the traditional system will help to locate the argument. For all grades, it was marked by stability. In view of the massive job losses since the war, this may sound surprising. But these losses were managed through a negotiating system that gave the unions considerable influence and that gave workers a sense of security and permanence. For the lower grades, this security, together with the availability of huge amounts of overtime, helped to balance the low wages. Moreover, changes in working practices were made only slowly, so that there was not a great deal of pressure on staff. For guards, the position was broadly similar. For drivers, the traditional system combined stability with pride in the work and a strong loyalty to the occupation: drivers had a more collective orientation to their work than the other groups, a difference which was still evident within our samples. Though well organized, drivers have never been militant in the sense of engaging in frequent strikes or using local bargaining power to push up wages above nationally agreed levels. The traditional system contained their militant potential by creating institutions which ensured that their interests were met. For example, the allocation of work was determined by seniority, in ways which have been well understood for decades; and individual grievances about the interpretation of an agreement have been handled through a bargaining system running from the local to the national levels. The conduct of work was thus regulated by a clear system of rules, and the need for militancy was largely removed.

Management has changed this system in many ways. The control of attendance is one, though it has received less attention than changing working practices. We begin with absence control before moving on to discipline, which has received more comment: a greater resort to punitive and corrective discipline has been noted by several observers, but there has been little assessment of practice at the shopfloor level. Managers have also tried to promote a sense of individual involvement through such things as better communication. We assess the effects of these before turning to negotiation of order in its micro aspects of fiddles. These various strands enable us, finally, to characterize the shopfloor regime. There was major change, notably in managerial concern about absence and in the use of discipline, which reflected authoritarian elements. But managers' continued dependence on the traditional system meant that managerialism had to date created a situation on the shopfloor which was less straightforwardly bleak than critics of the managerial offensive imply. We are not arguing simply that change had been limited, though that is certainly true. We also suggest that the new regime relied heavily on aspects of the old and that a pure commercial model might prove to be unworkable.

Absence

Management and the Control of Attendance

Controlling attendance was a major issue for managers. The Area Personnel Manager saw it as his most important task; a specific objective, set by the Area Manager, was to reduce the absence rate to single figures. There had been an increasing concern about absence over the previous three years. Various reasons were offered by managers including the costs of absence and claims that absence rates had been increasing, a tendency that some attributed to more generous sick pay arrangements. On the last point, at the time of the study (1988), the first day of absence attracted no sick pay, except in the case of workers with ten years' service and all drivers. This one 'waiting day' had recently replaced a system of two waiting days, and it was due to be abolished.

There was in fact little evidence that absence rates were a growing problem. As shown below, the only evidence that we could find pointed, if anything, to reductions in absence rates since 1981. Our data, and also the study by the Monopolies and Mergers Commission (MMC, 1980: 64), also show that rates were not very different from those in other organizations. Moreover, the ways in which managers discussed absence did not suggest that they saw absence rates as a major problem. Some defined the problem as being limited to a small minority of bad attenders, while others explained pressures to go absent in terms of awkward shift patterns or unpleasant working conditions.

Concern reflected neither a worsening absence problem nor a perception of such a problem. It was due, instead, to the climate in which absence was viewed. Growing attention to labour costs meant that absence was more salient to managers. This in turn reflected the decentralization of authority and the making of each Area responsible for its own budget. As an Area Manager interviewed by Ferner (1988: 120) put it, 'the budget is king'. In our Area, the manager had instituted campaigns to control the use of overtime, replacing previous practice wherein local managers gave out overtime freely. The link with absence is simply that absence is not only costly in itself but that, to the extent that it is covered by overtime, it makes a further dent in the budget. Budgetary pressures forced managers to think about absence, in many cases for the first time.

Since budgetary pressure is national, absence might similarly be expected to be a generic concern. The MMC (1987: 76) has noted that areas have been paying more attention to absence, and those of our managerial respondents who had worked in other regions mentioned that concern had been at least as marked there as in our Area. In terms of the origins of policy, this raises questions of function and level: how far has absence control been driven by the personnel specialist and how far by line managers; and was it a local or a higher level decision to act? On levels, management in the Region that covered our Area argued that absence was identified as an issue by a group on which all area personnel managers were represented and this then became policy. It does not appear to have been a matter of policy being imposed on local managers; there was, rather, a general awareness of the issue. As recent studies of managerial decision-making (Schilit, 1987; Marginson et al., 1988: 254) have argued, it is wrong to see decision-making in hierarchical terms, for managers often work in teams and produce joint decisions. A similar point applies to the role of line managers. It was not a matter of their demanding control with Personnel providing the procedural mechanisms; neither did personnel specialists impose a concern with absence on apathetic line managers. Both groups were responding to the new environment of budgetary pressure. Personnel were certainly left with the responsibility of devising procedures, but all the line managers to whom we spoke were actively concerned about absence and saw controlling it as part of their own jobs: they did not shuffle off responsibility to Personnel.

How, then, was control exercised? BR has kept the absence control system strictly separate from the formal disciplinary procedure. In our other case study firms, the same procedure involving a progression of warnings was used for all forms of misconduct; this is the case in most large organizations. BR's different practice has occasionally been noted, but not explained. It stems from the meaning of discipline on the railways: a disciplinary offence is a blameworthy breach of rules such as driving a train too fast or being rude to a passenger. BR managers wanted to approach attendance control without questioning the genuineness of a worker's reasons for absence. The control policy was therefore kept separate from the disciplinary procedure.

The policy was remarkably informal. Thus there were no generally-applied rules of thumb, such as those used in Multiplex, as to the number of spells of absence that warranted action. The manager at the cleaning depot had instituted his own system, based on three spells in a three-month period as the trigger. His ability to do so probably reflects the isolation of the depot: staff in other departments were in close contact with each other, and it is doubtful whether the train crew or the operations manager could have acted so freely. The depot's approach was, however, in line with the general one in its relative leniency. When the Multiplex standard of three spells in a year was put to them, BR managers said that this was far too strict: their concern was to deal with the minority of 'bad cases'. The system was for the personnel manager to check through absence records and to draw any problems to the attention of the relevant line manager, who would then see the worker concerned. Line managers were told that the first approach should involve counselling and avoid questioning the reasons for absence, though stressing that continued absence interfered with the running of a business and could lead to further action. Forms were returned on which managers dutifully stated that they had used the approved language.

Consistency is an obvious problem here: how can approaching 2,000 staff be monitored informally? The Personnel Manager's view was that this was not a problem, because there were only about 30 serious cases, which he could easily check. Moreover, set triggers for action were inappropriate because he had to take into account a pattern: someone regularly going absent on a particular shift, or on a day next to a rest day, needed picking up whereas with someone else, perhaps with a known medical problem, there might be no justification for action. Such arguments make it difficult to test whether arbitrariness had crept in: we could find two people with similar records, one who had been spoken to and one who had not, and argue that they had been treated differently, when a manager's knowledge might enable him to recognize the specific circumstances of individual cases. None the less, if the aim is to bring unacceptable records to workers' attention, and if the justification is the disruption caused by absence as such and not the justifiability of particular incidents such as an absence next to a rest day, one might expect workers with similar records at least to be subjected to an initial interview. From an examination of absence records, which contained notes as to when a worker had been 'seen', this appears not to have been the case, for there were several individuals who seem to have escaped being seen when others with similar records were warned.

The arbitrariness here should not be exaggerated. It did not seem to stem for prejudice, for example. Thus many of the guards and station staff were of Asian origin, and it would have been easy for an entirely white group of managers to develop racial stereotypes. In fact, none was evident. This cannot be written off as a refusal to talk to a researcher about such issues; in studies of absence (Edwards and Scullion, 1982) and recruitment (Jenkins, 1986) managers were only too eager to use such stereotypes. There was no evidence of bias against groups in the identification of bad attenders. The arbitrariness of the procedure illustrates simply the imprecise way in which rules were developed, so that there was an element of chance in whether or not a workers was 'seen'.

The usual form of control was an interview with the departmental manager, which could be followed up with further warnings. Managers generally felt that drawing an absence record to a worker's attention was sufficient to cause an improvement. A study of management records certainly pointed to cases in which being 'seen' was followed by a sharp reduction in the frequency of absence. In others, however, a series of warnings seemed to have little effect and, as shown below, the shopfloor reaction did not suggest a major attitude change. For managers, however, a major change from the past lay in the use of dismissal for absence. Several claimed that this had been unthinkable a few years previously but that there was now the will at the top to dismiss. Even if not literally true, this perception was important to managers themselves, in asserting a self-confidence that had been lacking: they now felt that they were in command. Some told us of key incidents that had effected a change. One, for example, said that in another Area a manager had caused amazement by dismissing a worker but had been upheld, the result being that other managers became alive to the situation.

Such semi-mythical events were important for managers in making sense of their world. But they were based in fact. In our Area, of nineteen dismissals in one year, twelve were for absence. (No data were available for previous years). As would be expected, most of these dismissals involved workers with BR for a very short time: four of the absence dismissals involved workers with less than six months' service. But five of them concerned workers with at least five years' service, pointing to a determination among managers not to let issues drift. In the clearest example of this, a worker whom we will call Singh was dismissed. He had worked for BR for ten years and had a record of long-term sickness. At his appeal, he asked to be made redundant, but was told that ill-health retirement was available only for very long-serving employees. The manager said that if he would guarantee to work, he would take him back. He asked Singh if he would return to work the next day. Singh replied that he was still ill, and the manager concluded that he plainly did not want to work for BR and that it was best if they 'parted company'.

This tough approach was widespread across BR. In March 1989 the *Locomotive Journal* (the monthly paper of the drivers' union ASLEF) reported a case of a driver with ten years' service sacked for absence; BR's alteration of the decision at an industrial tribunal was hailed as a major union victory. We also spoke to three NUR divisional organizers in various parts of the country, all of whom reported a stricter control of absence. From the unions' point of view, the managerial approach was unreasonable because there was little opportunity for a union representative to state a worker's case before a dismissal: if the formal procedures had been properly followed, it was hard to overturn a decision at a tribunal. This reaction might be written off as desire to cling to old cosy relationships. As noted above, moreover, part of the rationale for taking absence control out of the disciplinary procedure, in which union representatives can be involved from the first stage, was to avoid connotations of blame. The new absence control policy was not a straightforward attempt to ignore existing procedures. Yet neither should the rationale be taken at face value. The will to be more pro-active necessarily meant that workers were going to be dismissed when previously they would not have been. In our Area - and, as far as we could judge, in others too - there was, moreover, no effort to explain to the unions either the reasons for tighter absence control or the methods adopted. This left union representatives feeling powerless and aggrieved, and contributed to a worsening atmosphere.

Cases such as Singh's illustrate managerial toughness. Yet this still applied to particular cases and was not universal. As noted above, absence records that in Multiplex would call for instant action were not defined as a problem. And even in 'serious' cases the outcome was uncertain. In our Area one worker had become notorious. He had had eleven warnings for poor attendance in a ten-year period and he had yet to be dismissed.

Control was thus tighter than it had been, but it had not reached the level of a major crack-down. In many ways the approach remained much more caring than that in other organizations. On the type of absence that might qualify for sick pay, for example, a clerk in the personnel department explained that sick pay was formally only for personal illness but that someone going absent for some domestic crisis and explaining this to his manager might well be paid. Managers claimed that they were tightening up on excuses for sickness, but a degree of leniency remained. As shown in other chapters, managers in our other firms certainly exercised discretion in, say, letting people go home early to cope with some domestic crisis. But this did not extend to allowing sick pay for whole days off. The problem from the point of view of BR management, however, is that their generosity was not seen as such. It had slowly become taken for granted that it was reasonable to go absent for domestic needs: as shown below, BR workers were more likely than others to cite such needs as reasons for going absent, but they did not see this as a valued managerial concession.

A final dimension of absence control concerns the role of supervision. In a firm like Multiplex, it was the supervisor who was responsible for recording absence and for initiating the first stage in the control system. In BR, supervisors had no such role. This reflects the specific nature of supervision in the organization. As supervisors of platform staff put it, they saw themselves as working along with their workers and as dealing with such things as the allocation of work tasks; discipline was not one of their functions. The difference between a provider of work and an overseer was even clearer with train crew supervisors, whose tasks centred on ensuring that each train due to be worked had its appropriate crew. Formal discipline was handled through separate inspectors who dealt with incidents such as drivers passing signals at danger. Absence control rested with the manager of each department. Some managers saw this as a weakness, and bemoaned the quality of their supervisors. It certainly put a burden on the line manager, and meant that the control policy stayed at some distance from workers. From time to time, someone might be spoken to, but it was difficult for any more developed message to filter down to the work force. As will be seen, there was awareness of control, but little feeling that this was tight and little appreciation of its logic.

We may now put control in context by setting out the pattern of absence. We then consider the shopfloor reaction.

Absence Patterns

The comparative statistics assembled in Table A.4 show that BR did not have a widespread problem of absence. The proportion of workers going through a year with no spell of absence (31 per cent) was 'better' even than Multiplex. The overall severity index, at 16.6 days absent per worker per year, was, however, about a third higher than the Multiplex figure. Since the average spell of absence in the two organizations was of virtually identical length, the reason lies in the greater number of absences in BR. Although many workers were never absent, significant numbers were also absent a great deal: 16 per cent had more than five spells in a year, as against 5 per cent in Multiplex. BR also stands out in terms of the distribution of absence spells. Two-thirds lasted only one or two days. This proportion was similar to that at FinCo, but here very few workers had long spells of absence. BR's record thus comprised a moderate to high number of cases of long-term absence, together with a substantial minority of workers taking many short spells.

The breakdown of the BR figures by occupational group in Table 4.1 shows that the frequency of absence was similar across the four grades considered. There was no tendency for the lower grades of station staff and carriage cleaners to go absent particularly frequently; indeed, the high attendance record of the station staff was remarkable, with 46 per cent having no spell of absence. These workers also had a very low severity rate of 8.6 days per worker per year, better even than the FinCo figure. The carriage cleaners, however, recorded a rate of 28.9 days. This is consistent with the reputation of the depot as a major problem area for absence. This image was in fact undeserved. Workers with health problems were often re-deployed to the depot, and its record was due to this, and also to the presence there of a number of other older workers with long-standing health problems, and not to any culture of absence.

TABLE 4.1   Absence Patterns by Occupation, British Rail

Year	Drivers		Guards		Platform Staff	Carriage Cleaners
	1981/2	1987	1981/2	1987	1987	1987
Absence Frequency (per cent of workers with specified number of spells)						
None	16	28	14	20	46	31
1	13	17	20	16	14	22
2	9	10	18	15	10	11
3	15	12	10	14	5	8
4	5	5	4	8	5	2
5	7	11	9	10	7	6
6–10	23	16	14	12	10	16
11 and over	12	1	10	3	3	4
Absence Duration (per cent of absence spells of given duration)						
1–2 days	81	64	87	67	68	62
3–5 days	5	19	3	16	21	12
6–19 days	9	11	8	11	6	19
20 days and over	4	6	2	6	4	8
Severity Measures						
Mean number days absent per worker per year	20	13	11	17	9	29
Mean length (days) of each spell of absence	3.2	4.7	4.8	5.5	3.6	9.9

As noted above, in the case of train crew it was possible to obtain some time series data. The figures for a twelve-month period in 1981/2 show a reduction in absence for both groups. In the case of drivers this was dramatic: close to a halving of the number of spells per head. The obvious interpretation, that the control policy was working, does not in fact explain the decline. We also calculated data for 1984, and they show that the decline was under way before the policy was implemented. Few managers could throw much light on a fact which did not accord with their own experience. But one factor identified was the current practice of using rest day working, instead of overtime, to cover work that could not be completed in regular hours. This reduced the incentive to take a day of absence close to a rest day. We have no other hard evidence to explain a puzzling phenomenon. It may be that, in the aftermath of the dispute over flexible rostering in 1982, train drivers in particular felt vulnerable and that the control policy, instituted from 1985, sharpened this feeling. What is clear is that the growing awareness among managers of an absence problem cannot be attributed to a rise in absence rates.

Leaving aside the spells of long-term sickness, which can be explained in terms of the age of BR staff (with, for example, 36 per cent of the station staff sample being aged 55 or over), the absence pattern appears to reflect the interaction of the nature of the job and the traditional mode of control. Long and irregular hours of work heightened the need for a day or two of absence to gain some rest, while the informal control system allowed some workers to go absent frequently with little penalty. This picture may now be related to workers' attitudes and norms.

Shopfloor Attitudes

In thinking about the general acceptability of absence, BR workers took quite a strong anti-absence line. As Table A.5 shows, when asked to choose between the statements that workers should attend work when able to do so and that they should be free to take time off if they wished, the great majority (82 per cent) chose the former. Similarly, as shown in Chapter 2, BR workers were rather more likely than those elsewhere to give pro-attendance answers to our vignettes. And, in relation to their own behaviour, a larger proportion than in any of the other three organizations said that they had never consciously thought about not going in to work when they were able to attend: 37 per cent, compared with the average of 23 per cent (Table A.1).

How can this be reconciled with the actual pattern of absence? As noted in Chapter 1, the dominant tradition of absence research views replies to questionnaire instruments as having an invariant meaning. This has led to much fruitless debate as to whether or not job satisfaction, say, is related to absence. It seems likely that it is so related in some circumstances and not in others, the nature of the link depending on the pattern of relationships in which attitudes are embedded (Edwards and Scullion, 1984). The present case is a prime example of this point. The reason why BR workers had pro-attendance views and a rather higher absence rate than many other groups is that they seem to have given a particular meaning to the idea of being able to attend. If domestic demands stood in the way of attendance, BR workers seem likely to have placed them first. As Table A.2 shows, of those workers who had thought of staying away, 52 per cent cited family illness or domestic duties, with a further 24 per cent mentioning time with family or other social interests; these proportions were far higher than those in our other organizations. There were no major differences between occupations. As one man put it, he would stay away to attend to personal business, and when asked whether he had taken a day off when he had been able to get in, he said that he had done so because of family illness. The BR figures, moreover, contain replies from only six guards, the remaining eleven saying that they had never thought of staying away. Yet some of these eleven scored quite high on measures of absence frequency. Though we cannot be sure, we think it likely that these eleven, too, were prone to go absent where domestic needs demanded. Many of them were Asian men who would have taken a number of domestic responsibilities. An indication of the ways in which taking time off for such duties was taken for granted appeared in a discussion with the Train Crew Manager, who cited a case of a man who had gone absent because his washing machine had broken down. The manager was just starting a policy of refusing to accept claims for sick pay which were made after the actual absence itself, but he admitted that he was only just skirting round the 'hard cases'. He also stressed, in ways which managers in our other firms would probably not have done, that he would still look sympathetically at the 'genuine' cases.

It is not hard to see how acceptance of going absent for domestic duties grew up. The long and unsocial hours worked in BR make it hard for workers to deal with such duties. In the past, manning levels were relatively generous, and managers were probably not too worried at some absence. Indeed, tolerating it may have been part of the *quid pro quo* for workers continuing to work, particularly when labour markets were tight and better-paying jobs were readily available. One platform worker, who started with BR nine years previously, said that at that time managers had not bothered if a worker did not show up for work. As Lupton (1963) argues, in such labour market conditions, managers in piecework factories may tolerate a few fiddles of the payment system to cut down on labour turnover. BR, with its flat rate pay system, had fewer of these carrots, and may have used absence as an alternative. Such an interpretation is consistent with the widespread managerial feeling that it was only recently that attendance was being managed at all actively.

BR workers were less likely than other groups to mention boredom or general dislike of the job as reasons for staying away. The only substantial category under this heading was 'unpleasant features of work on a particular day', but this was mentioned by drivers in particular. The reason was that a driver knew for which turn of duty he was scheduled: certain local trips were considered to be very monotonous, and a day absent was a means of avoiding them. In general, however, BR workers retained a high degree of commitment to doing the work itself. They are thus one group in which one would probably not find any relationship between job satisfaction and absence, because going absent was driven by domestic demands and not by discontent with the work itself.

Before going further, we need to address some of the key differences within the BR sample. We have already alluded to ethnic origins. As shown in Table 4.2, a quarter of the sample were of West Indian origin while a sixth were Asian. But there were major occupational differences, with drivers being almost exclusively white while three-quarters of the guards were Asian. Attitudes towards attendance were strongly connected with ethnic origin: 61 per cent of Asians, and 48 per cent of West Indians, but only 25 per cent of whites, said that they had never consciously thought of taking a day off work. There was a similar pattern on the first two vignettes, with Asians giving the most clearly pro-attendance answers. We were not in a position to explore the reasons for these contrasts, though they may be connected to the individualized approach to work among the Asian guards that we describe below. Casual observation suggested that small groups of friends tended to sit together during rest periods, whereas among drivers there was more of a group atmosphere. Guards were reasonably satisfied with their work, and, as noted below, they felt a considerable degree of loyalty to the employer.

The current significance of this is two-fold. First, it moderates but does not destroy the argument that BR workers were remarkably pro-attendance. On the vignettes, leaving out the guards puts the BR sample on a par with the other groups whereas one might have expected FinCo workers, say, to be substantially more pro-attendance. Moreover, the drivers stand

TABLE 4.2   Sample Characteristics by Ethnic Origin, British Rail

Per Cent	White (N=47)	West Indian (N=22)	Asian (N=13)	Total (N=82)
Occupation				
Driver	40	4	0	24
Guard	10	9	77	21
Platform	21	40	23	27
Carriage cleaner	28	46	0	28
Whether had ever thought of taking a day off work				
Yes	75	52	39	63
No	25	48	61	37
Whether had taken a day off when able to get to work				
Yes	40	10	23	30
No	60	90	77	70

out in most respects as being more pro-absence than other BR workers. All but one of them (or 95 per cent) had thought of not going in to work, whereas only half the remaining BR groups had done so. The drivers' attitudes reflected some particular circumstances, and other groups retained a substantially pro-attendance view. Second, it underlines the diversity of attitudes within BR.

This point also comes out when we consider reasons to attend. As shown in Table 4.3, thirty per cent of BR workers, and fully half the drivers, mentioned enjoyment of the work as a reason for not staying away, proportions higher than those elsewhere. But an even more important reason was the potential loss of money, mentioned by 49 per cent of all BR staff and rather higher proportions of guards, platform staff, and cleaners. Though, as noted above, any worker with over ten years' service would receive sick pay from the first day of absence, this did not compensate for the loss of other earnings, in the case of train crew various mileage payments and bonuses and, for other workers, overtime. Several workers said that they could not afford to go absent. The large number of guards citing duty to the firm is also notable as a further indication of their distinctively pro-attendance views.

The fear of discipline was cited much less often, which supports the argument that attendance control had not yet cut very deep. Workers were certainly aware of it: 84 per cent said that management had recently

TABLE 4.3   Reasons For Not Staying Away

Per Cent Mentioning	Drivers (N=20)	Guards (N=17)	Platform Staff (N=21)	Cleaners (N=23)	All (N=81)
Duty to firm	15	41	19	13	21
Loss of money	30	58	52	57	49
Possibility of discipline	25	17	14	17	19
Duty to work mates	15	6	5	13	10
Expectation of family and friends	10	12	10	0	7
Enjoyment of job	50	41	19	13	30
Backlog of work	0	0	0	0	0
Personal responsibility	45	29	33	22	32
Other	0	12	14	4	7

changed its ways of dealing with absence, and that this had involved a stricter approach. This approach had had an impact in some cases. The worker who said that in the past management had not been bothered about absence went on to say that the pressure was now daunting and that he himself had gone in to work when ill for fear of being disciplined. He sympathized with managers' problems, and in general favoured tackling bad attendance, but he felt that managers were using a big stick instead of dealing with the problem sensibly. While sharing with others the criticism of managerial style, he was, however, unusual in seeing the control policy as having a direct effect on his own behaviour. Few other workers mentioned attending when ill. Though there was awareness of the tighter regime, with two-thirds of the sample being aware of managerial pressures to attend, most workers did not say anything about how it impinged on them directly. In view of the intent of the policy, namely to control the minority of 'bad cases', this is perhaps not surprising. It confirms that the pressures remained somewhat inchoate.

The views of one driver, whom managers saw as a problem case, illustrate the balance of pressures to go absent and to attend. He mentioned work on a particular day and travel problems as reasons not to attend, and he said that he had taken days off when able to get in. As he put it, he was not actually ill but he was sick in that he could not do his job properly: every day was an awkward shift, and from time to time he felt he had just had enough. But he also cited duty to the firm and enjoyment of the job as reasons to attend, and added that he felt a duty to the passengers. He argued that most workers were dedicated and that a few days off was the only way of escape. Managers were unsympathetic and did not understand the pressures that were placed on drivers. Absence for him was thus not an act of defiance or irresponsibility but a form of escape used more in sorrow than in anger.

Norms and Cultures

The traditionally relaxed approach by management to absence control left space for work group norms to develop. In addition to this permissive factor, the character of the occupation might be expected to encourage norms. As Salaman (1974: 103) has argued, railwaymen form an occupational community, isolated from other groups and with its own language and customs; many of his 'respondents boasted that they had never been late for work, or missed a day's work', a claim which he attributed to a sense of pride and responsibility in the job. The absence of a driver or guard, in particular, also means that the work has to be covered by others. One might thus expect duty to work mates to figure high among reasons for attendance, and the type of norm to be pro-attendance.

As noted in Chapter 1, research into norms has adopted indirect methods, either inferring their presence from patterns of absence or, in more recent studies, correlating absence rates with indices of work group cohesion. We also used these indices. But for a norm to have any weight there must be independent evidence of its operation, and the key here is the extent to which workers discuss both their own absence and that of others.

Using these measures indicates that there were no strongly developed group norms. Duty to work mates was mentioned as a reason to attend by only 10 per cent of our interview sample, and even among drivers the figure was only 15 per cent. As shown in Table A.8, moreover, 86 per cent said that they never discussed the idea of taking a day off with other workers, and 45 per cent never discussed the absence of fellow workers. These proportions are in fact higher than those in some of our other organizations, indicating that BR workers were, if anything, less likely than others to have any work group standards on attendance.

There was, however, one respect in which norms had developed. They were restricted to drivers. Among other groups, there was no particularly strong work group cohesion. Indeed, at the cleaning depot several workers commented on the mistrust which existed between them and their fellows. The drivers' norms operated, however, in a more subtle way than has hitherto been recognized. They did not directly promote absence. There were certainly differences from other groups. For example, 30 per cent of drivers said that they would discuss the idea of going absent with their work mates, compared with 8 per cent of the remainder of the BR sample (and none of the guards). But this still left a majority of drivers who never engaged in such discussions, suggesting that there was no direct, active cultural support for absence. Instead, the work group provided sympathy for those who felt the need to go absent. After asking whether they discussed the absence of their fellows, we asked workers what sort of things were discussed. Among drivers (and also a small number of guards) many workers said that people would admit that they had taken days off when they were not ill. Of the 23 train crew saying that they ever discussed others' absence, 17 gave such a reply. As one driver put it, someone on a 'rough job' might say that he was going to go sick; this was common 'cabin talk'. Another said that he himself did not discuss going absent but that he heard comments about it; for example, it was accepted practice for men who did not want to work a particular turn of duty to exchange this turn with one of their mates, and people would sometimes ask why the person wanting to make the swop did not simply go sick.

The nature of the relevant understandings may be considered further by looking at the associations with our measures of work group cohesion. In general, these did not have any link with the absence measures. In Multiplex, for example, there was no relationship between a worker's evaluation of how his or her work group compared with others and the extent of discussions of other workers' absence. In BR, however, there was a tendency for more discussions to take place where cohesion was felt to be higher. There was not, however, any link between cohesion and the type of discussion that took place. In other words, workers reporting cohesion were no more likely than others to say that fellow workers admitted going absent. But they were more likely to report that some sort of discussion took place. That is, the work group provided an atmosphere in which drivers felt free to talk about their feelings and to admit going absent, but it did not itself encourage this.

The nature of drivers' occupational culture will be clearer when we have considered discipline and morale. In brief, however, there was a very strong sense of distrust of management. Drivers felt that they had been singled out for attack by managers, and there was a sense of a deep gulf between the two sides. In this context, a driver could feel safe that admitting going absent would not be reported to management. His mates, moreover, were likely to be feeling the same pressures that he was under, and they could therefore understand the need to go absent. Work group solidarity provided a climate in which workers could confidently go absent, but it did not itself create any norms as to appropriate levels of absence. As has been seen, drivers displayed very different rates of absence. The culture was permissive but not causative.

Conclusions

In sum, there was no general problem of growing absence rates, managers were trying to control absence through informal means, workers continued to have a broadly pro-attendance orientation, and there were no norms directly governing attendance. Absence also illustrates some wider issues in the management of labour. Numerous studies have analysed the new managerialism in the public sector in general and in BR in particular, but few have drawn out the implications for workers other than by inference. We have shown that the reasons for managerial concern about absence did not stem primarily from absenteeism itself but reflected a greater concern with labour costs. Absence control was one part of a policy of establishing managerial authority. Yet we have also shown that it had not yet cut very deep into day-to-day behaviour and that traditional assumptions about, for example, going absent to deal with domestic duties continued to play a part.

The managerial approach is unlikely to have had much direct effect on absence levels, given that it was aimed only at the minority of 'bad attenders'. The obvious implication is that the 'new managerialism' has been less sweeping in its impact than many accounts would suggest. But this does not mean that there was simply no change. Workers were made aware of increased managerial interest in absence, and the direct impact on rates of behaviour may have been less important than the indirect effect: managers were saying that the business had to operate according to a new logic, and that it was they who were taking the lead. Acting on absence carried wider messages, a theme that we may pursue by considering discipline and the pattern of morale.

Discipline

Tighter discipline has been noted by writers such as Ferner (1988: 107) and also in press reports. A magazine article (Platt, 1989) has quoted sources in the (then) National Union of Railwaymen as saying that after 1983 managers 'became more willing to use disciplinary procedures to sort out problems, and to use the punishment of dismissal'; it quotes several workers who describe an atmosphere of fear. The NUR officials to whom we spoke painted a similar picture. One argued that the new, aggressive manager on BR was keen to use discipline to the level of dismissal if necessary, whereas the traditional manager had been more understanding and more likely to give workers the benefit of the doubt. Little firm evidence has, however, been produced on the extent to which discipline is used on a day-to-day basis. We focus on this below, but first need to explain the background of BR's disciplinary procedures.

Background of Railway Discipline

The railways have a long history of formal disciplinary systems, reflecting the need for a detailed set of regulations to cover a complex operating system on which the safety of passengers and staff depended. During the nineteenth century managements insisted on the absolute right to control discipline which they saw as essential if order was to be maintained; fines were a common form of punishment (Kingsford, 1970; McKenna, 1980). In some cases workers were permitted to appeal against a punishment, but whether or not to grant an appeal remained at management's discretion. Unions were seen as an interference, and the struggle for recognition was difficult (Bagwell, 1963).

The unions made a significant breakthrough in 1907 when a threatened national rail strike forced the companies to make concessions. The Conciliation Scheme that was introduced with the aid of the government was a compromise: it did not entail formal recognition of the unions, and instead set up conciliation boards for each grade of worker in each company. Discipline was expressly excluded from the terms of reference of these boards. This situation was endorsed by a Royal Commission set up in 1911 to investigate the 1907 scheme: 'we think that with their great responsibilities the Companies cannot and should not be expected to permit any intervention between them and their men on the subjects of discipline and management'. But the Commission did point to the unsatisfactory nature of a system in which workers could put their case only after punishment, and it recommended that workers be permitted to state their defence and to call witnesses before a final decision was reached (Royal Commission, 1911: paras 52, 31, 72). A wartime agreement of 1915 still formally excluded discipline, but it did provide for workers to state their defence to a charge, to call witnesses, and in serious cases to appeal, at which they could be defended by an advocate who could be a union official (Halverson, 1952: 369).

The divorce between discipline and other aspects of management-worker relations has continued to this day. When the railways were nationalized, they carried over this aspect of private company practice, even though principled opposition to union involvement could no longer be maintained. The present disciplinary procedure dates from 1956. It provides that workers be informed in writing of charges against them; that they may state a defence in writing or reserve their defence for a hearing; that they may call witnesses and be accompanied by a spokesman; and that they may appeal to a higher level of management. In cases of grave misconduct, management has the right of summary action. The statement of the charge is now done on a 'Form 1'; Form 2 states the punishment that has been applied.

In view of the age of BR's disciplinary mechanisms, it is curious that it was not until 1980 that a scale of punishments was formally given. Normal punishments start with a reprimand, and proceed through a serious reprimand, suspension, reduction in grade, transfer to another location, limitation of concessionary travel facilities, and dismissal. Something like this system would appear to have operated for many years. In a 1976 case a court held that demotion was not a repudiation of contract because it was an accepted custom and practice which amounted to an implied term in the contract (*Theedom v British Railways Board*, 1976 IRLR 137). Our study of the origins of railway discipline, discussed below, shows that the notion of a formal caution or reprimand certainly existed in 1939, and probably much earlier.

It was not until the 1970s that most large British companies developed formal disciplinary procedures that came anywhere close to BR's (Edwards, 1989), and the right to call witnesses and to be represented at the first stage of a disciplinary procedure is probably still unusual. Before the emergence of the new managerial hard line, BR workers could consider themselves to be much better protected against arbitrary action than other manual workers. Combined with well-established procedures on promotion, transfer, and redundancy, the disciplinary system gave workers a substantial degree of job security.

Yet some other consequences are also important. The separation of discipline and collective bargaining prevented any union incursion into the principles governing discipline. Union representatives have been able to defend workers as individuals, but they have had no means to question to general rules that are applied. The disciplinary procedure has also reduced the chance of using collective means to protest against the treatment of particular workers: it has become taken for granted that discipline is an individual matter. When managers choose to use discipline more and when a sense of injustice arises, workers are, as shown below, left curiously powerless to express this frustration.

The disciplinary system reflects its origins in a time when managements claimed absolute rights of authority. We studied these origins by examining reports of management-union discussions and official inquiries; we also analysed the use of disciplinary penalties on four railways over the period 1860-1930 (Edwards and Whitston, 1992). On the procedures, the BR case gives no support to those who have identified an evolution from a punitive to a corrective style, and even to a model of self-discipline (Ashdown and Baker, 1973; Henry, 1982). The move to correction allegedly means that discipline is no longer used to punish mistakes but is instead a means of teaching workers proper standards. Since disciplinary procedures have been formalized longer on the railways than in just about any other industry, evolution is most likely here. Yet workers are still charged with an offence in a quasi-military fashion, and by 1980 there were aspects where it had fallen behind current good practice. The system's procedures had in important respects remained frozen. Moreover, as we argue below, its practice in the 1980s had a great deal in common with that from earlier periods.

Tightening Disciplinary Practice

One by-product of the procedure is the very careful keeping of records. A worker's personal file contains details of all the Form 1 cases to which he or she has been subject, together with notes on other reprimands or warnings. We examined a sample of 316 files, drawn from the same grades as those from which the interview sample was drawn, though we made no attempt to include all of our interviewees. Any recorded case of discipline in an eleven-year period was noted. This may create some imprecision, in that managers may vary in the care with which they keep records, but we did not want to restrict attention simply to Form 1 cases. The method does not measure activity within our Area, since some disciplines against current employees will have been received in other Areas, and since other workers will have moved out of the Area. But we have a reasonable picture of the disciplinary histories of a substantial number of workers who do not appear to have been in any way atypical.

As Table 4.4 shows, approaching half of all staff had experienced at least one disciplinary action against them, with very little difference between grades. Taking each case of discipline, and not each worker, as the unit of analysis, Table 4.5 shows the distribution of issues and the timing of the discipline. Absence was the largest single category (except at the cleaning depot, where the figure for work performance issues is inflated by one incident where there was a collective refusal to work because the lighting to the carriage cleaning areas had failed, with all the workers involved receiving Form 1s). Verbal warnings were the main form of action against absence, though as late as 1986 Form 1s were being issued for absence, suggesting some managerial confusion as to the supposed separation of absence control from the disciplinary procedure. The significance of the other issues will be discussed below.

The key point from the table is the growth in disciplinary action in recent years. For drivers, for example, one-third of all cases occurred in

TABLE 4.4 Distribution of Disciplinary Action

Per Cent	Drivers (N=113)	Guards (N=89)	Platform Staff (N=69)	Cleaning Depot (N=45)	All (N=316)
None	52	56	49	60	54
1	31	26	17	31	27
2–3	7	11	20	7	11
4 or more	10	7	13	2	9

Note: A case of discipline is taken as any conversation recorded in management files. The category is thus much wider than formal (Form 1) discipline. Data relate to period 1976–87.
The numbers refer to numbers of workers, randomly selected from management files.

1986 alone. (This might be put down to a statistical artefact in that workers recruited in, say, 1985 can appear only in the records since that date. In fact, most workers had been with BR throughout the eleven-year period, and a cross-tabulation of number of disciplines with length of service showed that there was no significant association). As might be expected, the growth in action for absence was even sharper than that for other issues.

These data support managers' and workers' perceptions of tighter discipline. As noted above, managers, virtually without exception, noted a greater confidence and a willingness to take decisive action. We also took the opportunity of asking workers whether they felt that the use of discipline had increased in recent years. In all, 43 per cent said that there had been an increase, as against only 5 per cent noting a decrease, with the remaining 52 per cent saying that there had been no change or making no comment on the matter. There were marked differences between grades. As shown below, drivers stood out from the other groups in many respects, being particularly discontented and critical of management. This was reflected in their views on discipline, with 84 per cent of them identifying an increase in its use.

TABLE 4.5   Issue and Date of Discipline

Per Cent	Drivers (N=122)	Guards (N=76)	Platform Staff (N=88)	Cleaning Depot (N=28)	All (N=314)
Issue					
Absence	35	49	47	39	42
Late on duty/AWOL	6	4	2	4	4
Absent from place of work	7	3	7	7	6
Platform overrun, signal passed at danger, speeding	35	–	–	–	14
Other work performance issues	12	34	36	43	27
Booking off without permission, etc.	2	4	0	0	2
Other	2	7	9	7	5
Year					
1987	14	5	15	14	12
6	34	29	20	14	27
5	12	14	14	11	13
4	7	13	14	11	11
3	7	16	10	18	11
2	7	7	8	11	8
1	7	5	3	7	6
80	2	4	2	4	3
79	1	4	0	7	2
8	4	1	6	4	4
7	2	1	3	0	2
6	3	0	5	0	3

Note: The numbers refer to the number of separate cases of discipline recorded, i.e. the unit of observation is a case of discipline, not an individual worker.

The growing use of discipline did not, however, seem to be associated with any major change in the type of punishment dispensed. The overwhelming majority of cases involved only a verbal warning or a 'suitable serious conversation', a concept not specifically mentioned in the procedure which indicates that a manager talks to a worker about an error but does not record even the first formal step of a reprimand. The files also included several cases in which managers had taken an understanding approach. For example, in 1987 a driver passed a signal at danger and the manager gave the minimum possible punishment for this offence, a reprimand, in view of his good record. In 1986 another driver had initially been given a two-day suspension and a final warning for driving a train from the rear cab, but this was reduced to only a one-day suspension on the argument of the union representative that the evidence was hearsay and that the offence was not very great. The most severe punishment short of dismissal was given to a member of the station staff, who received five-day suspensions on two separate occasions. His record, however, suggested that in another organization he might have been dismissed even before the two relevant incidents. In 1984 he had a serious reprimand and a final warning for going absent without leave, that is for absenting himself without notification. A year later he received a two-day suspension for being rude to a passenger, and in 1986 the first of his five-day suspensions for being absent without leave for two days. This happened again the next year, and the manager agreed not to dismiss him on the pleas of his union representative that he had had a number of domestic difficulties.

A relatively relaxed approach was also evident in an area of some significance on the railways, namely leaving the place of work during a turn of duty. Train crew often have times when they are not actually working trains, and there was considerable temptation to slip outside to attend to personal business. For station staff, there are slack periods when they are unlikely to be missed. For carriage cleaners, there is the incentive to complete one's work allocation and go home early. These practices are discussed further below, but they also came within the remit of the disciplinary system from time to time. The approach adopted seems to have reflected widespread knowledge of their prevalence. For example, a guard admitted leaving work during his turn of duty for 3½ hours to do some shopping; he received only a verbal warning, along with loss of pay for the relevant time. When a station worker was disciplined for arguing with a superior it was noted without comment that he had gone for some tea and did not re-appear for 52 minutes. More generally, as a cleaning supervisor in particular argued, it was quite common for BR workers to absent themselves in this way, and sometimes for them to punch each others' clock cards: in other firms, he said, this would lead to instant dismissal but in BR it was left as a warning. In one case at the depot a worker booked sick, only to find that he had been clocked out by another worker. There were also cases of workers being found in a nearby pub, the penalty being a reprimand and loss of pay.

As shown below, there were limits on this behaviour, and there was much less disorder than a recitation of cases would suggest. The present significance of the cases is to point to an issue which has often been debated but on which clear evidence has been sparse. This is the connection between formal discipline and the day-to-day negotiation of order. Industrial sociology contains a mass of material on the latter, pointing, for example, to the ways in which shopfloor custom can amend formal rules. Foremen have been shown to co-operate with workers leaving early, using the incentive of tolerating this in order to gain co-operation in the production process (Ditton, 1979). Yet many discussions have treated custom as a world of its own, immune to other pressures. From the other side of the coin, studies of disciplinary procedures have looked at the kinds of behaviour for which workers are disciplined without relating such practice to the day-to-day control of work. In this case, we have been able to indicate the connections: fiddles of time were quite widespread, and on occasion they came to light and managers had to act, but they did so in the knowledge that the fiddles were part of established practice and that to crack down hard might lead to unpredictable results. The worlds of custom and formal discipline were not independent, but were defined in relation to each other.

The major exception to a continued low-key use of punishment was in dismissals. As already noted, the Area had 19 cases in one year, which gives a rate of dismissal of about 10 per 1,000 employees. This is close to the average for industry as a whole, but in establishments with more than 1,000 employees the rate in 1980 was only 4 per 1,000 (Daniel and Millward, 1983: 171). The Area thus had a much higher figure than comparable establishments, even though BR's developed procedures might lead one to expect that it would rely rather little on the ultimate weapon of dismissal. The lack of data for earlier years makes it impossible to judge trends, but it seems from managerial reports that dismissal was being used much more. The basic reason was a widespread feeling that in the past there had been a reluctance to take the final step, leaving a worker with a series of final warnings and eroding managerial credibility. The view now was that, where dismissal was justified and where there was no alternative, managers should no longer hold back.

There was thus a growth in the use of all forms of discipline and of dismissal. But, in general, the method of handling discipline had not been marked by a dramatic hardening. Discipline had attained a much higher profile in the conduct of workplace relations but some traditional elements of control remained in the way in which it was handled.

Workforce Reactions

The reactions of the workforce reflected the mix of change and continuity. Overall, 62 per cent of workers said that the strength of discipline was 'about right', with 26 per cent saying that it was too strict and only 5 per cent that it was too weak. Criticism of strictness was thus more intense than it was in our other organizations. There was, however, a dramatic variation between jobs in BR. None of the cleaners, and a fifth of the guards and platform staff, said that discipline was too strict, but 68 per cent of drivers took this view. Drivers were also the most likely to say that discipline was applied differently to different groups of workers. This reflected a strong view that it was drivers who were being chosen for particular attention and that managers were increasingly arbitrary and unreasonable in their approach. This view ran very deep among drivers, many of whom quoted cases where they felt that managers had acted completely unreasonably. One particular current case concerned a driver who had been disciplined for drinking; other drivers argued that this represented double standards, since managers themselves did the same, and an excessively harsh approach. Another example of double standards concerned the enforcement of rules that were often ignored. The railway rule book is so complex that to follow it to the letter would lead to chaos: not for nothing was the practice of working to rule invented on the railways (see Hudson, 1970). Drivers complained that they were in practice expected to ignore certain rules and that they were then penalized for doing so. One explained that he had been reprimanded for exceeding a speed limit in a station, even though breaking the limit was necessary if trains were to run to time: managers created pressures, such as keeping to schedules, which forced workers to break rules, and then turned round and applied disciplinary penalties.

The intensity of this resentment among drivers cannot be explained in terms of the rate at which discipline was applied for, as noted above, managers were not particularly likely to act against drivers. Indeed, among drivers and across the whole sample there was no relationship between attitudes to the disciplinary system and whether or not a worker said that he or she had been disciplined: criticism was not the product of personal experience but was general. The drivers' attitudes reflect several aspects of their situation. First, their occupational solidarity was greater than that of other groups. As one driver explained, they saw each other day and night, and stuck together. Thus a case of discipline against one driver would be discussed by all, whereas other groups adopted a much more individualized approach. Second, as shown below, drivers felt intense distrust in management, and their views on discipline were just one part of a much wider loss of confidence in management. Not surprisingly, there were strong associations between perceptions of discipline and our measures of trust in management, though much of this is due to the fact that it was drivers who were most critical of discipline and least trustful of management. This reflects the third feature, the feeling among drivers that they were an elite under threat, both directly through such things as flexible rostering and indirectly, through the traincrew concept which promised to erode the distinct character of the drivers' line of promotion.

Historical Parallels

Such reactions reflect, we have suggested, tighter financial pressures, which led through to a more frequent use of discipline by managers. This is more than just a plausible set of linkages. We have shown that managers were well aware of the commercial regime and that they underlined the need to tackle issues which, they felt, the previous regime had encouraged them to neglect. The argument is strengthened further by looking at some historical parallels. Price (1986: 120) has argued that at the end of the nineteenth century there was a tightening of discipline induced by growing financial pressures. Our study of staff records gives substantial support to this view: rates of discipline rose significantly at this period. We saw above that disciplinary procedures had a strong historical legacy. We have now seen that the dynamics of how discipline was actually used during the 1980s were similar to those of ninety years earlier.

A second parallel is the level of disciplinary activity. An evolutionary view would expect that punishment will be needed less frequently as procedures become established. In fact, rates of punishment recorded in the 1980s were of the same order of magnitude as those in the period 1860-1920. There were plainly differences: fines have disappeared, and peak levels of discipline during the nineteenth century were notably higher than those for the 1980s. But there was no qualitative shift in the extent to which disciplinary action took place.

Conclusions

We have seen, then, that the new commercialism of BR did have a clear effect on the use of discipline. Managers felt the pressure to act on matters that they might previously have let slide, and they were confident of their ability to do so. The perceptions of the unions on the extent of discipline were accurate, though in our Area the handling of cases at the higher stages of the procedure was not marked by a particularly aggressive style. There was, for example, no evidence of a greater use of the more severe punishments such as suspension.

Some managers saw a greater use of this discipline-as-control as part of a restoration of a sense of order, with workers now working more effectively and with BR itself having a clearer vision of its purpose. Better communication with staff was part of this approach. Relevant evidence would be awareness on the shopfloor of these efforts to improve communications and better 'morale'. In fact, as we proceed to show, workers saw discipline simply as punishment. BR had not re-shaped its workplace relations. In fact, the growth in the use of discipline can be seen as one of a number of episodes in which tighter commercial pressures led to the intensification of managerial control. Events in the 1980s were not novel, either in the sense that tighter discipline was a unique feature of the railways under Thatcherism or (still less) in the sense of a breakthrough to anything that could be called self-discipline.

Shopfloor Relations with Management

How far was management actually claiming an improvement in morale or the achievement of a new industrial relations? BR was certainly not arguing that it had created an entirely new atmosphere. But there were suggestions of moves in this direction. At national level, such things as the Customer Care campaign have been designed to heighten workers' awareness of the needs of passengers and to induce them to think of the railways as a business. Senior BR managers have also argued that a policy of individual involvement was being put in place, and that this was connected with the business strategy of decentralization in that reducing central control made it possible for workers to identify with a distinct operating unit. At the time when we were doing most of our interviews, *Railnews* (Feb. 1988), the BR house newspaper, printed the new policy on employee involvement, which includes a commitment to improving working relationships and encouraging workers to know how the business is performing. In asking workers about recent changes in management policy, we used this statement as a convenient focus: we were, in effect, directly putting in front of workers the idea that managers did care about shopfloor relations, and those who denied it were responding to some very definite cues.

Local managers' claims were mixed, but fell into three groups. First, there were the 'modernists', who felt that change had had to come and that workers had generally accepted this. The manager responsible for the smaller station that we studied, for example, said that there was an excellent working relationship with staff, who were highly committed to the job. Second were the 'sceptics', who were as keen on change as the modernists but who stressed the traditionalism of railway workers and the difficulty of making thorough-going change. Finally the traditionalists were unhappy with commercialism. One long-serving manager said that there was a lot of talk of communication, but BR was really managing through 'fear and rumour'; morale was low and, though discipline had brought people into line, this had not generated satisfaction. In his view, it was necessary to try to understand the worker's situation and to manage through an understanding approach. Managers were, then, far from united, and the further down the hierarchy that we went the more we found questioning of the new commercialism. None the less, all managers were aware of the general claims about communication and involvement, and we can reasonably take these as being the official view against which to set worker reaction.

In Table 4.6 replies to four of our standard questions about relations with management are set out, together with a classification of spontaneous critical comments. Two features stand out. First, the overall view of management was less favourable than in our other organizations, with the exception in some respects of the hospital. Not one BR worker said that there was complete trust between workers and management; more than half felt that the amount of trust had been declining; when asked about three possible productive functions that managers might perform more than a third said that BR managers carried out none of them; and just under half offered spontaneous critical comments. This last issue is illuminating. The question about management's functions often induced workers to talk with considerable feeling about managerial failings. A third of the whole sample argued that managers did not know the details of railway operation: young graduate trainees were being brought in who might know about balance sheets but who were ignorant of operating procedures. As one driver put it, managers were so concerned with their budgets that they cut down on such things as training, the result being that there was now a shortage of drivers capable of covering all the routes served by the depot. (Train crew managers in fact admitted that there had been a problem here, but claimed that they were now actively pursuing route and traction learning). A platform worker said that managers were

TABLE 4.6   Attitudes to Management

	Drivers	Guards	Platform	Cleaners	Total
Managers are:					
Very friendly	0	12	18	5	9
Quite friendly	20	35	41	55	38
Quite distant	30	24	23	23	25
Very distant	35	6	5	5	12
(Other)	15	24	14	14	16
Trust:					
Complete	0	0	0	0	0
Most of time	10	20	40	29	25
Fair amount	15	40	45	35	33
Not much	65	33	15	29	36
None	10	7	0	6	6
Trust has:					
Improved	10	21	35	18	21
Stayed same	15	36	24	36	26
Worsened	75	43	41	45	53
Functions performed by management:					
All three	0	18	9	12	10
Two	25	6	9	12	13
One	35	30	54	40	40
None	40	46	27	36	37

not really concerned with passengers, but only with budgets: trains were overcrowded or cancelled because the managerial concern was cost and not the quality of the service.

Second, there was a sharp difference between drivers and all the other groups. Three-quarters of drivers perceived a decline in trust, and 80 per cent argued that managers were technically incompetent. When set alongside drivers' views on discipline, this points to a profound sense of dissatisfaction and open resentment. Other groups were nothing like as discontented: the discontented were in a minority, and their discontent was expressed much less forcibly than was the case among drivers. An apathetic view was common, as we can see in looking at reactions to recent changes in the managerial approach.

As Table 4.7 shows, almost two-thirds of the BR workers who commented on recent changes said directly that there had been no improvement in the amount of communication from management. Only among platform staff was there a substantial number saying that communication had improved. Though the small numbers involved make gener-

TABLE 4.7   Reported Changes in Managerial Policy Towards Workers

Per Cent Mentioning	Drivers (N=20)	Guards (N=16)	Platform Staff (N=17)	Cleaners (N=15)	Total (N=68)
Stricter	55	44	35	20	40
Work harder	25	19	41	47	32
Work not harder	25	25	6	27	21
More communication	20	25	47	20	28
No more communication	70	75	53	47	62
Friendlier	0	0	0	0	0
Less friendly	0	0	0	0	0
Fairer	0	0	0	0	0

Base: All those present at least five years, and stating a clear view on recent
    changes.

alization difficult, there seemed to be a clear difference between platform workers in the small out station and in the main station. The general atmosphere certainly seemed to be different, with workers in the former feeling reasonably content while those in the latter saw managers as distant and the Customer Care campaign as an irrelevance. A typical comment was that it merely re-stated what any rail worker knew anyway. Other workers to whom we spoke more informally had similar feelings. It is likely that these differences among platform staff reflected a more general division. We were told of staff at the very small stations of the Area who took a pride in their work. They presumably felt in charge of what they were doing, a sense quite foreign to the majority of workers in the large, anonymous central station. One worker here told us that under the Customer Care scheme he was responsible for assisting handicapped passengers but that it was impossible to do this properly since he was supposed to cover a dozen busy platforms at once. He felt commitment to the job, but argued that staffing cuts had made it impossible to carry it out properly.

This links with the question of the effects of the cuts on effort levels. In view of their deep discontents, drivers might be expected to argue that they were being required to work harder. In fact, train crew were less likely than other groups in BR to say that work had become harder, and indeed less likely to say so even than Multiplex workers, in relation to whom managerial change had been much less dramatic than was the case in BR. It was probably true that actual work effort had not changed much.

Driving a train is driving a train, and there are few ways in which the effort demanded when a driver is actually at work can be increased. The key is the proportion of the working day spent in the cab. At our depot, drivers were clear that flexible rostering had not in general increased their working time. Some even argued that it had worked against management. For example, under the old system of an eight-hour turn a job might finish at, say, ten minutes before the end of the turn, with these ten minutes being paid at normal rates and with any delay to the train being covered by this time. Under the new system, if a train was delayed a worker might go straight on to overtime rates.

These are complex issues, and it was not part of our brief to investigate them in detail. What is relevant is that drivers did not report working harder. Indeed, the fact that they were not doing so was seen as a further example of managerial incompetence, for why did management go through all the bother of introducing flexible rostering for such limited gains? Pendleton's (1991a) findings cited at the start of the chapter - that the gains of flexible rostering have been highly variable and that the system has thrown up new problems of its own - bear out the impressions that we gained. Pendleton also notes that flexible rostering might have more of an impact on freight depots, where the exact timing of trains is not critical and where each journey tends to be lengthy, than on passenger ones, where the exigencies of passenger timetables make it difficult to make many savings through flexible rostering. The Monopolies and Mergers Commission (1980: 99; 1987: 84-6; 1989: 62-3) has also made several studies of this. In 1980, drivers on the Southern Region were estimated to spend 45 per cent of their working time actually driving trains, a proportion which had risen to only 47 per cent six years later. In 1988, however, drivers on Provincial services recorded a figure of 62 per cent. The MMC does not itself comment on these differences, which may well be due to longer journeys in the Provincial sector. Had the introduction of flexible rostering in 1982 had any major effect, a much sharper rise would have been expected between 1980 and 1986 than in fact occurred. The MMC also complained of the time taken in scrutinizing working arrangements. Traditionally, BR staff produce 'diagrams' for a programme of work, and these are studied by workers' representatives (the Local Departmental Committee). The MMC claimed that this scrutiny could take ten man-days per week and welcomed the fact that the easement of manning agreements had ended this practice. In our depot, however, there was no suggestion of such a change, and the drivers' LDC representatives were quite clear that they retained their established rights of scrutiny. In short, here at least train crew were not working significantly harder.

Larger proportions of platform staff and cleaners reported working harder. In the case of the former, this reflects staffing reductions. On most platforms on the large station the standard manning had been cut from three to two. Opinions were divided as to whether this directly meant more work, but the tendency was certainly in that direction: of the 17 platform staff stating a view on these changes, seven thought they were working harder and only one that work was less hard; the seven were, moreover, concentrated in the large station, where the manning cuts had been most obvious. Cleaners, too, felt that they were working harder, though there was no specific organizational change at the root of this: there was just a general feeling that they were expected to do more. This was probably more to do with the standard of their work than the literal amount: each cleaner was given a set number of carriages to clean, and this had not increased, though the standard of cleanliness expected may have increased.

Workers thus perceived the direction of managerial changes as being towards tighter discipline, less good working relationships, and more demanding work. Improved communications were given little weight. But discontent was certainly not universal. Among all the groups except drivers, significant numbers did not make major criticisms of management. Responses to our questions were often low-key and reflected a resigned acceptance of what was happening. There was certainly no eager acceptance of change, but neither was there overt, still less organized, opposition. We can understand this reaction by considering the pattern of detailed job control and how it had been changing.

The Control of Effort

Labour relations on the railways have traditionally been marked by a distinct balance of conflict and accommodation. In its evidence to the Donovan Royal Commission of 1965-8, the BR Board noted the industry's good strike record and the loyalty of staff in turning out for duty every day of the year and in having a high standard of service to the public (Donovan Commission, Minutes of Evidence 14, and oral question 2093). Yet the absence of overt conflict does not mean that the pattern of workplace behaviour suits management. At least since 1919, when the eight-hour day was won, the unions had been trying to secure their own interests. By the

1970s, there were well-established rules on promotion, transfer, and redundancy. We have also seen that train crew LDCs had gained considerable influence over the allocation of work. Critics saw the system as unduly rigid, and as allowing workers to cling to outmoded working practices such as having two drivers in the cab. Implicit in the criticism was the assumption that workers also enjoyed less formal means of influencing the effort bargain: they could work a few fiddles with little fear of penalty. The picture painted of the 1980s, by contrast, has management rigorously sweeping aside both formally agreed rights and informal fiddles. We begin by describing the state of workers' informal practices and considering how far their presence indicates change from the past. This enables us to draw together the various strands of our argument in relation to the issue of how workers were persuaded to work hard. Finally, we consider the implications: were the various discontents that we have described leading towards more overt conflict?

Fiddles and Informality

The work organization of our four grades of staff differed widely, which meant that the kinds of job controls open to them also differed. We thus need to discuss each in turn.

As noted above, train crew are not directly supervised. Their potential fiddles fall into two kinds: reducing effort when at work, and fiddling time. The former would include, for drivers, breaking speed restrictions and, for guards, not making as many or as thorough ticket inspections as were expected. For drivers, we found no evidence that their low morale had led to any major reductions of attention while they were working. There was discontent with management but still pride in the work. A traction inspector grasped this when discussing drivers' attitudes. He began by saying that they found their routine work on suburban services monotonous but then elaborated this to underline that this did not imply a lack of attention to the job or a withdrawal of interest in safety: drivers were still conscientious. As argued above, practices such as breaking speed limits were not fiddles in the sense of actions which benefited workers at the expense of management; they were jointly acknowledged customs. In terms of behaviour when driving trains, there seems to have been little change. For guards, our inquiries were not detailed enough to uncover workplace fiddles, but most guards remained relatively content, and certainly did not complain about an increase in their work load. It is thus unlikely that there was any significant change in their fiddles either.

Time fiddles are much more instructive. One aspect covered the time of booking on at the start of a shift. Train crew enjoyed considerable leeway here. Part of this was supplied by formal agreements, namely that they must have sufficient time between booking on and taking out a train to read notices containing new operating instructions. This reading time could be used by coming in a few minutes later than the official booking on time. More significant was the ability to come in much later than the few minutes that this fiddle permitted. Managers had the right to send anyone home if he reported late, but this was used very rarely. The general expectation was that anyone reporting late would be allowed to book on and would be given a new set of duties. To the extent that budget cuts were making train crew supervisors short of labour, commercialism was actually increasing workers' ability to get away with this fiddle because they knew that they were needed and that the risk of being sent home was remote.

The related practice of leaving the workplace when on duty has been mentioned above. This could be carried out by a worker assigned to train duties who had some empty time between two jobs or by a man who was 'spare', that is who was being used as cover in the event of absence or other contingencies. Such temporary leaving of the workplace was likely to come to light only if the supervisor required a worker. It would probably be dealt with by a 'quiet word' and not formal discipline. As one train crew supervisor explained, to take a hard line would cause him problems in the longer term. For example, there was formally a limit of twelve hours on the length of time that a worker could work continuously, together with a minimum rest period between the end of one turn of duty and the start of the next. In practice, workers were willing to bend these rules, for example doing thirteen hours one day and having one overtime hour recorded for the next day. The supervisor explained that he could gain this sort of co-operation only if he were willing to engage in some give and take with his workers. Or, as a worker said, managers were good to him and he was therefore willing to do overtime as and when he was asked. Disciplinary action for lateness or being absent from the place of work was likely only in exceptional circumstances. One such circumstance was being found away from work by a senior managers, and we were told one or two stories of what had happened in this event. Otherwise, something depended on the character of the individual supervisor: one or two had a reputation for favouritism and inconsistency. But otherwise the customary balance was well-established, and there was no discernible effort by management to alter it.

More changes were being made in some other areas. A key fiddle exercising train crew managers concerned the learning of new routes. It had come to light that some guards had been signing their cards to say that they had done a trip over a route when they had not in fact done it. A new procedure requiring them, and drivers, to have a managerial counter-signature at the far end of the route had been introduced. The manager argued that such practices had been allowed to grow up and that it was now necessary to attack the most obvious ones. A related case concerned a change in the ways in which workers were assigned to 'links' (that is, to teams of workers each of whom does part of the link's diagram, a depot having a number of links arranged by seniority, with the top link doing the most desirable work). Change had been necessary but previous managements had backed off, in the face of threats of industrial action, but management had now succeeded in pressing through the change.

There was thus no sweeping attack on every aspect of custom and practice. Managers were acting a little at a time in an opportunistic fashion. Most of the formal LDC rights, such as scrutinizing diagrams, remained in place, as did fiddles of time.

Platform staff and cleaners have always had a less powerful position than train crew, for they have lacked any strategic position in the production process. Their fiddles tended to be of a minor nature. Cleaners, for example, said that there were some tricks of the trade to speed up the work and that supervisors had their favourite areas of a carriage to check: depending on which supervisor was in charge, different parts of the work could be skimped. But no one questioned the right of a supervisor to insist that someone return to do again work found unsatisfactory. There was no idea that the definition of what was an acceptable standard of cleanliness be made an overt bargaining issue, and fiddles remained marginal, to be practised by an individual with the nerve to do so and not institutionalized into any customs.

A similar point applies to time fiddles. Given that cleaners were assigned a set number of carriages per shift, the obvious temptation was to finish the work and go home early. Whereas in the case of train crew we were given a more or less standard picture of booking fiddles, at the cleaning depot we received many different accounts. Some people, workers and supervisors alike, denied that there was any early leaving; others said that it might be permitted at certain times, for example Sunday shifts which were always relatively slack, but that it was always a concession granted on each occasion by a supervisor and not a practice which had attained the status of a right; and others saw it as a more regular occurrence. The most plausible interpretation is that the practice was, indeed, established only very weakly. Unlike the relatively understood use of time fiddles by bakery workers described by Ditton (1979), carriage cleaners seem to be been able to escape early on one or two occasions but this was far from being a general rule.

As for platform workers, their time fiddles, namely, slipping out during working hours, were more established. Supervisors recognized the practice, complaining only if workers disappeared without telling them where they were going. The disciplinary cases which arose seem to have arisen either in this circumstance, for example when a supervisor wanted a worker who had gone missing, or, as with train crew, when a worker was unfortunate enough to be spotted by a diligent senior manager.

Two general conclusions may be drawn. First, a number of informal practices were still in place: the situation was still a good way from the total rule by fear assumed in some accounts. But, second, the extent to which these practices interfered with managerial goals was only limited. They were most extensive among train crew, but even here behaviour such as coming in late and being given a different turn of duty still meant that the worker was working the hours he was paid for. Indeed, several workers argued that the practice helped management: if they woke up late, they would 'phone in and be told to 'keep coming', whereas if they knew that they would be sent home they would simply report sick. As one driver said, his aim was to make the system as tolerable as possible, but he would never take off a whole day without being ill. It was a balance of give and take which helped everyone.

The Organization of Consent

We may elaborate this point by looking at the elements which persuaded workers to work hard. A contrast between drivers and cleaners will be sufficient to make the general point. For drivers, the traditional system is not hard to understand. One of the key elements was the system of seniority that governed movement through the links and that was also used for promotion, transfer, and redundancy. This internal labour market operated in the manner identified by Burawoy (1979): it eliminated the possibility of arbitrary managerial action and gave workers a sense of security. The difference is that in Burawoy's case seniority was associated with a profound individualization of the work force, with the rights accruing to individuals tending to erode collective solidarity. In BR, this did not happen because, as part of the British system of industrial relations, its shopfloor relations were not regulated by the state. Seniority rules have not been connected with the legal enforceability of collective agreements or with tough 'management rights' clauses that give American firms largely unlimited freedom to change working practices. BR management has had to rely on negotiation.

In addition to seniority, drivers had the benefits of jobs that they enjoyed and of working away from direct supervision. If they carried out their jobs as expected, they would not be badgered by managers. They also knew that they were tied to BR because their skills were not transferable to other employers. When we asked for their reasons for staying with their present employer, half the drivers mentioned enjoyment of the work, with around a quarter citing the security of the job or the fact that they were too old to move (see Table 4.8). They did not like the new regime, but it still left them a degree of autonomy and there was in any event nowhere much else to go.

For carriage cleaners the issue is different: why did they work long hours, often in the cold and wet, for low wages? Part of the answer lies in the detailed way in which they were controlled. The manager of another cleaning depot said that the depot that we studied was 'over-managed' in that it had a large number of supervisors. As well as the supervisor himself, the supervisory personnel included on each shift a chargeman or woman and, for each group of cleaners, a leading rail(wo)man (LR), to use BR's convoluted terminology. The duties of the last included some specific tasks as well as generally keeping an eye on the cleaners and encouraging appropriate standards of work. Why, though, did someone only one rank above the bottom of the hierarchy take on the duties of surveillance? It cannot have been due to the monetary incentive of the job or the chance of further promotion, since the very best that most LRs could expect was a charge position. The essence of the answer is simply that if anything went wrong, it was the LR who was held to account, so that the easiest path was to try to ensure that work was done acceptably.

The approximately 110 cleaners, including LRs, were managed by four supervisors and four charge(wo)men, together with senior supervisors who covered maintenance workers as well as the cleaners and the depot

TABLE 4.8 Reasons for Staying with BR

Per Cent Mentioning	Driver	Guard	Platform	Cleaner	Total
Money	11	35	0	45	23
Security	28	29	40	9	26
Promotion chances	0	12	0	0	3
Nature of job	50	53	30	27	39
Near home, convenient	0	6	0	14	5
Friendly work mates	11	11	15	5	10
Too old to move	22	24	30	31	27

manager. They were thus fairly closely monitored. The main incentive has already been mentioned: the opportunity to finish early and to sit in the rest room once a specified set of duties had been completed. Our observations suggested that it was possible to complete one's duties without undue pressure. A job that, while monotonous, was not particularly pressurized, together with reasonable job security, kept cleaners sufficiently motivated.

To understand their position further, three situations need to be distinguished. First, there were the women, who comprised half the work force. Many of them were black and they had few other job opportunities; they tended to stress the convenience of the work, in that it was near home, as a reason for staying in it. Second, there were older men who had ended up at the depot either because of poor health or because they had found it hard to keep other jobs. As one manager unkindly put it, they were the dregs of the labour market, and they knew it. Finally came younger and enthusiastic men, and managers noted with satisfaction that they were able to take their pick from applicants. The motivation for these workers was simply that if they kept a good record they stood a good chance of moving to a guard's job fairly soon. As Table 4.8 shows, cleaners differed markedly from drivers in their reasons for staying with BR, with almost half of them seeing the level of wages as an attraction. They were, moreover, particularly unlikely to see friendly work mates as a reason for staying. The depot, because of the divisions between its workers and their low level of skill, lacked any tradition of workplace solidarity, and it was difficult for an alternative to managerial authority to be conceived.

For somewhat different reasons, therefore, each of these groups was willing to put in a level of effort of which managers were quite proud. In fact, the depot saw itself as one of the best, a view expressed with particular pride by one of the LDC representatives. This last fact says something about the possibilities of a shopfloor reaction to managerial commercialism, to which we now turn.

The Stability of the Shopfloor Regime

What are the implications of the shopfloor attitudes analysed above for the ability of managers to continue to re-assert their authority? Was the intensification of discipline de-stabilizing the shopfloor such that some form of reaction might be expected? Several considerations suggest that it was not.

First, there was no reservoir of discontent affecting all groups of workers. We have seen that many guards, platform staff, and cleaners had a grudging acceptance of changes in work practices and that they had a strongly individualized approach. This was most obvious at the cleaning depot, where several workers said that anyone making a stand would not be backed up by others. But it was true even of the guards. The questionnaire replies of one give the flavour. Though feeling that there was not much trust between management and workers, and that the situation had grown worse, he expressed no very strong criticisms of managers; he felt that discipline had become tighter, but was not very bothered by this; he could see why managers wanted to deal with bad attenders; and he did not think that workers worked together as groups. His set of attitudes did not form the basis for a strong reaction against management.

Of course, these attitudes could change, but for this to happen there would have to be a major effort at mobilization. This could come only from the LDCs. In general, however, the LDCs reflected the views of their constituents, with the drivers' representatives being outspoken in their condemnation of management and with others, with a few exceptions, taking a remarkably passive view. At the cleaning depot, for example, the representatives said that working relationships were reasonable and, though they complained at certain changes being pushed through, they accepted the outcome with little complaint. There was no idea at all of using, say, selective industrial action as a bargaining lever. When pressed on this, they pointed out that workers were highly individualistic and would not stand together; that industrial action hit workers most because they lost money; and that any action would have only a limited effect because managers could easily send trains out dirty if need be. Even the drivers' representatives said that militancy was usually counter-productive. They insisted that they could stop the depot almost when they chose, sometimes for formally legitimate reasons. For example, rosters for holiday periods were supposed to be published a certain number of days in advance. We were talking to them just before Easter and they could insist that no one work the rosters for Easter. But, they argued, sticking to their rights in this way would encourage managers to get their own back. For example, there had been a row some years previously about some week-end work, and management had ensured that subsequently the work was allocated to another depot. The possibility of an organized reaction against the managerial approach was not seen as a serious option.

The managerial changes themselves were also of a kind against which it was hard to mount an organized campaign. The tighter control of absence, for example, necessarily meant that workers were selected for treatment as individuals. It was hard for representatives to form any view of what was going on, since they had no formal role in the procedures and since some workers were likely to keep the matter to themselves. Similarly, representatives had no access to managerial records to argue about the fairness of acting against one worker and not another.

The situation could certainly change. Absence control was so far directed only at the 'bad cases', and if control came to be generalized it might provoke a wider reaction than had hitherto been the case. Similarly, workers have been left with some control of their own work lives through the lenient approach to time fiddles. If managers launched a determined attack on these, there could conceivably be a reaction. Managers implicitly relied on the legacy of the old ways of gaining consent: a belief in service to the customer and a commitment to formal procedures, and not spontaneous action, as a way of settling differences. To the extent that it continues to erode this legacy, it may also be generating an unstable set of shopfloor attitudes which could develop in unpredictable directions.

More generally, though managers could point with satisfaction to the changes that they had introduced, they could not claim to have generated a new constructive atmosphere on the shopfloor. They had forced through specific changes and thereby shifted the frontier of control in their own favour. But they had not generated a sense of commitment. Indeed, in the case of drivers in particular, the consequence was discontent on a massive scale. The state of workplace relations was new in so far as managerial power was enhanced, but the situation was not qualitatively different from the past: the ways in which consent was achieved had not been drastically re-structured, and such change as there had been involved a shift back towards a more autocratic management and the greater use of overt discipline, not the creation of self-discipline.

Conclusions

The central concern of this chapter has been the extent to which public sector commercialism has altered traditional patterns of shopfloor relations. There plainly was a major change in managerial approach, characterized by a greater self-confidence and assertiveness. The effects were, however, mixed. An increased willingness to dismiss went along with an acceptance of some traditional practices, such as going absent from the place of work, which was more than a conscious toleration and reflected an implicit acceptance that this was a normal activity. A greater use of discipline did not imply a more aggressive approach within the disciplinary procedure or a tendency to use tougher penalties. Closer attention to absenteeism was directed at only the small minority of 'bad attenders'.

And tightening up on workers' fiddles was directed at only a limited range of these practices.

It is not surprising that the image presented by managers themselves and also by union leaders, and, as we have seen, some groups of employees, was rather simpler. Managers have stressed efficiency improvements. Unions and workers, aware of the more intense use of discipline and of the *causes célèbres* which have arisen, have seen management as autocratic. There undoubtedly were some cases in which managers had adopted a very tough approach and which seemed to exemplify a uniformly authoritarian style. It is not, however, surprising that some such cases emerge or that they provoke a strong sense of injustice. Equally significant are those in which strong elements of traditionalism remained. Managers had not broken down old ways of working to produce a new commercial ethos on the shopfloor, but neither had they moved to a straightforwardly authoritarian style.

They relied, perhaps more than they would have liked to admit, on traditional assumptions. These ranged from the micro shopfloor level of give-and-take between workers and supervisors to the level of the national collective bargaining system. Workers steeped in the railway tradition took it for granted that grievances would be handled through the bargaining machinery and that direct action at the point of production was literally not to be contemplated. Loyalty to this system reflected some clear material benefits: it may not have done much for rail workers' wages relative to other groups, but it gave them stability and a degree of security. Throughout the 1980s managers challenged this understood world by pressing through new working practices and by altering the machinery of negotiation. By the time of our study, in 1988, they might well feel that they had been successful. At the start of the new approach, critics might have warned of the difficulties in the way. But the flexible rostering dispute had been won and many other changes were being pursued. And the data presented above, while pointing to massive discontent among drivers, suggest a much more limited response among other groups. More significantly for managers, perhaps, is not what workers think but what they do. Our data may be interesting to researchers, in showing that communication programmes had had little effect and that there was widespread scepticism about the new initiatives. But they also point to a very fragmented and limited response in terms of action; the absence control policy, for example, was not a central concern for most workers. Why, then, should managers worry?

The national rail strike of 1989 provides the most obvious answer. Workers demonstrated a substantial degree of solidarity and determination, and the outcome of the strike was widely seen as a victory for them and the unions, for they had wrung significant wage concessions from BR, had achieved a substantial degree of public sympathy, and had shown that a major public sector dispute could still be pursued successfully. Underlying the strike were some deep sources of discontent about the ways in which labour relations had been conducted in recent years. Strikers interviewed by the *Financial Times* (29 June 1989) complained of a tougher stance on discipline and attendance, of the lack of sufficient staff to cover the demands of Customer Care, and of a management more concerned with financial objectives than with providing a public service.

The strike was the most dramatic illustration of the limits to the new managerial style. We have also suggested that the pattern of shopfloor relations of the late 1980s rested to a significant degree on traditional forms of compliance. The further that managers go in dismantling traditionalism, the more they will have to find something to replace it. It may be that shopfloor relations become less predictable and more febrile, as traditional forms of order are eroded. This tendency could be heightened by changes in patterns of recruitment. Many managers to whom we spoke were proud that they were no longer reliant on the 'dregs of the labour market' for rail(wo)man posts. But more capable employees may begin to demand more than a secure job with plenty of overtime, and the celebrated demographic time-bomb may mean that BR's ability to pick and choose among applicants was only short-lived.

In describing BR as lying, somewhat uncomfortably, between traditionalism and commercialism, we do not mean to imply that there was a clear move towards a full-blown version of the latter. The system as we observed it had elements of both aspects, and we have analysed their connections. How far it was in transition to a different state we cannot say. What we can suggest is that the management of labour remained rooted in the past, in two senses. First, traditionalism was still observable. Second, the managerial attack on it had at least as much in common with the past as with the new world of human resource management: financial pressures were leading to tighter work standards and to stricter discipline, and not to anything approaching a high-commitment system. BR's workers were either thoroughly discontented or marked by resigned acceptance of the situation. There remained a residual pride in providing a public service, but the general view was that managerial change was making such a service more, and not less, difficult to provide. If BR managers wanted to promote commitment to the organization and an acceptance of change, it is this pride on which they might have built. The commercial path seemed to have found few friends on the shopfloor, and to have created its own tensions and uncertainties which may resolve themselves in unpredictable ways.

Finally, and more analytically, we have stressed that managerial action was often symbolic: acting against absence did not necessarily deal with a concrete absence problem but it demonstrated managers' active role and sent out messages about their more general approach to controlling the work force. This is a theme to which we return in the final chapter.

5

City General: Management Change and the Service Ethos in the NHS

The previous chapter showed that commercialism in BR was associated with a significant effort to change the handling of workplace relations but that the impact on practice was constrained by a need to rely on traditional ways of gaining consent. Our case study of a large urban acute hospital, which we call City General, develops the theme of variation within the public sector. Commercial pressures were as evident as they were in BR, and the consequences, notably a collapse of confidence in management, were profound. But the work process itself had been undergoing less dramatic change, and managers relied even more than did their BR counterparts on traditional ways of regulating work. There had not, for example, been the extensive action on absence that characterized BR. This reflected several factors, notably that core workers such as nurses were seen, to a large degree, as professionals, whereas the core BR workers tended to be seen by managers as a group which needed to be actively disciplined and regulated. This meant that managerial change in the hospital was taking place within the context of a developed service ethos which had particular effects on worker commitment and management style.

The hospital differed from BR in other important respects, principally arising from the experience of compulsory competitive tendering, and the many disputes surrounding nurse regrading. While these did not feature directly in the case study they not only reflected the broad thrust of commercialization, but also highlighted the problems of a management system in transition. Hospital management had traditionally been based on the demands and status of medical professionalism. At the hospital the new disciplines of commercialism were accompanied by the introduction of managers from outside the tight circles of health professionals. As a result, management change at the hospital tended to produce a fragmented system which, we argue, was only sustainable in the context of a traditional reliance on informal staff co-operation, even though this contradicted stated policy aims which emphasized formal managerial controls. There was thus a system of work relations in flux, subject to contradictory pressures arising from changes in the service ethos, struggling to find a new equilibrium within which staff commitment could be retained and reconciled to new organizational objectives. The overall theme of this chapter, then, is the continuation of workplace practice, albeit in a situation in which assumptions were changing.

The following sections examine the context of change in an organization steeped in a service ethos. The first section outlines the pressures for change, and how this affected the status of the 'care team'. The second asks how far health workers differed from others in our study, and concludes that the service ethos did not support a distinctive 'attendance culture'. The third section deals with how the management of attendance reflected the difficulties of a management in transition. The final section brings these factors together and tries to illuminate the apparent paradox of a work setting which combined high levels of staff commitment with low morale and distrust of management.

Managing Within a Public Sector Ethos

The Context Of Change

It would be difficult to overstate the extent and diversity of pressures for change in the NHS. While many of these changes have no direct impact on the individual employment relationship, in total they have important (and ongoing) implications for the whole culture of management in the service. At the time of this study the hospital sector of the NHS had gone through several changes, and there has since been no breathing space in the rate of change. It is not intended here to give any systematic overview of these processes, but a general consideration of the underlying logic of financial and management structures is necessary if the development of employment relations is to be understood.

The NHS occupied a unique place in the mixed economy that developed after 1945, a position that can best be seen in the special place it had in the political agenda of the Conservative governments of the 1980s. The NHS shared with other nationalized enterprises and services a highly structured and bureaucratic management system, and one in which external, political influences have been marked. It had this distinction, however, that it was the most politically sensitive area of public provision for the Conservatives; the maintenance of the claim that the NHS was 'safe in our hands' was a primary consideration of government policy in a way that never applied to the public utilities, or even local government provision.

Nevertheless, the NHS could not fail to be a target for change for governments which were determined on a threefold agenda which sought to cut public expenditure as a proportion of GDP, to liberalize the labour market and reduce the effectiveness of collectivism, and to introduce both the disciplines and forms of market structures into the sphere of public provision. If the political sensitivity of the NHS precluded straightforward privatization this did not reduce conservative determination to subject it to the terms of its broader agenda, and this determination was only increased by the financial pressures produced by the conjunction of demographic change and the advancement of medical technology which raised the spectre of the so called 'black hole' of health expenditure, or the existence of 'limitless demand'.

In its attempts to control escalating costs governments were concerned that long term efficiency gains would be impossible without deep changes to the management structures and style of the NHS. A series of measures were adopted to improve management information, planning, and cost effectiveness through regional reviews, the use of performance indicators, and option appraisal of investments (see Bach, 1989). More importantly, from the viewpoint of this study, was the impact of the so called 'Griffiths reforms', and in particular the introduction after 1983 of units of management under the control of General Managers.

This initiative had several implications. On the one hand it formed part of a strategy to curtail the influence of committee structures at area level (also to be achieved by 'freezing out' local authority and trade union representation), while, on the other it challenged the consensus management based on medical professionalism that had characterized the service previously, opening the way, it was hoped, to a wholesale reorganization of working practices. As Bach (1989:13) notes

The implementation of General Management has led to greater emphasis on individual decisions rather than committee decisions and has attempted to increase the power and status of management in the NHS and confer on it greater legitimacy in order to weaken the professional ethos that pervades the NHS.

This development coincided with the introduction of competitive tendering. Together they apparently spelled the end of the paternalistic management style of the NHS.

It is no easy matter, however, to transform management style in such a fundamental way without producing significant institutional frictions. At City General the changes had had two linked effects; firstly a new layer of management was introduced, and secondly there had been an influx of new managers recruited from the private sector often highly critical of what they saw as a lack of managerial professionalism amongst medical managers. 'Incomers' mentioned two aspects in particular which had formed in their view a managerial 'catch 22'; an unwillingness to delegate authority down the managerial line, combined with a reluctance to take decisions outside of a consensual framework.

It would be simplistic, however, to take these criticisms at their face value without taking into account the particular nature of NHS professionalism under challenge. There are two primary factors to consider. First, the pre-existing functional management structure placed considerable power in the hands of qualified medical staff whose chief concern was the development of services, and often the development of particular disciplines, developed in the days before substantial constraints on public expenditure. Any challenge to this style of management not only requires the use of different management methods, but different criteria for decision making which potentially reorders relative status amongst managers themselves. There were, in other words, always material differences amongst managers which reflected different institutional interests. These differences have been exacerbated by a shift towards commercial criteria for policy making and management within the NHS.

Second, the dominance of medical professionals had been accommodated within an industrial relations system based on the Whitley model, which, because of its highly centralized nature, effectively insulated units such as City General from pressures for the liberalization of pay and working conditions. Furthermore, the particular nature of the nursing trade unions, with their highly developed professional functions, reinforced the culture of a professionally based service ethos. This tradition had come under considerable pressure well before the Griffiths reforms as public spending controls began to conflict with the demands of the NHS and other public services. Such a system of consensual, professionally legitimated decision making runs contrary to the aims of the management reforms in hospitals, and it has been considerably eroded, not least by the removal of unit general management from the system, the introduction of short term contracts and performance related pay, and limitations on collective bargaining for the majority of employees. These changes were in their early stages at the time of the study, but the outlines of future developments were already clear to all.

Managers, Carers, and Professionalism

The study of City General was intended primarily to consider how changes in the control of work have affected the meaning of absence, and manager-worker relations more generally. It also enables some useful comparisons with other occupational settings. To understand the distinctive processes at work calls for a closer look at how the professional service ethos relates to the regulation of the individual, and the nature of work commitment that is generated. Management was widely distrusted, and in some doubt of its role, while having still largely resisted pressures for the more draconian approach favoured by some employers. What did seem to be of importance was they ways in which workers' attachment to the service aspect of their jobs interacted with management styles and objectives. Here, of course, it is necessary to differentiate between occupational groups; there is a different professional and material basis for the service ethos among highly qualified nursing staff than among, for example, the domestic service staff, the two groups which formed the basis of our study. We look, therefore, at the different components of what was termed, within City General itself, the caring team.

Carpenter(1977:190) has traced the underlying tensions in the development of the nursing profession from 'Ministering Angels' to modern professionalism, and in particular how its social and gender construction produced a contradictory amalgam of vocationalism and managerialism. Changing organization and the division of labour in hospitals, he suggested, had begun to undermine the position of nurses as an occupational elite, legitimated by 'total devotion', and produced new possibilities of reducing social distance from other health workers, especially ancillaries and, therefore, an increase in conflictual employment relations.

More recent work by Carpenter et. al. has compared nursing and social work, and concludes that important ambiguities persist in the social status and outlook of nurses, in which neither professionalization nor 'proletarianization' have become dominant. However, they note that, to a greater degree than social workers, 'Despite cutbacks, rationalisations and other difficulties, nurses generally still found confirmation of their own sense of social value' (Carpenter, 1987: 51). Cousins (1987: Ch.8) has also argued that public service employment shares the same social relations of exploitation as manufacturing, but that these are mediated by often conflicting public policy objectives which have become more important as Conservative administrations attempt to restructure the welfare state.

These ambiguities continue to affect the position of nurses, not only in terms of their social location, but also their role in management structures, and in the forms of labour control under which they work. Nursing is an occupation with distinct hierarchies in which relations with management take two forms which, while necessarily related, have distinct characteristics; firstly as a relation between waged labour and its managerial control, and secondly as between different levels of a professional occupational group. These different characteristics vary also according to the levels of qualification within nursing. At the time of the study this comprised three levels. At the top were the Registered General Nurses (RGNs), often called staff nurses. These were the most highly trained nurses who commonly looked towards specialization and postgraduate level studies as the expected route for career development which could lead to very senior and responsible posts. Below these were the State Enrolled Nurses, essentially the non-graduate-level generalists concentrating on 'bedside' nursing. A third, minority section, was the Auxiliary Nurse - the unskilled backup on the wards. Experience and qualification levels were central elements of an hierarchy not only between, but within these categories.

At City General nursing management was professionally based, and, as is the profession, dominated by women all of whom had come from the RGN grades. Under the Director and Assistant Directors of nursing were seven nursing managers who were effectively line managers of departments or specialisms. These managers were responsible for some 463 whole time equivalents, of whom one hundred and forty four were qualified RGNs. They were also responsible for a considerable number of student nurses, but these did not feature in our study. At ward level direct clinical management was in the hands of a ward sister, or occasionally a staff nurse, but these played only a limited role in discipline and personnel matters. It was the intention to develop the management role of ward sisters, and this is discussed below, but at the time of the study the management structure placed a considerable distance between nurses and managers, a distance that was amplified for non-RGN grades by their qualification levels.

There was a considerable degree of stability in work groups, although staff nurses were more mobile as they developed their careers. The development of specialisms, however, led to greater stability for more experienced RGNs. Ward sisters, SENs and auxiliaries tended to stay in stable posts. This led to a considerable identification with the ward, and the 'care team'. Senior nursing management stressed the need to make staff feel part of the hospital management. There were regular meetings between ward sisters and nursing managers, involving the Assistant Nursing Director 'when anything big is in the offing', and these were sometimes supplemented by ward meetings. The aim was for managers to 'get things down to ward level'.

Nevertheless, at ward level this management structure was viewed less sympathetically. Scepticism was widespread regarding the ability of nursing managers to appreciate conditions and problems at ward level, and the developing distance between nurses and nurse managers was also reflected in feelings that managers had become too far removed from clinical practice to fulfil adequately their role as professional mentors.

In short, management was experienced by nurses at distinct levels of discipline and professional control, and this ambiguity was increased by what was seen as the development of a managerialism less tied to nursing as a profession. The various communication levels did not seem to alter this, nor to reconstruct the era of consensualism. At the same time, it must be said, the particular nature of 'paternalism' in nursing had always been highly regimented (even, perhaps, regimental) and hierarchical, this discipline receiving its legitimacy from a professional ethos. The legitimacy of discipline was also therefore under a certain stress, although there was no evidence that this had led to overt resentment or conflict.

Ironically, senior nursing management shared some of the unease of the ward staff, although in their case discontent was directed upwards. Senior and non-medical management were often seen as unappreciative of clinical and care problems. 'Who cares for the carers?' was a question asked at all levels of nursing.

Ancillary and other grades in hospitals may have a less ambiguous social position than qualified nurses, but it would be wrong to imagine that they do not share the 'ideological commitment to the service' that Carpenter et al. (1987) identify as what 'remains different and exciting about state public service workers'. Yet the ancillary workers studied here have experienced perhaps more immediately the impact of managerialism introduced by the Griffiths Report and other measures. Bach points especially to the effects of cost cutting and competitive tendering, which had led to an estimated loss of 9,500 ancillary staff in the NHS by 1986, and their real pay is more than 40 per cent lower than it was in 1974 (Bach, 1989:5). Cousins (1987: 180) has also found evidence of a substantial restructuring of ancillary work which, while introducing more coercive forms of management, have failed to 'elicit the compliance of staff, since their trust and morale has been lowered'. Our own study also found distinct stresses operating amongst these levels of staff which may have a real impact on how employee attitudes to commitment and discipline are formed and develop.

It is important here to distinguish between the service ethos as experienced by ancillary staff and that of nurses, based as it is on a professional status. Indeed, the degree to which ancillary staff could really be considered part of the 'care team' must be in doubt, precisely because they were excluded from the professional solidarity of the wards. In addition, the management structures of these workers was more closely integrated into the new commercialism of the NHS, and indeed was the site of many of its newer practitioners.

The domestic services were run by a 'Performance Review Officer' who was recruited from private industry, and who oversaw the successful retention in-house of all services apart from window cleaning and garage maintenance across the entire area health authority. In doing so some services used economies of scale to operate outside the health area, and the laundry at City General was doing work for hospitals from the midlands to London. This determined commercialism had had one of its biggest impacts on the domestic staff. The Performance Review Officer regarded the domestic section as badly overstaffed, and numbers were cut very rapidly. As a result he was sure that workers were definitely working harder.

Cost cutting, competitive tendering, and a tighter, more industrial definition of job content and standards all conspired to undermine the perceived 'caring' element of domestic work at City General, and with it the domestics' precarious position within the care team. So much so that the domestic manager had recently introduced name badges for the staff - not as a customer friendly gesture à la the citizen's charter, but to 'stop people calling them hey you'. Nevertheless, there was distinct evidence that domestic workers defined their own work and purpose as within a framework of patient service, and that this perception had survived radical changes in their jobs.

These tensions generated by both external pressures and management driven change are further considered below. The next section deals with the salience of attendance in this changing context, and how far the service ethos at City General was reflected in workers' attitudes to absence.

Are Health Workers Different?

An Attendance Culture?

Medical workers, and especially nursing staff, have for long laboured under the 'Angels' label, as if their work experience, and their own attitudes, were sharply marked off from the more mundane world of industry and commerce. Since it is sometimes asked if an 'absence culture' exists in certain work settings (Johns and Nicholson, 1982: 127-72)ᐟ we were interested to see if there was anything at the hospital that could be described as an 'attendance culture'.

Sentiment apart, there were several features of work at City General which may have produced something resembling an attendance culture in the sense that workers' own attitudes would complement the demands of the institution. The most obvious of these is the consequence of absence on patient care, but this is not simply a matter of personal responsibility. Despite considerable industrial relations disruption in the 1980s health workers have shown a marked reluctance to take industrial action which would impinge on patients. The professional character of nursing organizations (and possibly also the hierarchical and regimented organization of nursing work) reinforce this reluctance to disturb the service provision.

Changes in work organization and workloads may tend to undermine this commitment, but, equally, they may reinforce it, if they can be linked to appeals to professionalism and service. We have already seen how competitive tendering had led to staff cuts and higher workloads for domestics at City General. Nursing staff had not had to face this process, but there was clear evidence of significant change. Increasing bed turnover, coupled with a falling pool of recruits, had changed employment patterns at the hospital, most notably by a shift from a reliance on full time staff to a predominance of part timers. As a result, we were told, management was much more dependant on staff flexibility with a 'whole multitude of working arrangements in which we have split some posts between three or four staff'.

Here again we found entrenched differences in management views of the process. Nursing managers often felt that higher management did not understand the stresses these changes had produced for the staff. Even allowing for changes in care routines managers insisted that nurses were having to work consistently harder. Managing these changes and attendant stresses was a constant challenge for line management, and one in which success was only possible through the enlistment of staff cooperation.

In this setting it was clear that attendance had a high degree of importance for City General, not merely in operational terms, but as an expression of successful management of change. It was soon apparent, however, that there was no discernible culture supporting high attendance. Absence rates were relatively high, and, while there was evidence of strong loyalty to the 'service', staff attitudes to attendance did not differ substantially from other workers we studied. The main elements affecting absence appeared to be work pressures, combined with low morale, but balanced by commitment to the job.

This is particularly important because little is known about attitudes and actions amongst health workers. Hackett (1986) asked a sample of Canadian nurses how much they wanted to go absent, and why. The main contributory factors for wanting time off were stress, tiredness, and health, which parallel our findings, but he did not investigate the managerial controls, and wider job attitudes which may have applied. Price and Mueller (1986) studied all the employees of five United States hospitals, but they did not investigate managerial control policies or shop floor culture, concentrating instead on testing a causal model. Significantly, a model containing 24 independent variables was able to explain only a tiny proportion of the variance of absence rates across individuals, suggesting that an enquiry into the social processes of absence might offer more fruitful lines of analysis. Chadwick-Jones et al.(1982) included two Canadian hospitals in their survey of 21 British and Canadian organizations, and in some of their firms they asked about peer group and supervisory pressures, but unfortunately the hospitals were not included. Turning to Britain, Clark (1975) has looked at absence data in a large hospital, but the data was collected over only a four week period, and employee interviews were limited to 20 student nurses. A press article reported a survey of student nurses, which found that 71 per cent of third years interviewed intended to leave the profession because of low pay and disillusion with the work (*Times Higher Education Supplement*, 2 Oct. 1987). Clearly, with rapid changes in job organisation, administration, and payment systems, hospital workers' own assessment of their role and commitment is an important factor in locating them within broader debates on commitment and motivation. This theme is pursued below, but first we turn to a consideration of the problem of absence at City General.

Accounting For Absence At City General

We have measured absence in terms of the number of absence spells, and the pattern of duration. There is little comparative information on health workers. Chadwick-Jones et al. ((1980: 120-1) feature a graph of absences for nurses only. From this it can be estimated that only 6 per cent had no absences at all in a year, while 39 per cent had over six spells. These figures compare relatively unfavourably with those presented in the table below.

The proportion of qualified nursing staff with no absences at all in a year varied between 18.8 per cent and 6.7 per cent by grade (see Table 5.1). From 1985 to 1987 this proneness to absence had increased, as fewer workers recorded no absences, and more were absent six or more times. Unqualified nurses and domestic staff were considerably less likely to have no spells of absence at all, but the extent of six or more spells of absence was more widely spread, with SENs being more prone to multiple absences than domestics.

There appears to be more uniformity amongst staff when the mean number of spells of absence is considered, but there are marked differences when both the average number of days per spell of absence, and the average number of days lost per worker is considered. The pattern for domestic ancillaries is the most notable, resulting in 41.4 days lost per worker, the highest in our studies. This was due to the large number of long spells of absence in this group: 14 per cent of spells lasted 20 days or more, and these accounted for fully 75 per cent of all days lost. Domestic ancillaries tended to have more spells of sickness absence, and these lasted longer on average, than among nurses. Although management saw brief absences of one or two days as a particular problem, absences of this sort were less common than, for example, amongst sisters. Between 1985/6 and 1987/8 the average number of absences per worker has in fact declined slightly, in contrast to nursing staff, but their average duration has risen by 60 per cent, and the average number of days lost per worker has risen by about 39 per cent.

TABLE 5.1   Absence Patterns by Occupation, Hospital

	Sisters	RGNs	SENs	Auxiliary	All Nurses	Ancillaries
Absence Frequency (per cent with given number of spells in a year)						
None	19	16	12	7	13	9
1	18	18	11	20	16	16
2-5	58	53	54	62	56	57
6 and over	6	13	22	12	14	19
Mean number days absent per worker per year	18	13	31	26	23	41
Mean length (days) of each spell of absence	8	5	8	9	7	13

Absence rates at City General tended to be higher for all grades of staff than was the case in the other studies reported here. This does not mean that there is an 'absenteeism problem', a term often used to imply that absence is without good cause, or has become part of an accepted pattern. There seemed to be no evidence of this. Staff did not say they were prone to take time off, or seem to treat attendance lightly.

While there was little difference in the mean number of absence spells between hospital staff and the other studies reported here, a generally higher rate of long term sickness resulted in a higher pattern of days lost per worker. Thus, while there was little difference in spells of absence, there were large variations in average duration. The main contributory factor was sickness spells lasting over 20 days, with ten per cent or less of absences accounting for over half of days lost.

Nevertheless, comparisons with other occupations are quite interesting. For example, qualified RGNs had a similar pattern of absence spells, and days lost per worker, to women production workers studied at Multiplex. Table A.4 establishes the general pattern of absences, comparing City General with our three other studies. This shows that workers at the hospital had the smallest percentage of workers taking no time off at all, and also, jointly with BR, the highest percentage of workers absent for six or more spells in any one year. While the number of spells accounted for by short absences of one or two days is relatively unexceptional, staff at the hospital were by far the most prone to absences of 6 days or above. They also led in terms of severity measures, with the highest scores for both the mean number of days lost per worker per year, at 27.9 and mean length of absence per spell, at 8.9 days. Table 6.1 in the following chapter shows comparative absence data for all women in the three of our studies where they formed a substantial proportion of the group. From this it can be seen that, once again, staff at City General led on both severity measures. Notable is the fact that the hospital workers, with a large number of staff which would be counted as professional, showed such a markedly higher score for severity of absence than white collar women at FinCo.

In general, there was some linkage between job status and attendance, but there were important exceptions. The mean number of days lost rose by grade, while the proportion of staff taking no time off in a year declined quite steeply by grade, with an 18.8 per cent figure for sisters, and 6.7 per cent for auxiliaries. However, nursing sisters were likely to have longer spells of absence than RGNs, and nursing auxiliaries tended to lose fewer days a year than SENs. Comparisons with other studies are also quite interesting; as discussed in Chapter 7, qualified RGNs, for example, had a similar pattern of absence spells, and days lost per worker, to those of women manual workers in an engineering company. In short, hospital workers were no less prone to absence than manual workers, who might be expected to display higher rates.

By themselves the data do not easily account for these differences. In the case of the ancillaries, one factor must be the make up of the workforce, with domestics having a much higher age profile than most of our sample, as well as the expected lower general standards of health associated with manual, unskilled labour. Many of the women employed had not only brought up families, but had spent years in industry or other employment before coming to the hospital. Although most worked part time, their earnings were often an important, if not the major source of family income. Their wages were, however, considerably below the EC decency threshold.

Attention must also be paid to the effects of changes in work organization following contract tendering. Over 60 per cent of respondents felt that the work had become considerably harder in that period. Staffing was halved under the new arrangement, and management claimed that some increase in long-term sickness resulted from the pressure of change. Workers agreed, citing new timings and extra stress as causes of increased sick absence. That seems to have continued, and in general, despite attempts to 'manage the problem properly', most absence indicators were up.

For many practitioners and academics there is a tendency to treat absence figures as some kind of measure of job satisfaction, or commitment, and this might be expected to influence attendance at City General. However, this is far too simple. A study by Edwards and Scullion (1982) has shown that 'good' attendance can result from harsh discipline in a harsh labour market, and that more relaxed attitudes can go with high productivity and good management-worker relations. It is also the case that ill health shows a class distribution, and that personal and family ill health can fall disproportionately on women, an effect particularly noticeable in Britain according to a report in The Times (1988, Feb 10).

Many factors may be involved, including externalities like family commitments, but work related questions such as shift patterns, and in particular stress, seemed of particular importance. Some nursing managers felt that higher managers did not always believe in the reality of stress effects arising from cuts and increasing workloads. They pointed to a 5 per cent increase in patient throughput per annum over the previous five years, with less staff to cover. This was said to lower resistance to infections, and some staff simply became tired; physically and mentally. This would tally with findings in a 1987 Canadian study of 162 hospital workers in which stress was related to absence frequency and duration, with an average of 4.7 spells per worker per year, and mean days lost of 14.8 (Léonard et al., 1987).

This question of stress was raised often by staff at all levels, but was largely discounted by managers coming from outside industry, who felt that work in the NHS was no more stressful than elsewhere, and that the statistics did not support the idea of stress as a serious factor. It should be noted, however, that the great majority of nurses interviewed felt that any mention of stress in accounting for sickness absence would be liable to get them into trouble, or to hinder their careers. The next section explores this and other questions of how the staff at City General viewed attendance matters.

Worker Attitudes To Attendance

The comparative review of attendance at City General has shown that, far from being restrained by a service ethos, the health workers studied were in fact more prone to absence than other groups. How then, did they see their own role in attending work, and what differences, if any, can be found between them and other workers in our study? We stated above that there was no evidence of an 'attendance culture' amongst hospital staff, and, in fact, general attitudes towards attendance were very similar to those found in our other case study companies. Nevertheless, there were significant differences in emphasis, especially in respect the nature of commitment to work. In this, adherence to the interests of the patients, and of the 'service', ranked high, as against concepts of responsibility to managers or the employer. This 'service' attitude was present throughout the organization, but much more in flux in a rapidly changing management structure.

There was no evidence from the staff of a casual attitude to attendance. When asked to choose between the statements that 'a worker should not stay away from work in any event, except when it is really necessary, as in the case of a genuine illness' and 'people have a right to take a day off if they want to' 82.5% chose the first response. This is in the mid-range of results in our other companies, but higher than results in previous studies (Edwards and Scullion, 1982: 109). Some indications do exist in respect of how this result may be compared within the study. Table A.6 shows the most important reasons given by workers for attending work. The hospital workers have the highest score (only FinCo's white collar workers come close) for duty to work mates as a reason for attending. It also shows a mid-range score for 'duty to the firm', but what the figures do not reveal is the near universal rephrasing used by these workers which emphasized the service, or patients in response to this question. This is reinforced by responses to questions asking staff their main reasons for staying in their current job, listed in Table A.12; of all our studies 'interest in the job' scored highest for City General respondents.

Obviously, in the abstract people may be expected to choose what sounds like the 'correct' answer. Also the question of what constitutes a genuine reason for absence will vary. Replies to the vignettes discussed in Chapter 2 may be particularly useful in tapping the `moral universe' of hospital workers. To remind the reader, the three questions concerned a man who had 'flu, who recovered by Thursday, but decided not to return until the following week; a single woman parent with a sick child who had to decide whether to report sick, or take unpaid leave; and a woman feeling very depressed at work who was thinking about taking a day off to escape the pressure.

Responses showed a strong sympathy for people's personal circumstances, and how workers themselves judged the necessity of an absence. A majority accepted staying away in the first case, and usually referred to the necessity for getting properly fit. Large minorities accepted staying away in the other two cases. As we saw in Chapter 2, hospital staff were no more likely than others to disapprove of absence; indeed their overall score on all three stories was the most sympathetic, with 93 per cent taking an 'understanding' view on at least one of the stories. All staff were more sympathetic to the woman suffering depression than workers in BR and Multiplex by a large margin. They were also all more sympathetic than a group of trainee health service managers who were asked the same questions. Table A.2 shows 27 per cent of hospital workers citing 'other' reasons for thinking of not attending, and these replies were overwhelmingly to do with tiredness or stress.

Staff were also asked if they themselves had a lot of time off. Most thought not, excepting some serious, long term illnesses. Staff were generally less likely to say that they had extended a period of sickness beyond recovery than the response to the mini-story would suggest. But this question of assessing health was clearly seen as a difficult issue, and people were ready to accept other choices than their own.

This should not be taken to mean that staff approved others taking time off, or that there was a culture which supported 'absenteeism'. Those supporting the idea of the right to take time off did not differ much from their colleagues when asked why they chose that response. Generally they simply put more emphasis on the range of events that would justify an absence, or placed less trust in the reasonableness of management to adapt to individuals' needs. That there was some abuse of the sick pay scheme was a widely held idea, and it was almost universally unpopular. Staff felt strongly that absence let down colleagues, but they were often reluctant to make judgements of individuals. When others' absence was discussed amongst staff, the tone tended to be mildly critical.

At Multiplex it soon became clear that many people would come into work when they were unwell. Reasons fell into two main categories: those who did so for reasons of their own (boredom, wanting to 'see it through'), and those who responded to perceived pressure from management. Many staff at the hospital also reported that they would come in when ill, but this was very rarely because they felt directly pressured by management. More often it was the pressure of the work itself, and a feeling of responsibility to patients and workmates. This is the other side of the decisions that people regularly make when they feel unwell, and it is clear that, where not simply incapacitated, many factors go into the choice of work or sickness absence.

This was an aspect of the question acknowledged by many managers, some of whom said they sent more staff home than they spoke to about absence, but this was not how staff saw it. Staff often felt that they were taken advantage of, and that criticisms were often unjust. Many staff felt that they were not believed when they phoned in sick, and some responded by coming in hoping to be sent home. In some respects there is clearly an element of ritual, or of forced, or half accepted dishonesty in some absence situations. One problem is finding a reason that 'sounds right', especially when minor illness coincides with tiredness, or some family problem. One manager reported a 'suspicious' spate of migraines among absentees, and used this in assessing genuine sickness. Certain sorts of complaint were regarded by staff almost as ciphers for less specific illnesses.

The necessity for this is highlighted by responses to the 'mini-story' of the single parent. Circumstances could force a worker to lie, and even those who would not themselves have taken time off in that circumstance thought it not very serious. The responses to the 'mini-story' on depression or stress show another side of this question. Staff plainly regarded their work as stressful, and thought that stress could be a contributory cause to sickness, or, less often, bad enough to justify absence. Some staff were asked how they would report such an absence; whether they would put 'stress', or 'stress related' onto a self certification form, and whether management would accept it. The idea was often greeted with hilarity, and it was generally viewed as a short cut to disciplinary action. Most said they would think of something 'acceptable' to put on forms. Amongst qualified staff there was also a widespread feeling that any absence due to stress would undermine a person's career prospects, as management would take it as a sign of weakness, or unsuitability. Some said that even if seeking a medical certificate they would ask their doctor not to mention stress as a cause or factor in illness because of these fears.

Frequent references to stress, and difficulties in dealing with it within both the culture of the hospital and the absence control procedures must cast doubt on frequent managerial disclaimers that it was a serious factor at General Hospital. A survey in Nursing Times (March 18, 1992) shows evidence that stress is a widespread problem amongst nursing staff, and that managerial responses are inadequate. Some 1,800 responded to the Nursing Times questionnaire. Of these, 64 per cent cited stress headaches, 62 per cent sleep problems, and 30 per cent stomach and bowel complaints. The causes for stress cited by respondents were equally interesting, as most thought that the problems were organizational, rather than being integral to nursing. 65 per cent blamed increased workloads, and 54 per cent lack of resources to do the job. More importantly from the point of view of organizational culture were the 61 per cent citing management related problems, including unclear lines of communications, and the 42 per cent citing changes within the profession.

Clearly staff have their own ways of establishing the necessity of an absence, but how do they see the factors which bring them into work? The most regular response concerned duties to patients and colleagues, and commitment to the service rather than to management as an employer. Enjoyment of the work also ranked highly, and not only amongst qualified staff. Domestic staff were often quite insistent on their commitment to the patients, and reported a loss of contact with them on reorganisation of the work. Nursing staff too often felt that work pressure or a lack of facilities hampered the human care aspect which they valued highly, and these pressures were clearly being felt by staff as a whole, and were expected to get worse rather than better.

Conclusions

Are health workers different? The answer would seem to be - not much. In terms of absence from work, workers at City General did not compare well with industrial workers, and even the highest levels of qualified nursing staff seemed more prone to time off than white collar workers at FinCo. Nor did the attitudes of the health workers mark them off from other occupational groups in very obvious ways. Yet there were differences, and these related mostly to the nature of the commitment to work, and in particular to patients. If there was no discernible attendance culture it is still clear that a service ethos informed many attitudes at City General. How was this ethos incorporated in the management of labour and attendance at the hospital, and what implications did the commercialization of the management context have for its role? The next section deals with these issues by looking in more detail at the process of managing attendance.

Bureaucratic Inclusiveness and Absence Control

While it is clear that the management of labour at City General was subject to the changing pressures described above, the formal system of attendance control and discipline remained firmly within the Whitley mould. As was argued in the chapter on Multiplex, typologies of management styles can be insensitive to specific institutional settings. This seems to be particularly true within the NHS. Management styles at City General clearly had a paternalistic element, although one modified by strict occupational hierarchies. They were also governed to a large extent by extensive, and highly centralized agreements generated through the Whitley system. These agreements do not, however, conform to the relatively rigid, rule based systems found in some areas of industry, not least because of the consensual tradition in the service.

For this reason we have used the term bureaucratic inclusiveness to describe the main elements of the management of labour at City General. By this is meant a system in which an extensive network of agreements, rules, and guidelines for best practice, largely generated at the higher levels of the organization, attempts to contain all aspects of the control of labour. This network, devised as a comprehensive regulatory framework, was an attempt to guide the operations of consensual management.

Here we view the operation of this management style through the lens of attendance control in both its formal structures and everyday practice. Two general themes emerge. The first is that changes in management style and practice had not become deeply rooted. The second is that the control of labour was in an uncomfortable transition as more 'industrial' attitudes to control were becoming embedded without any systematic re-evaluation of the methods and purposes of bureaucratic inclusiveness. As a result informality played a large role in relations between workers and managers, as it did in all our studies, but this informality was rooted more in the fragmentation of management practice than in any worker-driven demands.

Absence Control Policy

The personnel department at City General issued all managers with a comprehensive, nine page document on 'Handling Sickness Problems', including reference to further advice and guidance available from ten other sources. The emphasis of the guidance notes was on the need to manage absence actively while attempting to 'assist the employee ... to bring about a return to duty at the earliest opportunity'. The notes also emphasize 'reasonable and enlightened' treatment of staff, and point out that disciplinary measures should not be the normal method of dealing with sickness absence.

Management policy had three main elements: the careful monitoring of absence records; counselling and assistance to problem cases, involving where necessary the hospital's occupational health unit; and detailed advice on steps to be taken where problems persisted, ranging from disciplinary action to rehabilitation and retraining. Employers vary widely in the use of 'trigger points' for identifying absence problems. The guidance for managers at City General established such triggers for managers, but only 'as examples and not as maximum or minimum levels'. This is consistent with the general tone of the guidance notes, which were at once highly detailed, with consideration of a multitude of possible circumstances, while, at the same time, there was an emphasis on a personalized, consensual approach.

Personnel at City General did not play a central role in absence control, except in those rare cases which attracted disciplinary sanctions, or where long term absence raised questions of reallocation or termination. In general the aim was to make managers manage their own areas, although managers were encouraged to seek advice, and personnel would intervene where there was concern that managers were not 'playing by the book'; we were told 'its amazing how you get a feel for cases ... for managers who act sensibly and sensitively, and the inadequates.'

The guidance notes stress absence monitoring, not only as necessary to the maintenance of managerial control, but also to alert managers to any work or health factors which may be generating absence. The occupational health unit was to have played a role in this. Perhaps surprisingly, the unit had only been established for three years at City General, and was managed by a recruit from industry. It was plain that there had been resistance to the development of this unit. The unit manager put this down to the 'style of health service management, who want to do everything themselves, and distrust outsiders.' Line managers, she felt, had felt her as a threat to their authority, and had made staff nervous of approaching the unit. While this had improved over the three years, the wider role of the unit in absence management had not developed very much. When it was established, the manager wanted to use computerized records to investigate health patterns, but had found that information was patchy, ill distributed, and not widely used, and, as a result, 'all sorts of questions are simply not being asked'. She said

> 'I have to deal with thirty five managers at [City General]. I suspect that there are real problems, but I can't show it. Management seem to have no inclination to advance enquiries, either high or low.'

The procedures for reporting and monitoring absence were clear and widely understood, if sometimes resented by the staff. Staff had to report absences before, or at the start of, a shift, and also had to ring in to say when they expected to return. The return to work itself was not closely monitored, and the 'return to work interview' favoured by some employers was not used.

Management recorded absence on individual records on a seven day basis, and attendance figures were compiled from these figures. The method of monitoring had to serve a variety of purposes, from coverage, to SSP, to Whitley sick pay. The seven day basis of recording can, however, exaggerate the levels of absence, in some cases quite severely. For example, a 26-week absence of a worker on a 5-day week would show as 182 days lost, whereas actual shifts lost would be only 130. This would not matter much if management at all levels were clearly aware of the basis of figures. In general, however, management did not use absence data consistently, and they did not directly influence action taken in respect of individuals.

Attendance very rarely reached the higher levels of the disciplinary procedure. Managers tended to be informal in their approach to deciding what level of absence required action, relying on rule of thumb, and personal knowledge of individuals. The use of 'trigger points', whether of frequency or duration, were not a feature, although individual managers sometimes claimed to operate their own system. There were guidelines for action in policy, but these were not widely referred to, either by managers or staff, and seem to be important only in rare cases of discipline involving personnel.

Control in Practice

Nevertheless, there were clear pressures on managers to 'improve' on absence figures, whether these took the form of staffing problems or policy decisions. Work pressures can erode managers' patience with procedures, or, as some admitted, lead them to react to a particularly inconvenient absence. Some saw 'high' absence figures as a bad reflection on their abilities, even when they recognized causes beyond their control. While the control of attendance largely remained personal, rather than becoming a collective issue, pressures to improve absence figures did not seem to generate much resentment amongst staff, although they may have had a negative impact on standards of consistency and fairness. More importantly, however, both the personal approach and increased pressure for action on absence tended to produce a combative attitude amongst many managers. There were frequent references to 'coming down hard' on absentees, and 'giving them a bloody good fright'. Not only does this indicate a substantial erosion of official policy, it also cut across the emphasis placed on the stress inherent in much of the work at the hospital which we found amongst ward sisters and supervisors as well as staff.

Only among domestics had management adopted a policy which was widely seen as punitive. Domestics were attached to wards or departments, but there was also a pool of 'floaters', and this was widely regarded as the least enjoyable station. Management was removing staff from regular positions in the event of a long absence, and placing them in the pool on their return. This measure was widely unpopular.

A high level of informality did not seem to create substantial problems of consistency of treatment of individuals, but it could have important effects on attendance control overall. Recognizing commitment, while dealing with the everyday problems of absence, can produce conflicting pressures on managers. In all our studies, whether monitoring was sophisticated or not, managers claimed to know very well which members of staff were reliable, and which were a problem. Nursing managers often approached staff relations with a paternal/maternal attitude. Domestic managers, while generally more worried about attendance, pointed to low wages, and to the lack of regard for their staff in the hospital, and claimed a good job was being done under difficult circumstances. These attitudes were sincerely held, but they do not do away with material and staff constraints, which also affect management thinking and behaviour; nor were they always recognized by the workers themselves.

At the hospital, managers often displayed impatience with procedures, or a doubt in higher management's commitment to action, when faced with staffing problems arising from absence. One junior manager demonstrated this in his attitude to guidelines on absence. He claimed to follow the authority's guidelines strictly himself, but felt that for supervisors 'guidelines are not really in their day to day vocabulary of working practice' and he would only draw their attention to them if they 'were going astray.' At the same time he felt that workers should not know the guidelines, 'in case they work the system', although such a 'secret policy' would presumably conflict with the need to establish consistent and recognised standards.

Dissatisfaction with procedures can lead to pressure for a more aggressive style of management. This manager thought it 'too easy just to phone up sick, state a reason, and then stay off'. It was also reflected in feelings that line managers are expected to manage intractable problems without support from their superiors, especially when dealing with repeated or protracted absence. What is at issue here is not just a possible disagreement about the treatment of an individual, but conflicting messages in which personnel policy clashes with administrative and financial pressures.

Managers were themselves aware of these pressures and consequent contradictions. One line manager felt that sick pay 'encourages abuse, its seen as an entitlement, they use it as extra holidays.' At the same time this manager was very aware of the particular problems faced by women workers, and had a deal of sympathy for them, which she felt was not the case with higher management. Of particular importance for her was insensitivity towards staff's social problems, especially from male managers brought in from manufacturing, and who had a more coercive outlook.

Everyday management was therefore a matter of persistent informal negotiation and compromise. Amongst Domestics, changes in attendance control which abolished 'clocking' were welcomed by managers as allowing for this fact. One felt that 'When they were on the clock, then every minute off was docked. With time-sheets, we are more flexible ... There are trade offs in fact, informalities, I'm reluctant to admit it, but yes. We do our best for willing workers, supervisors know who and what.'

The same tensions between line and higher management can be discovered between line management and supervisors. One domestic supervisor describing the impact of competitive tendering emphasized increased pressures of work, especially on older workers, felt that people were 'frightened to phone in sick'. In her view 'Higher management understand its harder, but they take the attitude that you are lucky to have a job. I've got to be sympathetic, to get the work out.'

Amongst nursing managers many of these problems were less pronounced, if only because sick absence ran at a lower rate than amongst domestics, or because they felt themselves more secure in the hierarchy. Certainly they generally expressed confidence in their own handling of absence matters, but also they appeared less confident of the ability of ward sisters to take on wider supervisory functions. This was a common view amongst nursing managers, but was not echoed amongst the sisters we talked to. One commented that increased managerial responsibility had been on the cards for some time, but that nothing much really happened, perhaps because 'unit managers have been in charge for so long.'

As in many organizations we studied (Edwards and Whitston, 1989b), the focus for control of attendance was shifting towards supervisory staff, although in practice this had not proceeded very far as yet. In most cases domestic supervisors and ward sisters limited their intervention to the most informal level of a 'quiet word' preceding initial counselling. It was clearly management intention to go further, with at least the first stage of formal procedure put into the hands of first line supervision.

Senior nursing management were aware of this policy, but emphasized the continuing role of nurse managers who had, it was said, a better overview of the whole situation. 'Ward sisters may moan', we were told, 'but nurse managers take action'. In part nursing managers felt there was a difference, little understood by policy makers, between nursing and other disciplines. The role of the ward sister in supervision was sometimes felt to be too close to staff since relations were built around clinical matters and the care team. Ward sisters were also seen by some as poorly trained for this role, and 'not mature enough', being reluctant to approach colleagues as a manager.

Amongst ward sisters themselves there was a clear recognition that their supervisory profile would rise in the future. Many welcomed this growth in responsibility, but there was widespread nervousness about lack of training, and a feeling that they would simply be 'pushed into it without preparation.'

Among domestic staff things had been taken further. The senior manager, who had come from private industry, had always 'believed in supervisor power'. He felt that in the NHS there was a tendency for all decisions to be pushed to higher levels, and he had been determined to end this in his area of responsibility. Competitive tendering had provided the opportunity to build up the supervisors responsibilities. Training had played a major part in this, as had the establishment of 'job profiles' to enable supervisors to oversee any job on site. Supervisors had 'been in a mess' prior to this initiative, and had at first resented having their 'shortcomings highlighted', but the manager felt that considerable progress had been made.

In fact the increased role for supervisors in absence control was not new. One supervisor, who had been at City General for over twenty years, recalled having had her 'new' responsibilities many years earlier, but they had been 'clawed back' in the meantime. She saw it as a matter of managerial fashion. Nevertheless, the current reintroduction of supervisory control seemed more structured, and clearly owed much to an adaptation to a growing commercialization. Supervisors had much more paperwork to do regarding attendance, filling time sheets, and answering absence control queries from management.

These changes were mirrored in work organization and allocation. They had been made responsible for specified work checks on a daily basis, and the whole work process had been reorganized around a detailed task list and quality rates. Consequently supervisors had become far more concerned with the detailed control of individual workers. The style of control had shifted therefore into a pattern more closely resembling that common in private industry.

Some of these conflicting pressures are evident in workers' responses. As Table A.7 shows, hospital workers were at least as aware as those in our other studies of managerial pressures or expectations concerning attendance. But there was less awareness than there was in Multiplex or BR of a change in the managerial approach. This reflects the differing ways in which managerial behaviour was impacting. There were certainly managers adopting a more 'commercial' view, and this was the general drift of policy. But others did not follow this line, and how far it impacted on workers was mediated by traditional assumptions. Thus change was apparent, but it had not yet cut very deeply into practice.

Conclusions

Scepticism about non-medical managers ran deep amongst all nursing staff, from top to bottom, and more than one nursing manager commented that the administration 'floated out comments on figures' from time to time, but felt that they 'hadn't much of an idea of how it was really run on the ground'. On the wards, and in the departments, it was clear that the success of complicated shift patterns and difficulties over holiday allocation were solved often by a spirit of co-operation amongst the staff, which gave nurses a degree of flexibility, and which managers found extremely useful. While there was no suggestion of 'loose' management practices, the needs of individual staff were sometimes clearly accommodated at the expense of the formal rules. At the same time, however, nursing managers also applied appreciable pressure on absentees to account for their sickness, and to return to duty as early as possible. While they felt that in general they did this in ways which emphasized the importance of the staff contribution, many nurses complained of intrusive or distrustful responses to sick absence.

These contradictory pressures have important implications for the management of attendance. Informality can lead to incoherence in policy, and an unwillingness by line management to take direct responsibility. A reliance on 'moral suasion' as opposed to formal rules, can lead to friction with staff, while leaving the substantial problem unsolved, because of a lack of clarity regarding standards. The result is a degree of managerial 'drift'. At the same time there was clearly pressure to align control mechanisms more closely with those found in the private sector in ways which do not always engage with the positive elements of staff co-operation, and which are only very loosely connected with questions of work behaviour.

High Commitment, Low Morale: an NHS Paradox?

These changes in management approach, coupled with considerable external financial and political pressures, go a long way towards explaining the realities of day-to-day worker-management relations at City General. Demands on workers had increased over a number of years, and substantial institutional change meant that there was often little breathing space for adaption to the new commercialism. Workers showed little difference in attitude to those in other occupations, and there was a tangible absence problem compared to our other case study sites. Yet throughout our series of interviews, with both staff and managers, it was clear that staff commitment to the service was not only high, but essential to the running of the hospital. At the same time we encountered much evidence of dissatisfaction, if not disaffection, among staff. This section looks at how workers regarded both the control of their labour and their views on the management.

Worker Perceptions of the Control of Labour

Formal discipline played a relatively minor part in the control of labour at City General. Table A.7 shows worker perceptions of managerial control of attendance and discipline. From this it can be seen that the hospital workers were in no way exceptional in their views on the operation of the disciplinary system, feeling, for the most part, that the disciplinary regime was about right, but with a substantial minority unconvinced that rules were applied in an equitable way. At the same time, the experience of formal discipline was at the lower end of the range; such discipline was evidently much more likely to be experienced by manual workers at BR and Multiplex.

This may have been, in part, because of the professional nature of the nursing regime, and there was some anecdotal evidence that discipline played a more prominent role for support staff. The period following competitive tendering had produced some problems for the domestics. This was partly to do with the new emphasis on supervisory powers, and partly an adaption to more industrial standards of work measurement and control. One manual steward told us that for a period of about a year relations had reached rock bottom as the women on the wards took the brunt of the blame for difficulties in setting the new system in place, but this had improved with time and with more training for supervisors. He did feel that representation of members had become more difficult however, as discipline had become more rule based, and 'they keep rediscovering rules no one has heard of for years'.

Nevertheless, there was little evidence of systematic differences in the rigour of the disciplinary regime between domestic and nursing staff. On the wards relatively small workgroups, and common interest in clinical discipline, tended to produce a structure in which expectations of behaviour were relatively clear, and in which discipline was often contained in ways which avoided recourse to more formal methods. As noted earlier, the degree to which the domestic staff were included in this 'care team' approach is less clear, but it evidently remained a strong reality for most of the staff.

At the same time, as Table A.11 shows, hospital staff were much more likely than workers in our other case study sites to believe both that their work had got harder, and that management's approach was less friendly. This may also account for the fact that 54 per cent of staff interviewed had thought of leaving, again the highest proportion in our study. This may be accounted for in part by the expectations of qualified nursing staff who would look forward to moving hospitals to develop their careers, but Table A.9 shows that only 3 per cent of those who thought of leaving mentioned the need to gain wider experience, while 71 per cent mentioned 'other' causes. The variety of these replies precluded their tabulation, but very many of them related in one way or another to what were seen as threats to the patient-centred element of job satisfaction.

This was particularly clear among the domestics. The whole thrust of the reorganization of their work, and the substantial reduction in their numbers clearly limited the time they could spend in direct contact with patients. That this was so was clear not only from what the staff themselves said, but also the near unanimous verdict of their managers and supervisors. In the past a domestic on a ward would be able to find time to talk, and to perform minor tasks for patients (renewing water jugs, helping with meal distribution etc.), but the new work schedules had set strict limits to this role. Many supervisors, as well as staff, cited this as one reason for a decline in the 'happy atmosphere' that had typified the department in the past.

Among nursing staff the evidence was far less clear cut, but here too accelerated patient throughput on the wards, coupled with staffing restrictions, led to some complaints about lack of time to spend with individual patients. More common, however, was the complaint that nursing staff was being made to do too much with too restricted resources. This dissatisfaction could take many forms. One nurse complained that a lack of resources made it difficult to provide sufficient privacy for elderly patients on her ward, and felt that it was increasingly hard for her to 'continue doing a first class job in a third rate environment.' This kind of complaint was often aggravated by a feeling that financial savings were being made at the patients' expense, or by managers with little feel for what was required on the wards. It was impossible for us to know if these perceptions were accurate; the point is that their widespread expression indicated a deep-seated unhappiness with the realities of day to day work.

The service ethos, and the demands of professionalism amongst nursing staff, were important ingredients of the cement that held the 'care teams' together. At the same time, perceived obstacles to the expression of this ethos produced a marked negative effect on morale. This had some contradictory effects on how staff perceived management.

Worker Perceptions of Management

Staff were also asked questions about their relations with management; whether management were seen as friendly, whether management was trusted, and whether things were getting better or worse in this respect. These questions are more difficult than they seem. What does trust mean? The question was designed to ask about institutional trust, which has received some attention from academics and managers, but staff usually perceived it in more personal terms. Again, informal discussion was used to probe people's experience and the meanings they attached to them, and the results are reasonably reliable, and can be compared between groups and other workplaces.

One person put it this way; she would trust her manager to deal with her decently as an individual, to respect confidences and so on, but she would have little trust in management at any level to look after her interests, or to put them very high in their considerations. This was clear in the feelings of the domestic staff who saw most of the unsatisfactory aspects of their current position as due to changes connected with competitive tendering. While generally feeling that managers were approachable and friendly as people, they were very conscious of external pressures, and felt that not only had the work got harder, but that management was more demanding, and more inclined to pressurise staff.

Table A.10 shows how workers responded to questions on their managers. Over three quarters of staff saw management as very or quite friendly, a far higher proportion than workers at BR, but in line with results at Multiplex and FinCo. At the same time, nearly half of the staff felt that there was not much trust, or none at all between managers and workers, compared to between 20 and 25 per cent at Multiplex and FinCo. In those companies between 10 and 19 per cent felt there was complete trust, but only 4 per cent of staff at the hospital thought so. On this question they were much closer to respondents at BR, which had troubled industrial relations, and where no one expressed complete trust.

The lowest trust was expressed by the qualified nursing staff, especially RGNs, where over 60% expressed no trust at all. In all cases the higher management were seen as remote and ignorant of the true conditions and needs of staff. This critical view was also shared by those staff who thought that changes in work practices, a stricter attitude to financial waste, and more public accountability were overdue. Among nurses the grading issue was obviously seen as an irritation, but their distrust of management was also more widely based. It should be said, though, that a significant minority of staff thought things were improving in this respect, especially amongst newly qualified nurses.

The most striking element in staff attitudes was the contrast between approval of managers' personal approach, or friendliness, and the very deep distrust revealed, a pattern markedly different from that in other companies studied, including BR. A clue to why this is the case can be found in replies on staff's general attitudes to attendance. At the other sites, amongst those who answered positively on a duty to attend, duty to the employer, or management, came high in their list of reasons. At the hospital, by contrast, it was extremely rare for any reference to be made to a duty to the employer. Instead, answers focused on the service, or the patients, presenting, in extreme cases, almost a 'producers alliance' against the administration.

Table A.10 also shows how workers perceived the managerial function. Workers were asked to say if any of four attributes applied to their managers. At City General 30 per cent mentioned managers contributing through their knowledge and experience, 25 per cent that they were needed to make people work, and 79 per cent, the highest rating in our study, mentioned administrative matters. The comparisons with our other sites are instructive. The enforcement function was the least cited at the hospital, and knowledge and experience was also lowest, just behind responses from BR. At the same time 70 per cent mentioned only one of these functions, and this figure is much lower than at the other sites.

Workers at City General, it seemed, saw managers, functions in very narrow terms. The low score for the coercion function may well reflect the self motivating effects of the 'care team', but the low score for a contribution based on knowledge and experience is far more resonant of low morale. In a service ethos, backed by professionalism and a clinically graded hierarchy, much more emphasis might have been expected on knowledge and experience. The fact that it did not occur is partly due to the distrust of non-medical management, but also partly due to a deterioration in trust of nursing managers seen as too far removed from clinical disciplines and the reality of life on the wards. This seems to be a conclusion entirely in tune with the evidence recounted in earlier sections as a fractured management propels a transition from a service driven organization, to a more commercially driven environment. Seen in the light of both the nurse grading dispute and the effects of competitive tendering the apparent paradox dissolves: low morale, esteem for personal relations with managers, and high levels of distrust of management are understandable and rational responses.

Conclusions

Health service workers sit uneasily at the point of overlap of many characterizations of work and workers. Are nurses blue collar, or white collar, skilled or professionals, service oriented vocationals, or public sector drones? Of course, any close examination of their work quickly undermines such generalizations to the extent that labour in the health service is widely differentiated, with both internal clinical hierarchies, and wider divisions between professionals and support staff. But, nonetheless, can we identify particular characteristics of this workforce, and do they conform to any notion of the 'caring professions'?

The first point to emphasize is the closeness to other, industrial, workers in terms of attitude to attendance at work, and in those factors which come to bear on everyday decisions affecting attendance and absence. Most important here are the demands of personal and family life, but these cannot be entirely separated from the job setting, since, after all, they are common to workers who show very different patterns of action in respect of attendance at work, and organizational commitment. What seems more basic is the elaboration of a 'moral universe' of work which is singularly impervious to many of the new managerial strategies, so much so that the orchestration of 'commitment' can soon show its coercive face. This was certainly evident at the hospital. Changes, often justified in terms of some overarching notion of efficiency, were clearly seen as driven by politics and restrained resources, and the improved 'communications' so dear to managers' hearts seemed to have little impact on the minds of those to whom they were directed. For managers there remains an unacknowledged gulf between their need to control labour, and the limits of that control contained in not only collective agreements, but in the limited nature of employee consent. This gulf consequently becomes the breeding ground of illusions and ideology.

Having made these points it is still necessary to acknowledge the distinct setting of the hospital, and the continuing force of a public service ethos amongst the staff. The exact centre of this ethos may be difficult to locate at times. Some managers asked whether commitment was to the patients, as individuals, or to the 'service', so often mentioned by interviewees. It is possible that this is a nicety which is less important than the contradictory pressures on staff which are reflected in a disassociation between the 'service', and management as the immediate employer. In effect workers' commitment to their own estimation of the importance of their work provided the basis for a degree of self discipline, and of co-operation with management, which has largely enabled management to implement its own programme despite the deep-seated worries amongst many of the staff. Amongst qualified nurses this undoubtedly reflects to a degree, as Carpenter et al (1987: 51) argue, the concerns of 'proletarians who aspire to be middle class professionals', but, since the service attitude is widespread amongst unqualified and ancillary staff, this cannot be the whole answer. In effect, and despite the pressures of change, health service workers have accepted to some extent that they will police themselves, and leave managers considerable leeway for action. The general feeling amongst staff was that morale was low, but commitment to the job and the 'service' remained high. Although some staff felt they would be happier elsewhere, very few were actively considering leaving. Also, feelings of frustration did not seem to affect the kind of give and take between staff and managers that most saw as necessary for efficient operation. Managerial control of attendance reflected similar forces. The approach remained much less formal than it was in our other organizations and the contrast between the informal give-and-take at grassroots level and higher managerial policies was more marked. Though there have been massive pressures towards commercialism, day to day understandings on attendance continued to reflect long standing health service norms. Such co-operation may not, however, survive increasing commercial pressures. Management has so far been able to depend implicitly on traditional forms of loyalty. As the contradictions between these and commercialism are heightened, this loyalty may begin to erode.

6

FinCo: the Regulation of White-collar Work

FinCo is a well-known organization in the banking, insurance, and finance sector. It employs about 10,000 staff, of whom 2,000 work at its head office. We studied two departments at this office, employing between them about 300 workers. The great majority of the workers were routine clerical employees, and most were women. We chose this group deliberately, so as to maximize comparability with manual workers in our other studies: to have taken more senior grades would have been to study people with far more autonomy and responsibility than manual workers enjoy.

As indicated in Chapter 1, there were several reasons for studying the company. The most specific was to compare the control of absence and workers' attitudes to attendance with the situation among blue-collar workers. As we have seen in Chapter 2, FinCo workers did not differ from the other groups in their general views on the legitimacy of absence. This leaves open the issue of their actual behaviour and the ways in which management tried to control it. Traditionally, absence has not been a major concern in relation to white-collar workers, and we did not expect the issue to have the salience in day-to-day practice that it had in Multiplex or BR. And so it turned out: for FinCo supervisors, absence was not a central problem, and its control is not part of the story of how the shopfloor was regulated. There are, none the less, two important themes to pursue. First, how far was management making absence more of an issue, and if so why? Second, if the issue is not managed actively, and given that the workers had no particular moral commitment to regular attendance, just how often did they go absent and what sort of norms governed their behaviour?

The second interest in FinCo was its appraisal and performance-related pay system. We took it as an example of an attempt to promote a sense of commitment among workers. We did not study it in its own right: our aim was to assess its impact on the day-to-day conduct of the effort bargain. FinCo constitutes something of a critical test case. Many of its workers were newly recruited, so that there was no workplace tradition to interfere with the initiative; the company was not unionized, though it had a staff association; and white-collar workers may be expected to be less sceptical of managerial initiatives than are blue-collar employees.

This links with the third, most general, issue: the ways in which white-collar workers are persuaded to work. The labour process debate has stimulated interest in broad issues of the organization and control of clerical work. Most attention has focused on the question of skill: has new office technology removed traditional skills and increased management's ability to monitor levels of work effort, and have white-collar jobs therefore been proletarianized (Lane, 1988; McLoughlin and Clark, 1988)? This debate has several difficulties. In the strict sense, proletarianization implies that a group once enjoyed real authority in the labour process and that it has now lost it: since clerks probably never had such authority, to speak of proletarianization is to assume a historical process of doubtful validity (Kelly and Roslender, 1988). The assessment of skill is also a complex task (see Rolfe, 1986, and Crompton and Jones, 1984, for sensitive discussions). We did not set out to contribute directly to such debates, though there are points, for example the ability of management to use the new technology to monitor the output of workers, where we think we can usefully question some of the conventional wisdom. Instead, we looked more directly at the day-to-day production of compliance.

Surprisingly little attention has been given to the question of how white-collar workers are persuaded to work, and what happens if they resist such persuasion. Surveying recent literature, Lockwood (1989: 231) notes that 'how work is allocated and carried out is still a matter concerning which evidence is hardly more than anecdotal'. We aim to address this issue directly.

Some of the standard tools available in manual settings are rarely employed. They are not generally paid output-related bonuses, supervision is rarely close, and overt discipline is unusual. In some cases there may be implicit understandings that workers will be left alone as long as some acceptable level of performance is maintained. In situations where clerical workers are not the core producers – for example the wages office in a factory – managerial concern with work effort may be slight. But in organizations like FinCo clerks are the core group. We wanted to know how expectations of effort were established and maintained. In seeking an answer we found evidence that bears on the debate about skill. This evidence relates neither to workers' technical dexterity nor to their class position. It concerns the rationalization of clerical work. The tendency was towards the standardization of work tasks and the formal measurement of the quantity of work performed. Workers were thus being treated in ways which are more commonly associated with manual employees. At the same time, however, this was only a tendency, and there remained some distinctive aspects of the workplace regime. One was promotion, for it remained possible for a good many - but, as we will see, not all - workers realistically to aspire to more responsible jobs. A second was a culture in which supervision was imposed far less overtly than was the case in, say, Multiplex. Here, as in most factories, workers worked and supervisors told them what to do. In FinCo the distinction was blurred. Managers and workers worked alongside each other, and there was a shared set of assumptions, particularly about clearing each day's work, which encouraged the willing production of effort.

We were not in a position to make a detailed investigation of, say, the nature of skill or the culture of the work group. But this limitation was balanced by setting our material alongside that from other workplaces. A case study of white-collar employees would find it hard to establish just how distinctive the practices that it uncovered were. The comparatively rare approach of addressing the same issues of workplace behaviour among manual and non-manual staff helps us to understand why FinCo operated as it did.

We have suggested that in relation to the appraisal system FinCo may constitute a particularly relevant case: if workers here have not embraced a new model of shopfloor relations, it is unlikely that others will have done so. We make no such claim in relation to our more general results on the effort bargain. In the passage cited above, Lockwood, having noted the virtual absence of systematic study of the social organization of office work, remarks that 'what there is relates to very atypical situations'. These are large bureaucracies, whereas most clerical workers are employed in small workplaces. Our results are certainly not 'typical' of clerical labour as a whole. What we can do, however, is to add a distinctive dimension to the understanding of labour in large firms. More speculatively, our findings may indicate a trend: to the extent that work is being rationalized, one would expect the process to be most advanced in large firms where clerks are the core work force.

An important strand of the evidence relates to differences within the company. Clerical work is far from homogeneous, and in the case of FinCo there were differences between and within our two departments. We will call them Administration and Customer Services. The former, employing about 100 workers, was an archetype of routine clerical work. Its job was to store and retrieve documents and to process them in a fairly small number of standard ways. This standardization had permitted management to experiment with formal work quotas whereby workers on each section were expected to complete so many tasks per day. The rationalization of labour meant that workers were treated in ways which were qualitatively little different from the organization of manual work. The main division within the department was between those operating the computerized storage and retrieval system and the rest of the workers. About 20 part-timers worked on the system, doing work of a highly routine nature. Supervisory authority was most overt in their case, and work standards were most formalized.

Customer Services had one section with a similar arrangement, namely, the typing pool, where there were formal output quotas. The twenty or so typists were largely distinct from the rest of the department. Most workers did a variety of tasks such as registering customers' changes of address and administering pass books and a variety of cash cards. Though there were standard procedures and the work was routine, workers had to respond to queries over the telephone and to deal with a variety of different cases; it was hard to estimate how long any one task would take, and managers felt that the work did not lend itself to formal effort standards.

A feature of both departments was a very high level of supervision. A section manager could be responsible for as few as three or four staff, and rarely more than a dozen, in which case there was an assistant manager and sometimes also a 'senior clerk'. The computerized system in Administration had a supervisor and two team leaders. The section that included this system had a total of 13 full-time and 25 part-time clerks, who were supervised by the two team leaders, three senior clerks, five supervisors, one 'controller' and the section manager. As already indicated, these managerial personnel did not simply supervise the work of others: they handled the more difficult cases, advised staff who were uncertain about a procedure, and generally took on a proportion of their sections' work. None the less, their presence in numbers was an obvious part of the explanation of how workers were persuaded to work. There was little space, either physical or social, in which workers could create their own norms, and managerial assumptions about standards of performance were constantly evident.

One further feature of the two departments needs mention here. Both acted as ports of entry to the company, with workers who secured promotion moving on to departments offering more varied and interesting work. This might suggest that our sample was untypical of the company as a whole. We make no claim that our results apply to the more senior administrative and managerial posts, but there is no reason to suppose that our cross-section was in any way unrepresentative of people entering the lower clerical grades. We found some people who were, very reasonably, confident of progressing, but there were also others who plainly had no hope of escaping from the bottom levels. As Table A.12 shows, over a quarter of our sample had worked for the company for at least five years, and only ten per cent cited promotion chances as a reason for staying with the firm. Many workers could expect to remain in the more routine grades. The key point about mobility is that it helped to undermine any collective orientation which might otherwise have developed. This was a further factor in the lack of social space for workers to challenge managerial assumptions and arguments.

Before proceeding with the analysis, we need to deal with one obvious expectation, namely that differences in the rationalization of work between the two departments should be associated with differences in attitude. The more formalized approach in Administration might be expected to lead, for example, to criticism of management and to higher absence levels. In fact, there were no significant differences between departments on any of our questionnaire items or in patterns of absence. The main reason is probably that changes in work organization had not yet cut deep enough to have major effects on attitudes or behaviour. In Administration, formal work standards were only just being introduced and they had not led to any significant work re-organization. Conversely, in Customer Services several workers reported increasing work pressure. Moreover, this department was the more formally organized in some respects, notably the control of absence. These differing strands meant that there were no sharp differences between the departments. Formalization was a clear tendency, but its implications were perhaps more apparent to the outsider than to workers themselves.

The argument will proceed in three main stages, corresponding to three substantive topics. The first topic is absence. There were clear differences from manual workers in absence patterns, and the issue had a relatively low salience for managers, though even here the tendency was to give it more attention. Second, we consider whether the appraisal system had generated a new form of commitment. Concluding that it had not, we then turn to the organization of compliance at the point of production, arguing that the tendency was towards a heightened control of work by management.

Absence and Attendance Control

Absence Rates

One consequence of the rapid turnover of staff was that it was difficult to obtain a run of absence data for any one individual for the whole of a year. We eventually compiled information on 110 workers. The summary statistics are given in Table A.4. Since the great majority of the workers were women we also need to make comparisons with women workers in our other studies. The FinCo data are therefore reproduced in Table 6.1, along with the figures from the hospital and the data for women workers at Multiplex.

The obvious, and expected, feature of the figures is the low level of absence at FinCo when conventional time lost indices are used. The rate of 9.3 days lost per worker per year was dramatically below the rate at the hospital and substantially below the Multiplex rate. It translates into a percentage rate of around 4 per cent. Three per cent has been identified as the unavoidable minimum that most firms could expect (Huczynski and Fitzpatrick, 1989). Seen in these terms, absence was not a problem. The rate was, however, rather higher than those quoted for three Canadian banks by Chadwick-Jones et al. (1982: 19-21). Their figures imply a rate of days lost per worker per year of between 4.5 and 6.5 days. North American absence rates are, however, lower than those in Britain. Taylor (1979) gives a time-lost rate for all United States white-collar workers of 2.8 per cent, with 4.4 per cent for blue-collar employees, whereas in Britain the comparable figures are in the ranges of 3-4 per cent and 5-7 per cent respectively. In short, FinCo's figures seemed to be unexceptional.

None the less, the difference from Multiplex was, in view of obvious differences in work conditions, far from large. When we consider the frequency of absence spells, moreover, the differences are reversed. As Figure 2 (p. 76) shows, FinCo workers recorded fewer 'clean' years, and more cases of six or more spells, than did those in Multiplex. The hospital's

TABLE 6.1 Absence Data for Women Workers

	FinCo	Multiplex	Hosp.
Frequency (per cent of workers with given number of spells in a year)			
None	19	18	13
1	19	23	16
2	20	23	20
3	12	16	17
4	12	10	14
5	7	5	6
6–10	8	6	13
11 or more	3	(..)	3
Duration (per cent of spells lasting)			
1–2 days	67	35	52
3–5 days	24	42	21
6–19 days	7	23[a]	19
20 days and over	2		9
Severity measures			
Mean number days absent per worker per year	9.3	13.1	27.9
Mean length (days) of each spell of absence	3.4	6.3	8.9

Note: a. Relates to all 6 days and more spells.

record was not much 'worse' than FinCo's. All three groups, moreover, did rather 'better' than Chadwick-Jones et al.'s white-collar samples (1982: 120-21). Their charts for one bank show that only about 9 per cent of workers went through a year with no spell of absence; the figure for a hospital that they also studied was only 6 per cent; the FinCo figure was 19 per cent (with Multiplex on 17 and our hospital on 13).

Such differences suggest caution in evaluating Chadwick-Jones et al.'s generalization from their hospital and bank data: 'a "white-collar" pattern emerges as one of extremely widespread, very short, nonsickness absence' (p. 22). FinCo workers were absent less often than the Canadian white-collar groups, and their absences lasted longer. As we have already seen in Chapter 5, none of our hospital workers had a pattern of frequent, short, absences. Chadwick-Jones et al. offer no explanation of their patterns, and in particular they made no effort to explore the workplace regimes which gave rise to them. We doubt whether there is one white-collar pattern. Most obviously, the tensions and loss of morale that we noted in the hospital had no parallel in FinCo.

None the less, relative to our other organizations, the FinCo pattern was one of frequent, short, absences. Two-thirds of all absence spells lasted one or two days, and these accounted for a quarter of all days lost. We can consider the reasons underlying this 'white-collar pattern' by examining workers' reasons for wanting to take time off.

Attitudes towards Attendance

As we have already seen, FinCo workers' general views on the legitimacy of absence were indistinguishable from those of manual workers. The same point applies to our opening question as to whether workers should be free to take time off when they chose or whether they should attend whenever possible. As shown in Table A.5, the Finco sample, where 87 per cent chose the 'duty to attend option', fell between the BR and hospital samples at one end and the Multiplex sample at the other. Turning to reports of their own behaviour, there was again little difference in general attitude: as Table A.1 shows, the proportion who ever thought about going absent when they were able to attend fell within the range covered by the other samples. Such evidence suggests that no distinctive white-collar attitude lies at the basis of the frequently noted difference in absence rates between non-manual and manual employees. The difference is more likely to stem from the particular circumstances of white-collar work.

The main difference came in relation to reports about how far it had ever been necessary to act on a desire to go absent: a very high proportion (87 per cent) said that they had never taken a day off when they had been able to attend. This seems to have reflected several features of the scheduling of work. The company operated a flexitime system which meant that workers could deal with domestic contingencies without having to go absent. Several workers said that they valued this arrangement. For part-timers it was particularly valued, since many of them could vary their exact hours of work to suit themselves, starting at, say, 9.30 and not the official starting time of 9 a.m. and putting in an extra half hour at the end of the day. Interestingly, however, such flexibility was not permitted in the computerized section of Administration. Here, workers had to work 9-1 or 2-5; morning shift workers could not come later since the machines had to be free for the afternoon shift, who could not themselves start later because there would be no-one to supervise them after 5 p.m. Flexitime was not without its critics, however. As one worker put it, it suited the company more than her because use of it could be halted at managerial discretion. Indeed, it had been suspended in the Customer Services department during our study because of pressure of work. More generally, the limits to flexitime were quite strict: workers could not arrive after 10 a.m. or leave before 4 p.m., and each section had to ensure that it was staffed for the standard working day, which meant that workers could not choose the hours to suit them as individuals. More generally still, managements gain from flexitime to the extent that workers deal with domestic responsibilities in their own time and not through absence.

A second feature of working time was the ease with which holidays could be booked at short notice to deal with domestic problems. The need to use absence to cover such demands was thus reduced, though the value of the arrangement should not be exaggerated. It had the same limitations as flexitime, in particular the fact that it was discretionary and not a right.

Third, there was the use of part-timers. This could be expected to have two effects: such workers would deal with non-work problems in their own time, and hence would go absent less than full-timers for 'illegitimate' reasons; and, because they were at work for only a short time, they might be less likely to go absent as a result of boredom or other work-related factors. There is in fact no evidence to show that part-timers do indeed go absent less often, and there were too few part-timers in our FinCo sample to reach any conclusion on the issue. None the less, the tendency, particularly regarding taking time off for reasons other than ill-health, is likely to have been to depress the rate of absence.

There may also have been some distinctive encouragements to attend work. As Table A.6 shows, FinCo workers were, not surprisingly, very unlikely to cite the fear of discipline or the loss of income as reasons for attending. Perhaps more surprisingly, they were comparatively unlikely to cite enjoyment of the job, which suggests that it was not job satisfaction which made them attend work regularly. Their main reasons were duty to work mates (which they chose about as often as did hospital employees), a personal sense of responsibility, and the backlog of work if they stayed away. One third of them mentioned this last reason (though only 8 per cent said that it was their most important reason), a figure much higher than that in our other samples. Taken together, these replies point to a sense of duty to the work group and to the task but not particularly to the employer, for 'duty to the firm' was no more likely to be cited than it was by our other samples. Each section had a set amount of work to do, and if it was not done it built up the next day. Such obvious work pressures were absent in the other organizations. In BR, if trains do not run one day they plainly do not accumulate for the next day. Even in the warehouse at Multiplex, where there were set orders to be filled, work pressures were less immediate: workers were moved around between sections of high and low demand, and any worker going absent one day did not have a specific amount of work to be done by her on her return. In FinCo a backlog of work on a section was a perennial concern, and working as a group to minimize it was seen as important, not just in relation to absence but also, as we will see, in encouraging workers to work hard when they were actually at work.

Reasons for wanting to go absent (Table A.2) are also instructive. In line with the unimportance of enjoyment of the job as a reason to attend, FinCo workers quite frequently cited boredom as a reason to go absent; indeed, they chose this option more often than did BR or hospital workers. Family and domestic responsibilities also featured highly.

FinCo employees did not, then, exhibit particularly high levels of job satisfaction or commitment to the employer. To the extent that they were more prone than other workers to have pro-attendance attitudes, this was reflected in a sense of duty to fellow workers and in a belief that work tasks had to be fulfilled. Such attitudes did not, however, go as far as a workplace culture encouraging attendance. In response to our open-ended question about why most workers attend regularly, four people mentioned duty to fellow workers or friendly relations with work mates as reasons. The majority of the sample (57 per cent), however, said that they never discussed the amount of time off taken by other workers. The high degree of mobility and the low length of service of most workers, moreover, militated against strong work group norms.

We investigated this further by examining the relationship between attitudes to attendance and various measures of work group cohesion. It might be expected, for example, that people who get on well with their fellow workers, or who see a friendly work group as a very important reason for staying with the company, will also be aware of the absences of work mates and will discuss their absences with others. In fact, there were no associations of this kind in FinCo. Nor was there any link between measures of group cohesion and an individual's absence behaviour. There was thus no evidence of connections between attitudes to absence and loyalty to the work group.

FinCo workers were more likely than others to specify duty to the group as a reason to attend, but this view was not supported by anything that could be termed an attendance culture. And it was a fairly general statement of opinion which was not tied in to a closely-connected set of beliefs about the work group. These attitudes, together with the conditions of white-collar work provide part of the explanation of the place of absence in the workplace organization: workers felt some duty to attend, and work conditions reduced pressures to go absent. But managerial control was at least as important. We turn to this before summarizing the pattern and significance of absence.

Managerial Control

As might be expected, absence was not seen as a major issue by most managers. This was certainly the case at the departmental level, with most section managers saying that coping with absence or handling poor attenders was a rarity. There were no rules of thumb as to a level of absence that justified managerial action, simply because it was so rare for a problem of this kind to arise. There were, however, some differences between the two departments in the ways in which they had traditionally handled absence, and the issue had recently come to the fore within the personnel department. We discuss the traditional system before considering the reasons for change.

In Administration absence had had a low salience. No manager saw it as a problem. There was a system of seeing staff on their return to work from absence, with the self-certification form being completed in the presence of the section manager. In the great majority of cases, however, this was seen as no more than a formal requirement, and there was no system of detailed interviewing on the return.

In Customer Services absence had had a higher profile, as illustrated by the tradition, which reportedly went back several years, of giving a free lunch with the department manager to anyone going through a year with no spell of absence. The reason was claimed by managers to be no more than a small acknowledgement of good attendance: the scheme had not been introduced in response to any particular problem, nor was it felt to be a large enough incentive to have any effect on attendance. More substantially, two senior managers in the department took account of absence in awarding pay increases under the appraisal scheme. The system was for all appraisal forms to come to them, and they then added or subtracted small sums, generally around £10 or £20 a year, to the bonus that had been awarded. Including absence within the appraisal scheme appeared to be a practice peculiar to this department. It was explained partly in terms of a few people taking odd days off. But more important seemed to be the two managers' belief that people who went absent were not making a full contribution to the department's work, and should be penalized as a result. It was almost a moral statement rather than a carefully devised reaction to a specific problem, and it reflected the thinking of these two managers. The recently-appointed department manager seemed to take little interest in this aspect of policy.

The use of the appraisal scheme in this way could scarcely be anything other than symbolic. The sums involved were too small to be a major stick or carrot. When we asked workers about the system, there was a good deal of uncertainty. Some did not know about it at all, while others had a vague idea that something was done but they did not know exactly what. As the managers conceded, staff turnover since the scheme was introduced meant that new starters would be unlikely to know anything about it. The ways in which money was paid or withheld were, moreover, far from explicit. The managers were adamant that it was they, and not section managers, who decided the sums involved, and they said that the key criterion was the number of days absence each year. They also said, however, that someone away for a genuine reason might lose less than the frequent absentee. There was thus no clear formula for how much bonus a worker might expect. For all these reasons, the system was unlikely to have had any major effect on attendance, and for what it is worth there was no difference from Administration either in overall absence rates or in the frequency distribution of absences. The subjectivity and secrecy of the whole process also suggest that the system would not find a place in manuals of good personnel practice.

The fact that managers did not see absence as a major issue was reflected in workers' replies about the control of attendance. As shown in Table A.7, only 31 per cent of FinCo workers were aware of pressures or expectations from management concerning attendance, as against around 60 per cent in our other organizations. And only a fifth had noticed any change in methods of control. There were one or two instances where a hard line was evident. One worker said that she had been away from work with a succession of migraines and had been told that the next time she was away she would have to see the company doctor. Another had been away with a series of separate complaints and had been told that she could lose her job as a result. A third reported that managers' first reaction was one of distrust. She had a complaint which meant that she should not work on VDUs, and managers had at first not believed her. When she produced a letter from her own doctor she was moved from this work, but was then put back on it. She had felt powerless to complain, and had eventually been ill for a week as a result.

In a certain style of case study reporting, which rests solely on informal discussions with workers, such instances might be presented as typical and as illustrations of an increasingly harsh regime. By speaking to a larger sample, as well as to managers, we found that they were unusual. There was, moreover, no evidence that they were part of any deliberate policy, either at department level or at the level of personnel specialists, of tightening control. In general, the regime remained relaxed, though the fact that such cases could occur at all must not be forgotten: it may have been relaxed, but it did not prevent individual workers from feeling mistreated. We are of course unable to say whether similar cases could have been unearthed say five years before we did our study. But it is likely that they would have been less common. Broader changes in FinCo were certainly leading towards a more calculative view of the costs of labour and, as we report below, the general drift was for workers to report a more demanding and less friendly atmosphere. The three cases were not examples of a deliberate policy, but they may have been the unintended result of a rather tougher style of labour management.

Though the personnel department had not promulgated any 'get tough' directives on absence control, absence was just coming to attention as an issue. As one personnel manager explained, the business had been growing rapidly and it was hard to staff up to complement. Work had to be covered with temporary and agency staff, which added to costs. Absence was simply a further additional cost. The general view among personnel specialists was that managers in the operating departments did not take absence seriously enough, even to the extent of absence recording being substantially incomplete. As far as we could discover, this last concern was unfounded in relation to our two departments: section managers reported filling in the appropriate forms and, when we suggested that perhaps this was a piece of bureaucracy that the busy manager might sometimes ignore, they did not take the invitation to agree that form-filling was a waste of time. But it is true that absence was not very salient to them.

Surprisingly perhaps, personnel managers reported that absence control policies were more developed in FinCo's branches, their small size notwithstanding, than in the large head office. One senior manager had just moved to the head office from the branches. In the latter, she explained, there was a system of monitoring, whereby anyone with ten days' absence in a year would be noted for attention: in the first instance, a letter indicating concern was sent, and for subsequent cases workers were interviewed. In the head office, nothing had been done, largely, she felt, because attention had been focused on recruiting to match the growth in work. Absence was now being considered, though there were as yet no formal systems in place to control it. The general tendency, then, was for absence to be seen as an issue, though this had yet to reach the level of the manager in an operating department.

Conclusion

The as-yet limited attention to absence fits the character of the company. Senior managers were certainly aware that the business environment was increasingly competitive, as financial institutions competed for the same markets. But pressures on labour costs were relatively new and were much less severe than they were in, say, Multiplex or BR, two instances where there had been a decade of concern at meeting financial targets. In much of manufacturing the very survival of the business was in question during much of the 1980s. In FinCo such extreme concerns were wholly absent. This situation, combined with the low rates of absence, meant that managerial control could be exercised in a relaxed manner, though the tendency was certainly towards more concern about attendance.

With this approach to control, and with no strong work group pressures, we can explain the pattern of absence as occurring more or less by default. It is not the case that white-collar workers have a particularly moralistic orientation to attendance: on several key measures of attitudes FinCo employees were little different from manual workers. Nor did they cite enjoyment of the job itself as a major reason to attend. Without any strong managerial pressures, workers were free to take odd days off, and we can thus see why the frequency of absences was quite high. At the same time, the work force was relatively young, which reduced the incidence of long-term sickness, there was some feeling of duty to fellow workers to attend, and the working environment was not so stressful as to lead workers to need a great deal of time off. It was these contingencies of the workplace, and not anything distinctive in workers' attitudes, which explains the pattern of absence.

Appraising the Appraisal System

Character and Aims of the Appraisal Scheme

As we have said, a major reason for studying FinCo was its system of staff appraisal. This was linked to a bonus system, so that there was a direct monetary reward for a good appraisal. Some form of appraisal is increasingly common in Britain: between 1977 and 1985 the proportion of clerical and secretarial staff subject to it rose from 45 per cent to 66 per cent (Townley, 1989: 98). Surveys do not report in how many cases appraisal was linked to reward in the manner of FinCo, though one survey by ACAS showed that 24 per cent of the organizations sampled had introduced some form of merit pay between 1984 and 1987 (Sisson and Blissett 1989). There is, moreover, a widespread view that some form of performance-related pay is a desirable means of promoting efficiency. As Fowler (1988) notes, many organizations have introduced performance-related pay in the hope of creating a performance-conscious environment. 'What is missing from the growing volume of comment', he goes on, 'is any effective research into its impact on performance' (p. 34). We hope to throw some light on this issue.

In the FinCo system, someone achieving the top rating could receive a pay increase double the average, while an 'unacceptable' rating could mean no pay rise at all. The rating system was fairly straightforward, with employees being graded into five categories. In some schemes, there is a pre-determined distribution of employees between categories, the aim being to ensure that the total sum paid out does not exceed a specified limit. This creates the obvious problem that workers are not graded on their own merits (Fowler, 1988). FinCo avoided this difficulty by doing the gradings first, with no limit to the number who could be placed in any category; only then was a cash sum allocated to each grade. The sum was, however, fixed in advance, which meant that, while individual workers could gain from a high rating, it was impossible for workers as a whole to increase the total wage bill.

As noted above, in many ways, FinCo offers an ideal test case. In addition to general features of the organization, such as the absence of industrial relations problems, the scheme itself was a serious endeavour. The linking of appraisal to payment plainly offered workers an induce-ment to value the system. The scheme itself was sophisticated: as noted above, it avoided some of the pitfalls of restricting the grades that could be awarded; the appraisal form was detailed, and contained space for the appraisee's comments. There was an appeals mechanism, in which a case could be taken up by the staff association; the whole of the scheme had also been agreed with the association. Finally, substantial efforts were made to train appraisers and to explain the objectives of the scheme to workers.

It is worth stressing that senior personnel managers in FinCo did not have the inflated expectations of appraisal that are sometimes aired. They argued that money was not intended as the motivation: it was the process of being appraised which was important, with the link with pay being used only to focus the minds of both appraisers and appraisees and to encourage them to take the process seriously. Appraisal was thus not seen as a direct incentive to work hard. It had three rather different aims. First, there was a need to widen the range of pay in a given grade, particularly the lowest grades. Second, the company wished to be equitable, paying according to merit instead of giving the same increase to everyone. Particularly in the branches, individuals were aware of who were the good and bad performers, and there was a need to recognize this. Third, it was important to get the message across that, with growing competition in the sector, the performance of the company could not be taken for granted and that individuals' contribution made a difference. Appraisal was not seen as a panacea. Indeed, the present system replaced an earlier, relatively informal, one which was felt to have been unsatisfactory: managers recognized the problems of making a system work. They none the less invested a good deal of time in designing, implementing and explaining the new scheme. Senior management has been quoted as claiming that performance-related pay has played a 'significant part' in the development of the company. We can reasonably claim that they must have expected some measurable effect on the shopfloor.

Impact in Practice

In fact, the overwhelming reaction was one of scepticism, a response which embraced supervisors and managers as well as clerical workers. One senior departmental manager argued that there had been little effect on motivation because jobs had to be done in a set manner: the team leaders and supervisors were crucial in ensuring that proper procedures were carried out, and set against this detailed day-to-day activity the appraisal system was too distant to have any real effect. The manager of one of our departments felt that the system was trying to do too much at once: setting pay rises, establishing work targets, and evaluating performance. Other managers complained at the amount of time that appraisals took and at what they saw as the excessive detail which was required in completing appraisal forms.

Workers were equally unhappy. In each interview we asked a general question about appraisal and followed it up by pursuing each respondent's concerns. We have categorized the answers in terms of individuals' own views and the impact that they believed appraisal had had on motivation and morale. As shown in Table 6.2, those disliking the scheme were in a clear majority. As to the effects, almost half the sample thought that there had been no discernible impact, and rather more perceived deleterious than identified beneficial effects.

The most common complaint was that appraisal was not appropriate to routine jobs: the system was supposed to evaluate past performance and to establish future objectives, but performance was already assessed on a day-to-day basis while the objectives were often meaningless. Workers complained of being given aims such as keeping their desks tidy or answering the telephone before it rang three times. Others noted that it might be sensible to set objectives once but that it became increasingly difficult to find new aims that meant anything. Even one worker who felt that the system was generally useful, in that it gave the opportunity to talk things through with the supervisor, complained that the system was hard to understand. Other complaints turned on the pay arrangements. The basic idea was that everyone in the same job grade who achieved the same evaluation should be paid the same cash sum. But there was also some fine-tuning so that workers placed in the same overall band were then rated into other groupings. Workers expressed some uncertainty as to how this was done, and some said that it had led to some resentment when awards became known, though also saying that this had been short-lived.

TABLE 6.2   Attitudes to the Appraisal System

	Per Cent of:	
	Whole Sample	*Those Stating an Opinion*
Personal reaction (N=66)		
Keen acceptance	14	15
Qualified acceptance	22	24
Dislike	36	39
Extreme dislike	15	17
No personal experience yet	4	5
Don't know/no reply	8	–
Views on effects (N=57)		
Raises motivation/a good effect	18	23
No effect	36	46
Causes resentment	17	21
Counter productive/does more harm than good	8	11
Don't know	3	–
No reply	18	–

A second common complaint was that it was impossible to find the time to meet objectives. A worker might be given the aim of improving her knowledge of departmental procedures, only to find that there was no time to do so as day-to-day demands took precedence. Several workers argued that objectives effectively became meaningless since there was no time to pursue them. If appraisal is supposed to contribute to an awareness of the needs of the business as a whole, workers need to be convinced that objective-setting is taken seriously by management. For several FinCo workers, the inability to pursue objectives encouraged scepticism about the whole system and about managers' commitment to developing their skills.

A problem running though any appraisal scheme is that of objectivity: can workers' performance be evaluated fairly? Most workers did not seem very worried about this, and seemed to accept that, in broad terms at least, evaluations were fair. Six people remarked on the system's unfairness, however, in particular on the difficulty of having an appeal taken seriously. One long-serving employee said that objective-setting was a 'fait accompli' and that questioning an assignment would get her nowhere: she felt isolated and powerless when faced with the whole weight of management. Another worker had questioned an assessment but had felt that there was no-one to whom she could turn for help; she had felt so upset that she had thought of resigning. The force of these reactions may have been unusual, but it probably reflected a wider phenomenon. We looked through all the completed appraisal forms in our two departments, and found that hardly any worker had made any comment, even where appraisers had made unfavourable remarks or even given a 'less than effective' grading. This suggests that workers generally felt unable to affect the process, though most seemed to be unconcerned about this.

Six is not a large number, but it does represent one-twelfth of our sample, and if our results are in any way representative they point to quite a sizable number of people who felt deeply hurt by the system. Since there was an appeals system, how can this be explained? We did not look at the system itself, but we were told by personnel managers that it was quite common for appeals to be upheld, and the two appeals against 'less than effective' ratings that we found in our departments were both amended on appeal to 'effective'. It may be that the appeals mechanism worked for the 'big' cases in which a clear injustice could be shown. These, however, were the minority. In many more, workers felt a nagging sense that they had not been treated fairly, but it was difficult for them to act. To question an appraisal would mean challenging a superior, and workers lacked the self-confidence to do so. The staff association could offer only limited help. As two senior officials admitted when we put this to them, many staff felt that there was no-one to whom they could turn for friendly advice: making an appeal was hard, and workers lacked the skills and experience to write an effective challenge to an evaluation. Though we did not question workers systematically about their views of the association, spontaneous comments pointed to the distance of the association officials from their own immediate concerns. In Administration there was no association representative, while in Consumer Services the representative was a section manager, who might well be seen more as a manager than as someone likely to sympathize with a lowly clerk. Workers thus felt isolated and powerless.

As far as we could judge, criticism of appraisal was quite general. There was no tendency for it to be concentrated among longer-serving workers. A slight tendency could be discerned for those critical of management in general to have unfavourable views of appraisal. On the question about trust, for example, 16 of the 28 people (57 per cent) saying that there was complete trust or trust most of the time held broadly favourable views of appraisal, whereas only 5 of the 16 (or 31 per cent) of those identifying low amounts held such views. This difference was not, however, large enough to meet conventional standards of statistical significance. Criticism of appraisal was not, therefore, concentrated within a particular sub-group of workers. It was general, which adds weight to the view that the effect of the system on shopfloor attitudes was on balance negative.

More general aspects of the system also suggest that its motivational effects must have been limited. The first was the cash basis of the system. Managers explained that this had been chosen deliberately: workers in the same grade and evaluated the same should be rewarded identically. The effect, though, was to make the proportionate increase for those at the top of a pay scale smaller than the increase for those at the bottom. We looked at a sample of workers and found that there was indeed a significant tendency for the size of pay increases to be inversely related to current salary. Second, and more important, were general pay rises. Though a worker's rise was supposedly dependent on individual performance, in fact labour market pressures were forcing the company to make general wage increases for the lower grades of staff. The great majority of workers were graded as 'effective'. For those towards the bottom of a pay scale, the general wage increase was larger than that awarded for effective performance. For those towards the top, the position was reversed, and workers at the very top of a grade received no general increase (their merit pay being a one-off bonus that took them above the scale maximum and which did not contribute to pensionable pay). The result was a compression of pay differentials, and not the intended widening. For example, before the wage round a long-serving Grade 2 clerk enjoyed a 25 per cent differential over a colleague with only two years' service. After the general wage increase the differential had been cut to 15 per cent. Workers themselves were not necessarily well aware of this, though one did comment that the system did not reward long-term loyalty. But, since total percentage wage increases owed more to being towards the bottom of a job grade than to performance, the impact of the system on efficiency was questionable.

We have shown that the appraisal scheme did not improve shopfloor morale. Yet we have also shown that the scheme had some significant limitations, notably its operation alongside general wage increases and the consequent breaking of a strong link between performance and pay. It is thus open to supporters of performance-related pay to argue that the FinCo scheme was not a good test case. Several considerations suggest that such an argument is invalid. First, some very general claims have been made about the desirability of appraisal and performance-related pay. If it now turns out that these claims are to be made only in respect of schemes operating in special conditions, the general argument is put into question. Second, and relatedly, such schemes do not work in a world in which everything else is unchanged. FinCo faced labour market pressures, and amended its pay levels accordingly. The value of performance-related pay has to be judged in the light of such real world conditions and not against some ideal standard. Third, as indicated at the start of the discussion, FinCo was in many respects an ideal testing ground for appraisal. Experience here cannot be written off as a special case, and it is for advocates of performance-related pay to demonstrate their claims.

We do not suggest that our findings offer particularly strong evidence on the issue highlighted by Fowler, namely, the effects of performance pay on performance. FinCo is only one case, and we were looking more at workers' attitudes than at measures of output per employee. But we are not aware of any evidence in FinCo showing that specific output measures had changed as a result of the appraisal system, and workers' reactions certainly suggested that they themselves had not been motivated to perform differently. In short, our material tends support to those who question universalistic claims about performance pay. If it was a relatively minor addition to the regulation of work, how in fact was consent generated on the office floor?

The Regulation of the Office Floor

Formal Discipline

The most obvious way to control workers is through a formal system of rules together with penalties for their infraction. There was a formal disciplinary procedure, which had been agreed with the staff association three years before our study. This was a standard four-stage procedure, with an employee having the right to be represented by the association at all stages other than the first. There was no salary penalty associated with discipline, though any warnings could be taken into account in the appraisal system.

Not surprisingly, overt discipline was used very rarely. According to management, in the whole of the company only about 15 cases a year went as far as Stage 3 of the procedure. Most of these were for theft on which, again unsurprisingly, a very firm line was taken, with dismissal being the standard policy except where the evidence was questionable. In our two departments, we came across only two cases of overt discipline. In one, a probationary employee whose attendance had been irregular was not kept on to join the permanent staff. In the other, three workers took a day's leave to go to a race meeting but failed to report the next day. They were given a verbal warning for failing to notify their absence, which they explained as the result of a car breakdown, and for not making sufficient effort to attend. They were required to take their extra day's absence as annual leave. Both cases were seen as exceptional.

As shown in Table A.7, only 16 per cent of our sample of FinCo workers said that they had ever been disciplined. Most of these instances were relatively minor, for example cases where workers had been warned for talking too much. Our analysis of the appraisal records also pointed to a degree of managerial concern about chatting. One worker was said to become involved in petty squabbles, which she denied, and another was said to indulge in 'excessive socializing'.

Yet the relative lightness of discipline did not mean that workers were happy with the system. Eighteen per cent felt that rules were applied too rigidly, a proportion equal to that in the hospital and higher than that in Multiplex. Moreover, FinCo workers were more likely than our other samples to feel that rules were applied differently to different groups of workers. The main complaint here was that other departments were put under less pressure and enjoyed a more relaxed atmosphere. One worker, for example, said that workers in other departments were free to come and go as they pleased whereas she and her colleagues had their flexitime strictly controlled. We spoke to supervisors about this in some detail. It certainly appeared to be the case that flexitime was carefully monitored. One possibility, for example, is that workers can fiddle time by stretching a lunch break and claiming, if challenged, that any extra minutes should be put down as flexitime. Supervisors might be ignorant of the practice or they might tacitly collude with it.In fact, they, and the workers to whom we spoke on the subject, confirmed that such fiddles were non-existent. They were assisted in this by the fact that each supervised a small group and could easily tell if someone was absent.

Whether matters were in fact any different elsewhere we cannot say, but there was a feeling in our departments that they were the most closely regulated. This may have had some basis in fact in that the departments handled the most routine work. Elsewhere, workers had more responsibility, and it is likely that they were granted more freedom to come and go. Feelings hardly amounted to major discontent, however. There were some niggles about being told off, and some resentment about 'Other Departments', but there was no deep sense of dissatisfaction. Thus stories about other departments tended to be told in general terms without any profound outrage. Overt discipline did not, then, figure heavily in the shopfloor culture. Yet, as with attitudes to absence, workers did not stand out sharply from our manual samples. Their distinctive views can be explained in terms of the way in which their labour was organized, but we need first to consider the nature of these views in more detail.

Attitudes towards Management

As shown in Table A.10, attitudes to management were not markedly different from those in Multiplex. Thus 81 per cent of FinCo workers said managers were friendly or very friendly, as compared with 77 per cent in Multiplex. Three-quarters, in both FinCo and Multiplex, said that there was at least a fair amount of trust. As indicated in previous chapters, the low amounts of trust in management in the two public sector organizations reflect the specific circumstances of these two cases: it is not that FinCo workers stand out as having a high level of confidence in management, but rather that confidence was especially low in BR and the hospital. As Figures 3 and 4 (pp. 82 and 83) underline, the overall attitude profile in FinCo was very similar to that in Multiplex.

A substantial minority of workers expressed some scepticism about managers. A quarter felt that there was not much or no trust between management and workers. When invited to choose among three useful functions performed by managers, only ten per cent cited all three, with 15 per cent specifying none. Because of rapid staff turnover, only 36 FinCo workers answered the question about changes in trust, and as many of them (22 per cent) said that trust had declined as said that it had improved. There was an interesting variation according to length of service (albeit one that was not statistically significant because of the small numbers involved): of the ten FinCo workers with at least ten years' service, six perceived a worsening of relationships, whereas only one of the 18 with between two and five years' service gave this reply.

The interviews with the long-serving workers pointed to a sense of dissatisfaction which was much deeper than that regarding the disciplinary system. Workers argued that managers had become more distant and that work pressures were intensifying. Some spoke with considerable feeling about a rigid and bureaucratic atmosphere. One Grade 1 clerk with eleven years' service complained that in the past there had been a tea break on her section to allow relief from working with VDUs, but this had been removed and it was now difficult to obtain the necessary relief; managers were less approachable than they had been in the past. Another, with 24 years' experience, complained that managers no longer cared about their staff and had become anonymous.

Only 25 workers were able to answer the question about general changes in managerial approaches to workers. The pattern of replies (Table A.11) suggests, though, that there was a significant strand of dissatisfaction: more said that work was harder or that managers were less friendly than felt that work was less hard or perceived an increase in friendliness. Workers were, however, prepared to concede that there was more communication with staff than there had been in the past. Managers' views interestingly paralleled these opinions. All the long-serving managers to whom we spoke agreed that work had become harder. One said that in the past there had been quiet periods, but now the pace was unrelenting. Another noted that his department was always operating below its official staffing figure, and that this intensified demands on workers. The size of the problem can be judged from the department's planned and actual staffing levels. Over a year, the average planned level was 88 full-time equivalents, against an average actual figure of 81. Managers and workers thus agreed that the workplace environment was changing.

This was not, however, the dominant impression within the work force as a whole. The pattern of replies suggests four broad groupings. First, there were young and ambitious workers who were happy with the system and who, quite reasonably, expected to rise through the ranks. One young man, for example, although currently doing a mundane job, was quite content. He had worked for FinCo for less than a year, and expected promotion soon. He found the appraisal system fair and useful, saw FinCo as a good place to work, and thought that he had every opportunity to better himself by working hard. Second came other short-service workers who did not expect or necessarily seek promotion but who saw it as a reasonable job. A couple of workers, for example, had come from another company where monitoring of performance had been very strict; they found FinCo a perfectly satisfactory place to work. Third, other short-service workers expressed a degree of dissatisfaction. Some said that they found the work to be highly pressurized, particularly at first, but they were willing to stick it out. Finally, longer-serving workers were more likely to feel deeper discontent but also to feel trapped: as they, and indeed some other workers, said, their main reason for staying with FinCo was the cheap mortgage facilities that it offered, which meant that they could not afford to leave.

Discontent was far from rare, but at the same time it was not general and it tended to be highly individualized. Workers responded to the situation in their own ways, and two people could react very differently according to how they felt about the demands of work and the pressures that it placed on them.

This pattern illustrates something of the differences from our manual samples. White-collar workers in FinCo were far from being uncritical of management and, as noted above, they did not place 'duty to the employer' particularly high among their list of reasons to attend. At the same time, overt discipline was rare and resentment was moderate in tone. In short, workers were not qualitatively different from those elsewhere in terms of the expectations of work, but their experience of day-to-day control was sufficiently different to lead to a different atmosphere.

The Management of Effort

In many ways there was nothing mysterious about this day-to-day control. We have mentioned the high ratio of supervisors, team leaders, and senior clerks to Grade 1 and 2 clerks. These managerial personnel certainly did not spend all their time in overseeing work: one team leader estimated that supervision took up perhaps 25 per cent of his time, with the rest of his work being concerned with operating the computer software. But their presence made it reasonably easy for standards of effort to be promulgated and monitored. As discussed below, in the typing and computerized storage sections, explicit criteria were set and measured. The present concern is the majority of the workforce, for whom work standards were less formally established.

The informality of these standards is indicated by one worker who said that managers did not make a big issue of achieving them and that she was just generally aware that they were there. Another said that when she joined a year previously she just tried out the work with no formal standards being imposed, but she also noted that there was a certain amount of pressure and that managers did not always appreciate how hard workers had to work. In effect, workers slowly learned what was expected of them without managers having to lay down formal expectations.

A second factor was the arrival of work in each day's post, with clearing this work being established as a clear and understandable objective. A similar process was observed by Crozier (1964: 18) in his study of a clerical agency in Paris: 'one principle is followed, as a sort of golden rule: all the traffic arriving on time must be handled the same day'. In this case, discipline was harsh, and Crozier likens the work organization to a military system. The FinCo environment was certainly not militaristic, but the importance of meeting the demands of each day's work was generally accepted. But how were these demands enforced? The work group was as important as direct managerial control here. Workers seemed to take it for granted that the work had to be done, and that, if it was not, the people who would suffer would be fellow workers. This is not to say that they were clear effort standards policed by the group. The situation was more amorphous than this, and correspondingly difficult to grasp and to describe. But several comments from workers indicate how some, albeit loose, standard of effort was established.

One worker explained that on her section there was a great deal of work on the telephone, so that set standards, such as might apply to routine paperwork, could not be laid down. Managers seemed to have some implicit view as to what was reasonable. As for workers, they varied a great deal, and there was a degree of work group pressure on the slower ones to maintain an acceptable pace, because it was unfair to others not to be trying. A second worker, who had worked on a section with more paperwork for a year, explained that work was delivered on trolleys. Anyone with a difficult trolley would be helped, because everyone knew that all the rest of the section was making a genuine effort; but if someone was felt to be unjustified in needing help she would be told so directly. A third said simply that workers expected each other to do their bit.

There were thus no strong group norms on output. The sample split roughly evenly on our question as to whether there were shared ideas on how hard people should work, suggesting that norms were lacking: half of the workers saw no shared ideas while the half who did perceive such ideas were thinking of some general notions and not clear norms. Several workers commented on the differences in effort between individuals. As noted above, there might be some group pressure on those not pulling their weight, but there seemed to be no norms as to the maximum amount of work that someone might do. The impact of work standards also varied. Some workers reported that they were hard to achieve, others that there were times when they were difficult but that in general they were reachable, and yet others that they posed no problem.

What this suggests is a disparate situation: standards existed but were not exact; work groups had some ideas of duties to colleagues but no clear norms; and workers varied in their subjective feelings. Implicit ideas of a 'fair day's work' seemed to be sufficient to ensure that workers put in the effort which managers and fellow workers found to be acceptable. The tacit nature of the process is notable in view of the short service of many of the workers. In a workplace where most people have been there for years, like BR or Multiplex, it is not surprising that workers cannot articulate exactly how they came to learn the standards expected of them. But many of the FinCo workers whom we have quoted had been there only a year or two. They had slipped into a workplace culture without having to think explicitly about its construction.

Rules, Fiddles and Informality

It is none the less possible that they found ways to reconstruct it in ways which suited themselves. Apart from Crozier, the classic source on white-collar workplace behaviour is Blau (1963), who showed in the case of a group of American law-enforcement agents that workers developed their own rules which in significant respects subverted those of management. In manual work settings it is in principle easy for supervisors to see whether workers are working to correct procedures, but dealing with paperwork is a more private activity which is hard to monitor. We needed to know whether workers found ways of cutting corners, or otherwise turning the effort bargain in their own favour.

We have already seen that the fiddling of time was agreed by supervisors and workers not to be an issue. Turning to short cuts within work itself, one worker cited a few possible practices. To check the closure of an account, for example, was supposed to involve looking back through every year for which the account was open, but in practice it was possible to check without going through the whole procedure. She stressed, however, that when she trained other workers (such training being an interesting issue on which we comment below) she followed proper procedures. Thus there was no means for informal practices to become generalized: in some workplaces, the norm is for workers to say, 'this is what the rules say, but you really do it this way', but in FinCo this practice was absent. The worker explained, moreover, that it was impossible to cut many corners since the section's work was scrutinized by independent auditors who would find errors. In the particular work she was doing at present, she just had to stick to procedures. Another worker noted that people were taught the correct methods when they joined the company and that supervisors checked work to ensure that there was no slippage.

Managers confirmed the monitoring systems in force. One section manager explained that all financial calculations were double-checked within the section and that anyone dealing with correspondence with the public was also monitored by a manager. Auditors also carried out very careful checks every month. Another manager reported using random checks on all aspects of her section's work. Knowledge of procedures was also assessed during training programmes and in the appraisal system so that a worker might be asked to outline the correct procedure for a particular transaction. In any event, she argued, short cuts were not really in workers' interests: for example, if someone failed to record a transaction this would be picked up later by monitoring procedures, the result being twice as much work in checking back to find the error than would have been involved in doing the work correctly in the first place.

Audits, random checks, and the sheer presence of a large number of managers thus tightly constrained the space in which fiddles could occur. The need for them was, in any event, limited. The assumption in much of the literature seems to be that there is an inherent tendency for workers to alter formal rules. But how far they do so will depend on a variety of factors such as their collective solidarity. But one factor is simply the nature of the work task. Blau's federal agents subverted the rules in order to get the job done effectively. They were, for example, forbidden to talk to each other about their cases, but they found that following this rule made it hard for them to develop a real understanding of when it was appropriate to prosecute a firm breaking the law. A different example comes from Blau's other case study, of an employment agency. Here, workers were measured by the number of job vacancies that they filled, and they used illicit practices to inflate the number of vacancies filled (for example by counting someone as having worked at a job even when he or she had merely done an aptitude test) and to keep the best openings to themselves (by hiding from other workers requests from employers). At FinCo pressures of this sort were absent. The set procedures worked well enough, and there was no benefit in claiming to do more work than had in fact been done or in competing for work with other workers.

A final area of informality concerns the extra-contractual expectations that managers were able to rely on. The essence of fiddles practised by workers is that the employment relationship is imprecise: obligations cannot be specified in total, and workers can therefore amend the terms of the effort bargain. As Armstrong and Goodman (1979) note, however, this imprecision can be used by managers as much as by workers. They give as an example of what they call managerial custom and practice an arrangement in a footwear factory. The collective agreement stipulated that management had to give notice if workers were to be laid off, but managers were able to evade this obligation: they could send workers home at short notice, and the workers, lacking the collective means to resist and in any event appreciating the chance to escape from the factory, complied. In FinCo managerial conduct did not really constitute custom and practice, that is, a generally recognized rule, but was more informal.

One area concerned work effort. As discussed below, on some sections managers were establishing fixed standards of work to be done per day. These standards contained the danger that they could be treated as maxima by workers. When asked about this, managers did not see it as a significant issue, arguing that workers would generally do the amount of work each day that had to be done. The standard was just that: a baseline figure which the competent worker could reasonably be expected to exceed. In such a case, the formal obligations that management itself laid down were not treated as fixed but were open to implicit negotiation. The point also applied, albeit in a less clear-cut way, in areas without set standards, for again managers had created the understanding that they could call for varying amounts of effort and that this effort would be forthcoming.

A second issue which caused us some surprise was training. Even Grade 1 clerks who had joined the company recently took it as part of normal routine that they would train recruits. This was not extra-contractual, since there was nothing in writing to say that they would not train. But it was surprising because one would not expect workers at the bottom of the wage hierarchy to be responsible training, particularly where this involved teaching detailed procedure. For workers themselves, there was nothing odd about this, and no one said that it was a problem, let alone an issue that had been raised explicitly with management. The case is interesting precisely because of this, in indicating the extent to which managers could take for granted a high degree of compliance with their expectations even when workers in other companies might begin to argue about what they were and were not contractually required to do.

The case of rules and fiddles thus illustrates further the informal ways in which workers were persuaded to work. Day-to-day practice was characterized by what one may call the normality of co-operation. Work had to be done, and there was an established way of doing it. There was little space for the idea of a bargain about effort to become manifest. That effort was none the less an issue was indicated by the fact that workers were well aware that certain standards were expected, and by the existence on some sections of explicit definitions of what these standards were. We now turn to these definitions.

The Operation and Monitoring of Work Standards

There are two topics under this head: the operation, in the computerized storage section of the Administration department and in the typing section of Customer Services, of rigid output quotas; and the development in the whole of Administration of formal work standards. The essence of the first was simple. On the storage section, workers were expected to achieve a set number of tasks per day, and the equipment recorded how much each operator had in fact done. In typing, there was a standard norm of 700 lines per day. Audio typists completed sheets for each piece of work that they handled, and they also logged the number of each piece on a computer system. The section supervisor had reports which indicated, from the computer data, each worker's duties and the time taken to complete them. These figures were compared with targets that had been set by work study for each type of job so that a measure of efficiency could be produced.

The conventional wisdom on such computerized monitoring is that managements do not use the potential of the machine to monitor work closely. Storey (1986) reports from his study of three insurance offices that only in the most technically advanced office were workers required to enter their own code number into the computer. This was not even used to monitor individual performance, the managerial tactic being to have it known that this facility was available but not to use it. Lane (1987: 68), summarizing research in Britain and Germany, notes that researchers accept that the control potential of new technology is 'not systematically utilised and that old forms of control - both the personal and the bureaucratic kind – are still very prevalent and continue to distinguish office from manual work'. The continuation of traditional modes of control is important, but the dismissal of the role of new technology has been rather too easy. As Rose and colleagues (1986) note, the desire to avoid any taint of technological determinism has led some researchers to the opposite extreme of denying any role for technology.

The technology can surely be used as a control device without this having to occur on a day-by-day basis. If Storey's workers knew that they could be monitored, and if this knowledge produced the behaviour that managers wanted, then actually to carry out the monitoring would have been redundant. Storey in fact concedes that output per day increased after computerization, and adds that managements may have been holding back from pressing through the full implications of the new technology until it had become fully operational. Noon (1989) has shown how this possibility may be made manifest. In the provincial newspaper industry the introduction of computerized systems was accompanied by new technology agreements that met many of the aims of the National Union of Journalists, but managements have subsequently pressed through sweeping changes, including in several cases the removal of the union's negotiating rights.

At FinCo nothing as dramatic as this had happened, but the technology was contributing to control. As the computer systems supervisor in Administration explained, output was recorded each day. It was not actively monitored daily, but if a worker appeared to be consistently falling behind standards, the data could be used to check back on what she had in fact done. For the odd day below standard, he was not bothered, but if a worker began to slip back over a week or so he would take action. In one case, for example, a worker had consistently been doing about twenty files fewer than the others, and she had been persuaded to 'buck up'. What he saw as real problem cases also emerged from time to time, generally because people were simply not suited to the work. On the whole, he said, they just tended to resign.

A broader feature of the control system on this section was reflected in the fact that it was now staffed entirely by part-timers. Managers said that it had been hard to persuade full-time staff to tolerate the extreme tedium of the work, and it had been decided to go for part-timers, who would accept the system more willingly.

The workers themselves were certainly well aware of being monitored. One said, 'they do notice if things are wrong with your work. But they never tell you when your work is OK'. She was not bothered about being monitored. Another explained that the system could track errors, and that management would check up on these if necessary, with any mistake being brought to a worker's attention. She found the standards quite demanding. Workers were certainly not being checked every minute of the day, but they knew that they had to keep up an acceptable standard in the long-run. Other, traditional, modes of control also kept them at their tasks. They complained, for example, that their times for starting and finishing work and for tea breaks were closely checked. The supervisor explained that workers would not be allowed to leave early even if all their work had been completed; he thought that this was silly, but would get a black mark from his manager if he were to permit it. The fact, moreover, that the whole section was easily in view of his desk and that of the team leader meant that workers could not easily wander about or talk to each other.

The situation in the typing section was essentially similar. As one worker explained, the standards are reasonable and were not checked particularly closely, but 'you definitely notice that work is being monitored and that management know what we are doing'. Another said that she certainly felt the pressure to work and that everyone feared falling behind everyone else. 'You know when you've had a good day'. The idea of a 'good day' is interesting. It was certainly open to workers to take it easy occasionally in the knowledge that they would not be penalized immediately. But they also knew that they had to keep up an overall standard. They were thus keen to put in a 'good day' because this would give them a reserve when, for whatever reason, they found it hard to keep to standards. In short, the need to maintain the work pace was well established.

It could of course be argued that workers on these two sections were not qualitatively different from others: on other sections, too, workers knew what was required of them. It would be wrong to exaggerate the differences. As has been stressed by those wishing to deny the effects of technical change, new technology is embedded in a set of existing relationships. Yet they seem to have set unduly high criteria for the identification of an effect. At FinCo computerized systems were used to monitor work. These systems did not mark a total break with existing modes of control, and indeed operated literally alongside non-computerized methods. But they were one part of means of controlling some workers, with effects of which the workers themselves were plainly aware. The impact was certainly not so great as to distinguish these workers from others in terms of their overall attitudes to work. These attitudes were shaped by a wide variety of factors. There were, none the less, indicative tendencies. In Administration, some workers on the computerized equipment complained that they lacked others' freedom to take coffee breaks and to move around the department. Such feelings were not universal, but they intimate a way in which computerization was affecting traditional modes of control.

A wider move in the same direction was the development of formal effort standards throughout Administration. These were in essence simple: on one section, for example, workers were expected to deal with 150 pieces of work per day. It would be easy to imply that these standards were part of a systematic move towards the 'white-collar factory': the imposition of explicit effort norms on a de-skilled work force. In fact, matters were more complex than this. Most importantly, the development of formal standards was not part of a deliberate policy at the higher levels of the company: there was no general strategy of introducing standards. Indeed, as we have seen, managers in Customer Services dismissed the relevance of formal work quotas. What had happened was that the previous manager of the Administration department, who had come from a background in business systems, had decided that explicit measurement of performance would help to give proper targets as to the amount of work that was expected. Some managers argued that the appraisal system had encouraged formality, because appraisal called for explicit criteria against which people could be assessed. There is plainly no direct link between appraisal and performance standards established on a daily basis: appraisal was designed not to summarize the meeting of detailed targets but to evaluate long-term performance and a whole range of skills. But it may well have been that appraisal helped to give a rationale for the standards. The current department manager certainly felt that it was hard to run an appraisal system without formal standards.

As with computerized monitoring, it would be wrong to see the standards as making a sharp break from former practice. One or two section supervisors said that, though they had set some definitions of job content for each post, they did not take the idea of fixed norms very seriously. As one in particular argued, she worked alongside her staff and the main thing was to complete the section's work and not to worry about whether people were attaining specific targets each day. Workers, too, did not make a major issue of the standards as such. As one said, targets had not been forced on them too firmly, and she remained free to use her own initiative in how to do the work. As we have seen, there were no major differences from Customer Services in attitudes to work.

The standards were thus not part of a company-wide policy; nor had they cut deep into the organization of work. They were, none the less, significant. Though not part of company policy, they were not against policy either, and no efforts had been made to eliminate them. The manager who introduced them was arguably working in a way consistent with policy in that he was concerned with measuring and controlling labour costs. As his successor explained, the firm had become much more business-like in the past few years, and she was having to become tougher in insisting on changing work practices. A major aim, for example, was to train staff to work in a wider range of jobs across the whole department; though uncertain at present, staff would welcome this once they had become accustomed to it. The improvement in work practices was not, she stressed, a direct demand of her own superiors, but was part of a general recognition of a need to be more efficient.

This point helps to explain similarities with Customer Services. Here, too, there was a general pressure to use labour more effectively, as indicated by workers' and managers' views that work had become harder. But the particular device of formal standards was more applicable to the more routinized environment of Administration. These standards can thus be seen as a particular reflection of a more general approach. This approach had not reached the stage of being explicit policy. But managers at all levels of the organization were increasingly stressing the need for efficiency, and productivity was now coming on to the managerial agenda. The change was slow but unmistakable.

Conclusions

We have noted other aspects of the changing managerial approach in the attention being given to the control of absence; in the willingness to go to the trouble and expense of the appraisal scheme, with its aim of creating a performance-conscious organization; and in the attention to effort standards. It did not, to repeat, constitute a self-conscious drive, or one that had as yet cut very deep. Many of the traditional aspects of the labour regime remained in place. We have seen how these constrained the space within which fiddles could develop and how a mixture of closeness to supervisors, work group expectations, and the presence of workers with differing objectives and expectations ensured that work was done. But to the outside observer the logic of the situation - an increasingly competitive business environment and an organization which had hitherto had to give little attention to labour costs - seemed plain. The control of the labour force was moving in the direction of rationalization and the formal measurement of standards.

Conclusions

We can draw together the implications of this analysis by considering an issue that we had in mind in seeking a study of a white-collar environment: how far was it a white-collar factory, that is, how similar were patterns of work organization and workers' attitudes to those characteristic of manual labour? There were some evident similarities. The workplace was large, hierarchical and bureaucratic. Workers laboured at clearly defined tasks under the control of supervisors. Some institutional devices such as the disciplinary procedure were indistinguishable from those used in factories; more interestingly, the fact that there was a felt need for a procedure points to the formalization of the employment relationship. Workers' attitudes were not qualitatively different from those in our other companies. FinCo workers did not, for example, display alleged white-collar characteristics of a strong sense of duty to the employer. We do not find this surprising. The bulk of our sample were carrying out routine work, and their chances of promotion were small. Indeed, one or two even complained that managers were asking them to take on new work: all they wanted was to do a fair day's work at a defined job, and they were not interested in learning new skills or taking on new challenges. The idea that the divide between blue- and white-collar workers necessarily constitutes a major break in terms of work attitudes has always been a questionable one. Our evidence simply underlines what ought to have been familiar.

That it is not familiar is illustrated by Blau's (1963: 184-5) comments on the two groups of white-collar workers that he studied. He observed some collective effort norms but argued that such norms were imposed half-heartedly because the workers remained committed to middle-class beliefs in individual success. Manual workers, though, can be no less, and indeed sometimes more, individualized (Edwards, 1988: 198). It is not the collar divide as such which is important but the ways in which workers are controlled. There were differences of degree between FinCo workers and our manual samples. These included a higher level of job security, for lay-offs and redundancies were unheard of; the possibility, for a minority, of promotion; the absence of a clear divide between workers and supervisors; and the rarity of overt discipline. When the particular factor of a high rate of labour mobility is added to these general characteristics, it is not hard to see why workers lacked the collective orientation of even Blau's workers.

The overall 'atmosphere' was thus much different from that in a factory. The idea that effort was something that could be made the subject of overt bargaining was foreign. The lack of managerial concern that work standards might become maxima or that workers might begin to stick rigidly to task descriptions is perhaps the clearest illustration of this. Another indication is the role of the staff association. In some respects, it was quite an influential body. Managers expressed respect for the way in which disciplinary cases were handled and plainly did not see the association as in any way their creature. On the other hand, the association played virtually no role at all at office floor level. On some issues, for example the setting of work standards or the computerized monitoring of output, on which we as outsiders might expect some shopfloor bargaining, workers seemed to take the individualized nature of the process for granted. The situation in relation to the appraisal scheme was thus particularly notable, for here workers complained that they had no one to whom they could turn to express their worries and fears. Here was one explicit source of concern on which a shopfloor organization could conceivably start to build.

Such a development would also be consistent with wider changes in FinCo. We have argued that several strands, when taken together, pointed towards a rationalization of labour control. They included the beginnings of managerial attention to the costs of absence and a more developed approach to the control of effort levels within the workplace. This trend is consistent with the more sensitive arguments concerning the de-skilling of white-collar work (Crompton and Jones, 1984; Armstrong, 1988). As against simplistic models of de-skilling, which expect the destruction of all technical competence and ingenuity and which neglect the fact that de-skilling is only one tendency among many, these authors have argued that the process can be held up by other tendencies and that it is a long-term trend. In particular, they underline the control elements of the process. De-skilling is not to be equated with the loss of technical ability or of the power to plan the whole production tasks. Though we did not set out to examine these aspects in detail, we can be reasonably certain that FinCo workers retained, and in fact had probably enhanced, technical skills and that they had never enjoyed wider influence over the aims and organization of work. They retained some skills and had never had others. Yet when we look at the regulation of work, we can see clear tendencies towards rationalization. The most obvious was the use of explicit work standards, but moves in absence control pointed in a similar direction. The efficient use of labour power was increasingly on the agenda.

This development was not part of a coherent managerial strategy. But, as Armstrong (1988: 156) in particular has argued, to stress strategy is to miss the point: if managerial motivations are to demolish a de-skilling thesis, these motivations must be incompatible with de-skilling, must dominate the decision-making process, and must not endanger the long-run survival of the business. If these stringent conditions do not hold, then motivations are irrelevant. In the case of FinCo, the tightening of effort standards was compatible with the broad objective of increased business efficiency. De-skilling was consistent with other aims. One could argue, moreover, that the long-run survival of the business was dependent on containing labour costs and that this pre-disposed managers towards policies of rationalization. In short, the logic of the business created a climate in which local managers might well promote de-skilling, and this was the tendency even though there was no overt strategy.

How far this tendency will go is hard to establish. We have stressed that developments had yet to have any deep effect on work organization or on workers' attitudes, though the discontents of long-serving workers were an interesting indication of the direction of change. To the extent, moreover, that managers stressed the variety of work tasks and the impossibility of measuring output, rationalization may be contained. A factor working in the same direction might be fears that the old image of the organization as a caring institution might be endangered by rationalization. As Armstrong would argue, however, such fears would have to dominate decision-making and be compatible with business survival if they were to have any more than a transitional effect. We would expect that the tendencies that we have identified would continue to operate, albeit at a slow and uneven pace. A clear prediction would therefore emerge: in the case of FinCo itself, we would expect concern with attendance and with effort standards to grow, and formality to increase correspondingly; similar tendencies would also be predicted in those large financial services organizations subject to increasing market competition; and in smaller firms, the trends would be less marked but perhaps evident in the longer term. The accuracy of such predictions will help to assess whether the conventional 'no-skilling' thesis or the alternative 'rationalization of control' thesis is correct.

At the time of our study rationalizing tendencies had not developed far enough for widespread effects on workers' attitudes. But we have shown that longer-serving workers were aware of them. More generally, we found that white-collar workers did not differ substantially from manual ones in terms of their views on attendance or their opinions of management. Nor did FinCo's performance-related pay scheme generate any new sense of commitment on the shopfloor. In itself, it had, at most, a marginal impact. Set alongside other trends, it was less salient to workers than day-to-day effort standards. All of this suggests that there was little evidence of the generation of a qualitatively new system of labour regulation. This is one issue which we consider in the final chapter.

7

Conclusions

This final chapter draws out the implications of our studies and relates them to debates about the nature of workplace relations in contemporary Britain. It does not summarize the detailed findings from the case studies, for the conclusions to each chapter already do so. Instead, we pursue some common themes and inferences. In doing so, it will be helpful to recapitulate the objectives of the study. The overall focus was the management of labour at the point of production. This was chosen to complement studies from two traditions. The first examines changes in the institutions of industrial relations and in collective relations between workers and managers; it does not cover the micro level of the effort bargain or consider the relationship between the individual and collective aspects of the employment relationship. The second approach, drawing on the debate about human resource management, has focused on the individual aspects, for example in analysing systems of communication. But much of the debate has been conceptual, considering such issues as whether HRM is different from personnel management, or descriptive, and where there has been serious analysis it has rarely been at the level of the shopfloor. Yet the shopfloor is crucial for HRM, for it is here that its techniques actually have to work. This level is also central to the industrial relations tradition, in that there is a strong presumption that changes in collective relations will work through to alteration of the effort bargain.

We chose the management of attendance as an empirical focus because of the general neglect of the subject and because we hoped that it would point to one way in which the individual aspect of the control of labour was undergoing change. This focus, we argued, is important in its own right, but it was also possible that there would be connections with other aspects of the effort bargain. This proved to be the case. In two of the case studies, Multiplex and BR, the control of attendance was a central element in the re-organization of the shopfloor. In the other two cases, there had been less substantial change in the area, but it had attracted managerial attention as part of a more commercial orientation. One important implication, pursued below, is that action regarding attendance can have much wider symbolic results.

In addition to attendance, or how workers are persuaded to turn up for work, we considered the effort bargain, or what happens within the workplace. One key aspect is discipline, in the senses of punishment and self-discipline. This plainly links with the widest question, namely, how patterns of consent have been changing. The conclusions to the study may thus be examined under the three heads of the management of absence and attendance, the nature of disciplinary regimes, and the changing pattern of shopfloor order. Though the first section is the longest, it is not the case that we have most to say about absenteeism as such. Absence was studied as one key element of the wider issue, and the discussion of this section begins to consider the theme of shopfloor re-structuring which is then taken further in the second two sections.

Managing Attendance

Though we were not concerned with absence as such, our findings throw light on several topics within existing debates on the subject. We begin with these before looking at the less discussed issue of the managerial role in the control of attendance.

Workers: the Problem?

As noted in Chapter 1, absence is often discussed in terms of the characteristics of the individual absentee, with moral panics about excessive absenteeism or even about a collapse of the work ethic punctuating periods in which the issue is neglected. This study did not follow the dominant analytical paradigm of absence research, and accordingly has little to say about the determinants of absence at the level of the individual worker. The motivation to attend work or to go absent stems not from individual predilections but from the interaction between the worker and his or her environment. We are not surprised that studies seeking an 'explanation' in terms of workers' attitudes and demographic characteristics have met with scant success. They neglect structural constraints on behaviour and the social meanings which are generated through the interactions of workers with each other and with managers.

There are, none the less, three aspects of workers' views on which we can throw some light. In increasing order of what we may term their collectiveness, they are the link between attitudes and behaviour, the role of work group norms, and the extent of the work ethic. Consideration of these issues assumes that it is possible to generalize from the four case studies because these studies illustrate the operation of principles that will be present in any work organization. A fourth topic is the comparability of our cases with other firms, that is how 'typical' the cases were and how far it is possible to discern change by comparing them with other information.

Attitudes and Behaviour. Since we collected data on absence behaviour and on a range of attitudinal measures, we felt that we should at least consider whether there were any connections between attitudes and rates of absence. We looked in particular at the links which might be expected from the literature on work groups and absence cultures. As discussed in Chapter 1, the general idea that groups can shape absence rates has received some endorsement, and in particular it has been argued that a combination of strong groups and pro-managerial sentiments will lower absence rates, while strong groups together with distrust in management will tend to raise absence levels.

We were able to investigate such arguments in two ways. First, we related absence rates to measures of work group cohesion and to indices which captured the interaction between such cohesion and trust in management. The limitation is that such measures will be shaped by workers' past experiences. A FinCo worker might feel that there was a high degree of group cohesion and solidarity while a BR worker scored low, whereas to the outside observer the collective traditions of BR were evidently much stronger than those of the other organizations. Our second approach was thus to include organization as an explanatory variable. The logic here is two-fold. Organization might be standing as a proxy for group norms and attitudes to management. And it can also be seen as a 'control variable', that is as one which controls for extraneous influences and allows the specific effects of work group norms or attitudinal factors to be measured. In effect, in the latter instance the test is whether, within each organization, workers' views on group solidarity had any effect on their absence behaviour.

The short answer is that they did not. We examined three measures of absence: the total number of spells during a year; the number of short spells (namely, those lasting one or two days); and the rate of days lost during the year. We used regression analysis to assess their relationship with a range of independent variables. Group solidarity was measured as both a continuous variable and a binary variable distinguishing cases where very high solidarity was mentioned from the remainder. The reason for the latter was that it is possible that there is some kind of threshold effect, with only high degrees of group cohesiveness affecting absence. Interaction effects were captured through a continuous variable, which multiplied the solidarity score by a score on our question about trust in management, and through a binary variable identifying those with high cohesiveness and high levels of trust.[1] None of these measures had any relationship with absence rates, either on their own or in combination with other influences.

Of the variables representing each of our organizations, those standing for the hospital and BR were significantly associated with absence rates. A worker in either organization was likely to have a higher absence frequency than a worker in the other two, and hospital workers had a higher rate of days lost than those in the other three. The result for BR in particular might be taken as evidence for the importance of work groups. There was, however, no evidence of such an effect within BR. The group which was the most cohesive and most distrustful of managers was the drivers, who did not have particular high absence rates. How could we explain, moreover, the very low absence levels among platform staff? The answer probably lies in long-standing tradition of commitment to the railway service among such groups. But such an analysis would take us away from the search for specific work group norms about absence towards a wider understanding of workplace relations. Such an understanding moves outside hypotheses concerning group solidarity and trust: these would have to explain low absence levels as the result of high solidarity and high trust, whereas platform staff had neither characteristic. There was little evidence of any strong group norms on absence, even in BR. We therefore reject the idea that such norms are direct influences on absence rates.

We also looked at other possible correlations between attitudes and behaviour. In general, associations were weak or absent. Thus it might be expected that workers noting a tightening of managerial control of attendance would go absent less often than others. We found no tendency in this direction; the implications of this result for managerial action are discussed below. Nor did we find much of a relationship between how often a worker thought of not going to work and absence behaviour. There was some tendency for those saying that they never thought of going absent to have the lowest absence frequency, but this did not remain significant when other variables were taken into account.

This lack of association at the level of the individual worker is not very surprising. Decisions to go absent reflect a wide range of factors. Moreover, as discussed in Chapter 2, what is defined as a legitimate, and hence to a degree an unavoidable, reason for absence is variable. Workers' general opinions about absence and their reports on how they themselves behave do not correlate strongly with absence rates because taking a day off for a legitimate reason may not be defined as going absent, because there are many contingencies that come between overall views and the decision whether to stay away on a given day, and because attitudes are in any event not a good predictor of behaviour.

Norms. Turning to the more collective issue of work group norms, as noted above they played no role in explaining absence rates. Arguably, however, they were more significant in shaping the social meanings of going absent. In three of our organizations there was no evidence of any substantial work group norms or understandings. This might be expected in FinCo, though even here one could argue that white-collar workers might be expected to have pro-attendance expectations, and that in this particular case the fact that workers worked as groups and saw duty to the group as an important reason to attend regularly might promote dislike of 'skivers'. Multiplex, with its paternalistic traditions, might also be expected to have some kind of pro-attendance norm. The hospital would be expected to have an even stronger norm. In the fourth, BR, some sort of norm was detectable among drivers, but this operated only indirectly. There was a strong common identity among drivers which meant that anyone who took time off could feel free to talk about it with his mates without fear of being reported to managers; moreover, the common identity meant that other drivers could fully understand why someone might take a day off. The key reason was the combination of demanding shift schedules with profound discontent with the work. But group norms only offered support to anyone who felt that these pressures justified time off; they did not actively promote absence, and plainly the majority of drivers went absent only rarely.

The main reason why absence was not driven by norms was two-fold: workers saw control as the responsibility of management, and they did not have any collective norms which impinged directly on most fellow workers' behaviour. There was plainly some generalized dislike of skiving. Even at this abstract level, however, this norm has to be set alongside the sympathy for absence revealed through the vignette technique: general attitudes were deeply ambiguous. When it came down to the day-to-day level, workers might disapprove of the few who were felt to abuse the system but, more or less definitionally, these workers had cut themselves off from group sanctions. As for the majority, an occasional absence would not be a sufficiently obvious or significant act to occasion group disapproval. In short, there were few norms even where they might have been expected. There may be cases where they are important, but these are likely to be very special situations where absence is particularly salient to the group and where very strong group codes operate.

What does this imply for the literature on absence norms? We should set it in context by noting that it was a reaction to the dominant individualistic paradigm of absence research. Nicholson and Johns (1982) offered an extended critique of this tradition, together with an alternative programme of research. In criticizing the particular weight which they placed on norms, we are not rejecting the programme as a whole. On the contrary, their argument that absence needs to be seen in its organizational and social context, and not treated as a homogeneous phenomenon, is plainly in tune with our own approach. As we have shown, in each of our organizations the pattern and meaning of absence could be connected to the nature of the workplace order. In FinCo, for example, the lack of major sources of job discontent together with hours of work that did not create clashes between work and non-work demands generated few forces encouraging absence. The climate of close working relationships and of little overt managerial attention to absence meant that managers did not see absence as a reflection of workers' irresponsibility while workers did not see absence as in any way a protest. None the less, managerial permissiveness allowed quite a high rate of short absences, as workers as individuals interpreted the relaxed approach as permitting a little time off. The social climate around absence could thus be identified in ways which are broadly consistent with Nicholson and Johns's analysis.

The Work Ethic. Even if workers do not have specific collective norms, it is possible that they share in wider social understandings. Thus during the 1960s and 1970s there was widespread concern that the work ethic was eroding and that growing absence rates were a result: even without direct work group pressures, workers were responding to similar forces in similar ways. At the time, these forces were felt to include affluence and a lack of traditional loyalties among 'new workers'. Having assessed the limited evidence on such claims and noted that absence rates appeared to have risen during the 1970s and levelled off subsequently, Rose (1985: 68) reached a cautious conclusion:

> this trend is consistent either with the hypothesis that a traditional set of values about regular attendance was being discarded, or with the hypothesis that workers never really possessed such values but simply exploited new opportunities provided by higher income and job security rights to indulge preferences that had previously been suppressed.

But, he added (at p. 75), continuing high absence rates suggest 'how little "Victorian Values" about work seem so far to have been revived'. We prefer Rose's second hypothesis, that opportunities were increasing up to the 1970s, for two reasons: there was little independent evidence of a loss of traditional values, and the invocation of some vague trend to explain a very particular phenomenon is always questionable. As for Victorian values, it is of course debatable whether these really characterized the Victorian period. To the extent that evidence is available, it suggests that regular attendance was less, and not more, firmly established during the nineteenth century than it is now: as studies cited in Chapter 1 indicate, attendance was often sporadic.

Our own evidence, particularly that reviewed in Chapter 2, suggests that workers did not embrace a deep sense of duty to attend work: extending a spell of illness or dealing with domestic responsibilities was widely accepted as legitimate. What they did accept was the routine nature of attendance. Those who expressed a view to our question as to why most workers attend regularly replied in terms of habit or of practices which had been inculcated since school days. There was neither strong moralistic commitment nor a rejection of the work ethic. Work was just a reality. We would see the escape from it not in terms of major changes in social values but as a reaction to highly specific circumstances. As we have seen, patterns and meanings of absence varied in ways which such gross concepts as the work ethic cannot grasp.

The Comparative Dimension

The previous section considered general lessons. But where did the four cases fit within existing knowledge of the control of attendance? Were they unusual in any way? In particular, do they offer any clues as to how rates of absence and patterns of control differed between the 1980s and earlier periods?

The short answer is that it is very hard to say. First, few studies have examined patterns of absence and endeavoured to relate them to the social organization of work. Second, the few that have done so examined particular types of firm, so that any differences from our cases could be due to differences between organizations and not to change over time. Some limited comparisons are, however, possible within Britain and internationally.

On the former, previous chapters drew comparisons with an earlier study, conducted between 1978 and 1980 (Edwards and Scullion, 1982). In terms of general attitudes, our cases seem to be distinctive in the extent of pro-attendance views. Table 7.1 summarizes some of the present results and sets them alongside data extracted from the earlier study. As can be seen, the proportions of workers in the present study saying that workers should go absent only when really necessary were higher than in any of the earlier samples. They are even higher than those in a study of farm workers, who might be expected to be particularly pro-attendance but only two-thirds of whom in fact made the 'really necessary' choice

ABLE 7.1 Comparative Attitudinal Data on Absence

r Cent	Choosing 'Genuine Sickness' Option	Feeling Like Day Off	Ever Taken Day Off	Ever Though of Leaving
78–80 study				
Engineering firms: men[a]	54	80	40	58
Clothing firms : men[b]	78	57	14	45
: women[b]	31	94	68	53
Process factory : men	60	79	33	41
Average[c]	55	78	40	49
esent study				
Multiplex	91	67	21	39
BR	82	63	30	44
Hospital	83	91	37	54
FinCo	87	72	13	26
Unweighted mean	86	77	26	40

urce: Edwards and Scullion (1982: Tables 3.10, 4.6, 4.7).

tes: a. Averages from 2 engineering plants.
   b. Averages from 2 plants.
   c. Unweighted mean from 5 plants.

(Newby, 1977: 313). These differences are probably differences of organization, not time. The FinCo and hospital samples might be expected to have some pro-attendance orientation; there are no comparable data from other studies. In the case of BR, we argued that aspects of railway tradition promoted a belief in regular attendance, a view noted in other studies (Salaman, 1974). The Multiplex sample, comprising semi-skilled factory workers, offers the closest parallels with other studies. Yet there are good reasons to expect pro-attendance replies, namely, the firm's paternalism combined with the tradition of a relatively undemanding work pace. Such differences may suggest that our organizations were very special, thereby making generalization dangerous. Several considerations suggest otherwise. First, their nature makes them critical cases rather than exceptional ones. In the analysis of the legitimacy of absence, the fact that workers tended to select the 'really necessary' option heightens the significance of their taking a sympathetic view of absence: if these workers were so sympathetic, others will be even more likely to be so. As noted above, a parallel point applies to absence norms: there were strong grounds to expect such norms here if they were to be found anywhere.

Second, general opinions are a poor guide to behaviour. This can be seen when we consider workers' reports of their own behaviour. In the earlier study an average of 40 per cent of workers said that they had ever taken time off when they had been able to attend work. Our BR and hospital samples were close to this figure. Multiplex returned a lower figure, as might be expected from what we know about the organization. The even lower figure for FinCo can be attributed to the lack of pressures leading to the need to go absent when a white-collar environment is set alongside blue-collar ones. Our samples may have had some distinctive general views on attendance, but they were not very unusual in terms of reports of their own behaviour.

Third, in BR and the hospital in particular, general pro-attendance views went along with some very critical attitudes towards management. Their views on attendance reflect specific features of work experience but do not make the workers holding them some sort of distinctive moralist.

Turning to behaviour, comparative absence data are assembled in Table 7.2. Those from Chadwick-Jones and colleagues (1982) are drawn from studies of four firms in each of the four sectors studied, presumably at some time during the 1970s; the authors report only the highest and lowest figures for each industry. Our workers seem to have fallen within the lower end of the range of absence levels. Compare for example the predominantly female sample from Multiplex with the figures for women

TABLE 7.2 Comparative Absence Rates

		Rates per Worker per Year		Per Cent of Workers with No
		Spells	Days Lost	Spell of Absence in a Year
1978–80				
Engineering	: men[a]	3.4	14.1	22.6
	: women[b]	6.1	19.3	5.2
Clothing	: men[c]	1.8	8.5	38.9
	: women[c]	7.1	21.8	4.5
Process	: men	2.3	12.9	18.6
Chadwick-Jones et al.[d]				
Clothing firms		4.1–7.7	18.8–31.9	n.a.
Foundries		4.1–4.8	19.2–39.4	n.a.
Process firms		0.7–3.7	6.1–19.5	n.a.
Public transport		3.1–5.7	21.3–38.9	n.a.
Present study				
Multiplex		2.1	12.5	22
BR		2.9	16.6	31
Hospital		3.4	27.9	13
FinCo		2.9	9.3	19

Sources: Edwards and Scullion (1982: Table 4.1); Chadwick-Jones et al. (1982: 19–21).

Notes: a. Means from four plants.
b. Data from one plant.
c. Means from 2 plants.
d. Data are ranges, from 4 plants in each industry; figure recalculated to be consistent with present definitions.

in engineering plants in the Edwards and Scullion study. The firm studied there had some things in common with Multiplex such as a relatively cosy shopfloor atmosphere and the lack of any tradition of militancy. Yet absence rates were higher. Yet rates lower than ours have also been recorded, notably in the process plants studied by Chadwick-Jones et al.

What inferences can be drawn? First, and most importantly, our firms were plainly not those with 'absence problems'. To the extent, therefore, that managements were acting on absence here, it is likely that other firms will also do so at least as keenly: our estimates of the relevance of absence to shopfloor management in the 1980s will then be on the conservative side. Could it not be, however, that we have observed the effects of managerial action: that managements have deployed tighter control, and therefore reduced absence levels? As discussed below, with the exception of Multiplex, control methods are unlikely to have had a major effect on overall rates. There is more likelihood that in Multiplex control had restricted absence frequency. This may have played some part, but is unlikely to explain the whole of the difference from other cases. Our organizations seem to have had a distinctive but not unusual place within the range of absence patterns.

Second, it is very difficult to infer trends: as the Chadwick-Jones et al. data show, even within one industry at one point in time there are great variations in absence levels. But it does at least seem that there has been no clear trend up or down. A rise in absence levels might be expected from more generous sick pay entitlements or from the observation that firms have given more attention to control. A fall would follow from arguments about the work ethic or the re-assertion of managerial control. We have seen, within our case studies, that there was little evidence to support either expectation. The comparative data support this view.

Not only were there great variations within Britain, but there are also considerable national differences in absence rates. Data here are scarce, and those that exist are often not comparable. One study, however, did calculate absence in ways similar to our methods, and it did so using records at the level of the factory, so that results should be fairly comparable. Prins and de Graaf (1986) produced data from eleven factories in three countries; the factories were from four industries, paints, margarine, frozen food, and tins. The data appear to include manual and white-collar workers. Table 7.3 presents their key figures. It is plain that the frequency of absence was higher in Britain but that the duration of absences and hence the number of days absent per worker was much

TABLE 7.3 International Comparative Absence Data

| | Rates per Worker per Year | | Duration per Spell (days) |
	Spells	Days Lost	
Belgium	1.40	21.2	14.6
Germany	1.89	31.4	16.1
Netherlands	2.14	32.9	15.5
U.K.[a]	2.81	16.6	6.1
Multiplex	2.07	12.5	6.0
BR	2.89	16.6	5.9
Hospital	3.42	27.9	8.9
FinCo	2.87	9.3	3.4

Note: a. Unweighted average of figures from the four organizations.
Source: Prins and de Graaf (1986: Tables 5 and 6).

higher in all three of their countries. Countries such as Italy and Sweden are also reputed to have high absence levels. Britain plainly does not have a distinct absence problem.

In considering variations between their three countries, Prins and de Graaf give most weight to differences in sickness payment systems. State sickness benefit in the Netherlands, the country with the highest absence rate, was 80 per cent of average earnings, and collective agreements generally raised this to 100 per cent, whereas in Belgium the figure was only 60 per cent. Preliminary enquiries suggested few differences in managerial control systems, which would strengthen the explanation in terms of national characteristics. Some of the differences between Britain as a whole and these countries could also be explained in this way, since the ratio of Statutory Sick Pay to average earnings is much lower than the figure even for Belgium. Yet in most large organizations company schemes pay sick pay at rates at or near 100 per cent. The one obvious feature, however, is that such schemes are a direct cost to the individual employer, whereas in the other three countries, and in Sweden for example, sick pay is funded by the state. It costs employers a good deal of money, and efforts to reduce its costs have provoked debate in the Netherlands and in Sweden. But there is little incentive for any one firm to control the absence of its workers. It is thus possible that British firms have a greater incentive to control absence, and that this helps to explain the relatively low levels in Britain.

British workers do not, then, seem to produce an absence problem in general. Nor did we find much evidence of that other managerial favourite, the 'hard core' absentee. There certainly were workers with high rates of absence but, as some managers recognized, they were often to be seen as inadequate rather than malingerers: people who found organizing their lives difficult and who did not 'fit in'. We also found people who quite cheerfully said that they took time off when it suited them, but their actual absence rates were not often high. Those with 'inappropriate' attitudes were not necessarily those with high absence levels, and vice versa.

In short, to understand variations in absence behaviour and the significance of the phenomenon it is unsatisfactory to follow the literature in focusing on workers. Instead, throughout this study we have given particular attention to managerial definitions of the problem and policies of control.

Management: Definitions, Control, and Consequences

Definitions of the Problem. As noted in Chapter 1, renewed managerial attention to absence control has been remarked from time to time but little systematic analysis had been undertaken of the reasons or consequences. In all four of our organizations managers were giving more attention to absence control than they had done in the past. The main motivation was similar: the control of labour costs in the face of financial pressures. The nature of these pressures naturally varied: in FinCo they remained relatively modest while in BR they were particularly acute. Such pressures did not, however, have direct consequences on managerial behaviour. Comparing our two public sector organizations, BR managers appear to have responded to commercial pressures by eagerly setting out to restructure their labour relations. This embraced the well-known area of relations with trade unions as well as discipline and attendance control. In the hospital, by contrast, the response to similar pressures was more muted, and systems of attendance control had not been tightened to the same extent. The variability of managerial responses was illustrated perhaps even more clearly by the differing ways in which Multiplex managers in the factory and the warehouse operated their control procedures: within the same company there were clear differences of approach, even though absence rates, and for that matter worker attitudes more generally, did not differ.

The fact that managements can and do interpret external pressures in different ways is important enough. But more interesting is the question of how these variations can be explained. BR managers were eager to act because they saw workers as a problem, as illustrated by their belief, which their own data in fact belied, that absenteeism had been increasing. Such attitudes were much weaker in the hospital, where the distance between managers and workers was smaller and where there was more of a sense that, say, a nurse and a nurse manager were part of a team. In BR, managers were clearly separated from workers. As we saw, a sense of a growing divorce between manager and worker, and of priorities being driven respectively by financial exigencies and by public service, was central to workers' understanding of their relations with management. Managerial views about attendance connected with their wider understanding of the shopfloor: restrictive practices were a major refrain in BR but not in the health service. In short, existing views of the 'worker problem' shaped how far external pressures were amplified or moderated by managerial actions. In the case of variations within Multiplex, the explanation turns on specific aspects of managerial organization. As discussed in Chapter 3, the warehouse had relatively large numbers of supervisors and probably had more need for formal rules than did the factory, where a small number of managers could ensure that they were applying similar standards.

This example also allows us to draw together our findings on one point that we raised in Chapter 1, namely, whether there are differences between levels of management in the way in which the absence problem is viewed and in the degree to which absence is tolerated; one or two studies have, for example, suggested that supervisors tolerate absence if they believe that work is particularly boring. We found little evidence of this. In Multiplex and FinCo there were concerns in the personnel department that supervisors gave little thought to absence and hence did not even keep proper records. As far as we could discover, these fears were groundless. In Multiplex in particular we talked to supervisors at some length about how they defined good and bad attendance and when they might permit time off to deal with, say, a domestic crisis. Individual judgements were plainly involved, but these operated only at the margins, and in cases where any significant time off was involved supervisors would seek higher approval. The hypothesis about boredom seems poorly specified. The workers managed by one supervisor will be doing similar tasks, and the general factor of boredom will not enable a supervisor to rationalize the absence of one worker rather than another. In any event, supervisors generally denied that work was boring, or at least boring enough to warrant absence. They certainly spoke about the conditions of the job, notably demanding shift schedules in BR and the hospital, and the impact of these on workers' ability to attend. But this was a matter of the general understanding of the occupation which did not affect how absence was managed. Managerial policy was not significantly subverted by supervisory acts of omission or commission.

Control. The case study chapters offer more detail on why each management acted as it did. The key point to address here concerns the consequences. The direct results, in terms of reducing absence rates, are unlikely to have been great but it is likely that there were significant indirect outcomes. Some of these turned on the messages which shopfloor workers received and others, perhaps even more important, impinged on managers' own self-confidence. Much managerial action was symbolic. But this is not to write it off, for symbols are often powerful ways of seeing the world. We can order our organizations according to the strength of their concern about absence. The hospital and FinCo had introduced relatively few control mechanisms, BR was bringing in some, and Multiplex had the most thorough-going system. In the first two, we would not expect much effect on absence levels though such evidence as was available suggested that any impact was indeed slight: the two FinCo departments, employing similar workers in similar tasks, had virtually identical absence profiles despite quite significant, albeit detailed, differences in control policies. In the cases of Multiplex and BR it is, of course, hard to measure the effects: Multiplex lacked long-term data on absence rates, and many other factors may also have played a role. What we can say is that many workers were aware of tightening control. But, as noted above, there was no tendency for these workers to go absent less often than those perceiving no change. When we asked some workers directly about the effect on their own behaviour, most denied that there had been any. More generally, any such effects are bound to be minor when set against the main determinants of absence rates, notably long-term sickness.

These conclusions are consistent with those from the literature on the control of absence. Wooden (1988) has reviewed studies of various forms of managerial intervention. Interestingly, he could find only five analyses of sanctions and disciplinary methods, and they produced little evidence of clear effects. Reviewing wider managerial initiatives in such areas as job enrichment and worker commitment, Staw (1986) concludes that there is little evidence of any link between job satisfaction and worker performance or of either side of the equation being amenable to change by management. Perhaps the most important point is also the most obvious: if academic analysts have found it hard to discern clear results, managements are unlikely to have such evidence either. Yet managers in our organizations generally believed that their policies were working. And they are unlikely to have been particularly prone to self-delusion: it is a managerial truism that clear and consistent policies will deal with the problem.

Success depends on what the problem is. Arguably, it is not really the rate of absence at all. It is the climate of the workplace and in particular managers' self-image. A weak or inconsistent policy on absence contributes to an atmosphere of drift, with the occasional individual who abuses the system spectacularly gaining a mythical status. Managerial action is a way of saying that there is an ordered approach to attendance control. This may have no direct effect, either on absence rates or on productivity, but it tells workers that managers are 'in control'.

Symbols and Meanings. Such an approach also says the same thing to managers themselves. Controlling absence is one of the ways in which managers tell themselves that they are not just making the best of a difficult situation or keeping the lid on a problem but are actively running the enterprise. Many of our managers felt that their organizations were going somewhere and that managers themselves were making things happen. This was perhaps least evident in the hospital. In FinCo, it was a matter of continuing what had always been seen as a well-managed business, with the new merit pay system being presented as a further device to promote worker loyalty. In the other two cases, change was a more evident theme: in Multiplex from a harmonious but undynamic system to one more attuned to modern business needs; and in BR from a situation of managerial abdication of responsibility to one in which change was being forced through.

Absence control formed part of this world of symbols which produced for managers stories and accounts which gave meaning to their own activities. These stories need not be literally true. Their role is to offer interpretations and a body of belief, and they function in this respect just as myths function in pre-industrial society. To give just one example. A BR manager explained the renewed willingness of managers to tackle absence by reference to a named Area Manager who had sacked a worker for excessive absence; such a dismissal had allegedly been unheard of, but it showed to all other managers what they could do. In short, it offered an inspiring example and demonstrated that managers could manage.

Several writers have recently stressed the importance of symbols. Guest (1990), reviewing the human resource management fad in the United States, cites Staw to argue that the concrete effects of HRM initiatives may be slight. He also suggests that few firms may in reality use them. So why has HRM been so influential? Because, says Guest, it fits in with the American Dream of opportunity and business success: HRM may be more important in terms of managerial self-belief than as a technique. Storey (1992) develops this point in his study of HRM in fifteen British organizations: there was a widespread sense of change and of managerial self-confidence, with managers feeling that they could now shape how the enterprise operated and where it was going. Ferner (1990), in his study of privatization, has shown how the fact of being privatized gave managements the means to re-define their labour relations, with the symbols of the market being important devices in establishing their agendas.

Reference to symbols might be taken as meaning that nothing of substance has changed: that what happened was 'only symbolic'. We do not mean this, as can be seen by considering Ahlstrand's (1990) analysis. He studied the famous Fawley oil refinery, argued that productivity bargaining had not met its stated aims of increasing efficiency, and thus asked why managers continued to claim that it had been a success. He offered (1990: 213) three symbolic functions: the enhancement to managerial careers of being associated with such an important initiative; giving the impression to senior managers that something was being done; and creating meanings for managers facing an uncertain environment. We would define the first two as cynical rather than symbolic: giving the impression to one's superiors of managing an issue while in fact conniving in custom and practice is a time-honoured device. A symbol, by contrast, involves the creation of meanings and the use of action in one sphere to stand for what really matters in another. Ahlstrand shows that this was important at Fawley, as managers used productivity bargaining as a symbol of their ability to effect change and to control the organization.

To stress the symbolic aspects of change is not to argue that nothing had happened or that what happened was of little practical import. Plainly, some things happened in the literal sense that, in Multiplex and BR at least, workers were warned about their attendance more often and that some were dismissed when it is possible that they would have avoided this ultimate sanction in the past. In Multiplex in particular, attendance control was having demonstrable effects on workers in so far as they felt under pressure to attend when they were ill. As Wooden (1988: 21) comments, 'the use of discipline and punishment may have deleterious side effects for morale, industrial relations, and job satisfaction which could adversely affect work performance'.

We have aimed to question only the expectations that absence control policies have direct effects on aggregate absence rates and that such effects are necessarily the managerial objective. Being seen to tackle absence contributes to managers' self-confidence in that there is a sense that a problem is being managed. In the earlier study, there seemed to be quite a widespread fatalism, particularly among supervisors: absence reflected a loss of order or a lack of responsibility in society in general, and there was nothing much that could be done about it (Edwards and Scullion, 1982). We found less of this sense. The actual absence problem, as measured by the rate of absence, was not the important thing; what was important was a sense that the problem was under control.

This may help to explain managerial 'moral panics' about absence. As noted in Chapter 1, these panics can occur without any 'real' absence problem. They arguably stem from a deep-seated concern about worker irresponsibility. Having a control policy and acting on it can help to allay fears and to create meanings among managers. They do not emerge autonomously. In wartime, they reflected a heightened concern for production in an environment in which 'new' and potentially trouble-some workers were being employed and in which long hours created pressures for leisure. In our cases it was financial pressure which was the prime motive force. But once absence has come to managerial attention, a moral panic may ensue and thus help to explain the keenness with which control is undertaken. In our cases, 'panic' was relatively limited, being absent in the hospital and FinCo, present only among some personnel specialists in Multiplex, and being observable patchily in BR. This reflects the fact that managers who had chosen to act felt that they were doing so successfully, whereas in situations where workers are apparently power-ful managers may feel that they have lost control.

We can put some flesh on this argument by reference to Marshall's (1987) study of absence rates and control policies in a manufacturing plant employing about 1200 men in metal fabrication. Actual absence rates were not unusually high: the mean number of absence spells per year, at 3.18, was not much above our FinCo or BR figures (2.87 and 2.89). But there was a moral panic, with managers feeling powerless and blaming workers for taking time off unreasonably. It was said, for example, that a worker delayed on returning home from holiday would take it for granted that he could stay away and be paid by the company. This atmosphere was related to a bold move to harmonize terms and conditions some eight years previously: managers felt that shopfloor workers were abusing their new privileges, and they claimed that absence rates were worsening whereas examination of patterns from 1980 showed no clear trend. Fatalism was widespread in 1987. But when we last spoke to managers there two years later they claimed a transformation of attitudes stemming from some new initiatives. Such a turn-round is conceivable, but it is likely that, just as the problem was exaggerated in 1987, so the solution was talked up. Symbolic change is often greater than actual change, as managers generate a belief that they are now 'in control'.

The final role of symbolism concerns the effects of control policies on workers. The message which workers were receiving was that managers were now in command: there was no longer to be looseness as to when workers were expected to report for duty, and the expectation now was that only genuine illness was a reason for absence. And the message went beyond absence itself to underline wider arguments about the need for efficiency in a harsh environment. Controlling absence did not necessarily affect workers directly, but it said something very clear about the conduct of shopfloor relations. This point connects with the changing nature of shopfloor order, which is the concern of the following two sections.

Disciplinary Practice and Procedure

The Evolution of Discipline?

One evident implication of our findings relates to evolutionary models of discipline. It will be recalled that they posit a move from punishment-based to corrective modes of discipline, with some writers also detecting a recent further move towards 'self-discipline'. They have been heavily criticized (Henry, 1983; Edwards, 1989) but they continue to underpin the work of those personnel management specialists who identify a move away from corrective methods.

We found little support for any move away from corrective approaches towards 'self-discipline'. On the contrary, punishment, in the shape of disciplinary warnings and dismissal, was more in evidence. As argued in Chapter 1, moreover, some claimed cases of self-discipline contain rather more managerial domination than meets the eye. The strong attendance rules, and the fact that it was management which determined them, at Toshiba is a case in point (Trevor, 1988). A recent claim to have moved away from punishment to 'positive discipline' unwittingly makes the point (Osigweh and Hutchison, 1989 and 1990). At Union Carbide plants in the United States, it was felt that traditional discipline dealt only with the negative aspects of behaviour. The positive approach involves three stages: an oral reminder, a written reminder, and a paid day's leave for the worker to contemplate his or her future. This last requires 'the problem employee to make a choice: to become either a committed employee or an ex-employee' (1990: 30). The situation could hardly be clearer: workers are brought up against the demands of conformity rapidly, and they either accept the rules or quit. Just what is positive about this, or for that matter how it shifts the emphasis away from the negative aspects, is far from clear. The language of being positive can simply disguise the fact that the rules are enforced more rigourously. As the authors point out, their system means that the old reliance on lengthy disciplinary suspensions was eliminated, and replaced with something much quicker.

Such contemporary developments can be put in context by looking at the history of discipline. Evolutionary theories tended to chart an alleged shift in discipline as though this was a natural, automatic trend. As Jacoby (1990: 325-6) has recently noted, transactions cost economics offers some explanation. It argues that as firms grew larger towards the end of the nineteenth century indiscipline became more costly to employers; at the same time, traditional methods of control, notably the foreman's arbitrary authority, became less reliable. Employers increasingly limited the use of this authority: by imposing rules on themselves, they ensured that workers knew that they would be dismissed only for 'just cause' and thereby helped to strengthen workers' commitment to the firm. The problem with this account, says Jacoby, is that is fails to fit the facts. The emergence of large firms pre-dated such devices as formal disciplinary procedures by several decades. In the United States the emergence of defined rules on dismissal occurred during the 1940s and 1950s, and not from the late nineteenth century. Such devices had 'less to do with employer control than with employee preferences . . . and shifts in power and social norms'. Finally, internal labour markets and bureaucratic rules did not emerge gradually or spontaneously but arose as a response to specific crises, suggesting that 'external pressure was critical in the shift to more structured employment practices, whose putative efficiency incentives many managers remained sceptical of'.

Jacoby shows, then, that rules in areas such as discipline emerged not because of an inherent logic of managerial control structures but because of pressures from employees and from the labour market. Employers did not necessarily become convinced of the benefits of formality but accepted that it might be necessary in conditions of tight labour markets and trade union influence. The contemporary significance of this is obvious: if these conditions alter, employers may return to more traditional forms of authority. The evolutionists cannot explain why a firm should resort to stricter discipline, other than to see this as an aberration. If we see rules as historically contingent, however, we can understand how their use is variable.

This is not, however, to suggest that there has been a simple return to previous forms of control. Firms have not torn up their disciplinary procedures. Though punishment is important it is not based on the arbitrary power of the foreman. But because it is procedurally fair it may be more effective than arbitrary action. As studies of unfair dismissal have stressed, having to comply with some standard of fairness does not in fact reduce the freedom of the employer to dismiss (except in cases of pure spite or personal dislike) while making it harder for workers to question the reasons for a dismissal (Dickens et al., 1985). We certainly found no active questioning of disciplinary procedures: in FinCo and the hospital these were hardly an issue; in Multiplex shop stewards appeared to accept their logic without question; and in BR there were complaints about managerial high-handedness, but, union representatives said, if the rules had been followed there was very little that they could do.

Rather than any simple shift back to punishment, or for that matter forward to self-discipline, there has been a reconstitution of the elements of disciplinary regimes. Discipline is achieved through a mix of formal sanctions (of both punitive and corrective kinds), economic incentives, efforts to promote a sense of responsibility, and managerial accommodations to workers' own definitions of 'the rules'. Claims to have established self-discipline can be questioned, on the grounds that they often mask a managerially-determined order which denies any real space to workers, but should not be written off as mere rhetoric. They help to generate a particular type of workplace order in which certain definitions of responsibility are established. But even here punishment plainly has not been eliminated: it remains at the boundaries of the system, and though it may not need to be used very often, its presence makes clear to workers the limits of acceptable behaviour.

Our organizations did not seriously claim to have instituted self-discipline, though as discussed below they did feel that some wider efforts had been made to promote worker commitment. In terms of discipline in the specific sense of the rules and sanctions of the workplace, punishment was one increasingly evident strand. As for correction, the situation is less easily summarized, since instances of corrective discipline cannot be counted like dismissals. If we take correction to mean methods to keep employee behaviour within acceptable limits without overt penalties, we can, however, suggest that the limits were being made clearer. In FinCo, the introduction of effort standards in one department pointed to the use of more exact and more explicit expectations. Actual corrective action by a supervisor, in the shape of an indication that a worker's behaviour was coming close to the limits, was rare but the possibility of its use was plain, as were the expectations inscribed in the effort standards. In Multiplex, formal work measurement in the warehouse was producing staffing norms for each section, which were in turn leading supervisors to identify performance standards for each worker. In the factory, though, systems were largely unchanged. Similarly, in BR and the hospital there were no specific new performance standards. Disciplinary standards were felt to be tighter here too, but this was more a matter of re-defining existing expectations than establishing new ones; BR workers, for example, commented on greater managerial attention to the wearing of the correct uniform.

The Negotiation of Order

In addition to the punitive and corrective aspects of discipline, Henry (1987) speaks of accommodative-participative and celebrative-collective models. The last is not important, except in so far as it comes under the rubric of self-discipline (Edwards and Whitston, 1989a: 5). The accommodative-participative model refers to workers' ways of devising their own rules and the common tendency for managements to tolerate this practice and to contribute to the emergence of custom and practice rules. One curiosity about the extant literature is that these rules, which were at one time the stuff of debates about workplace industrial relations, have received little comment. The re-structuring of workplace relations has been discussed in more general terms, with the details of the negotiation of order on the shopfloor receiving only passing attention.

There have been suggestions as to what has happened to custom and practice. Metcalf's (1989) paper entitled 'Water Notes Dry Up' refers to the arrangement in the coal industry whereby workers in wet parts of a mine were granted 'notes' to leave early; Metcalf argues that custom and practice had in the past led to the granting of notes even when an area was not wet, and he uses their drying up as a metaphor for the elimination of cognate practices throughout industry. Although there may have been a broad drift in this direction, there is a significant issue of evidence and method here. It is very easy to produce stories that at some time in the past a certain practice existed, with the implication sometimes being that it was universal in scope and frequent in occurrence, when in fact it was much more limited. Park's (1962: 124-7) ethnography of a Scottish coal mine at the end of the 1950s, for example, mentions water notes, here called wet lines, but does not suggest that they were used at all widely for 'improper' purposes. Or consider our evidence on leaving early from the BR cleaning depot. It plainly happened, in the shape of individual workers slipping away and of more collective visits to the nearby pub. But it was hardly a daily occurrence, and the conflicting stories that we were told suggested that its collective manifestations were restricted to the maintenance department (which we did not study) and that its individual forms were scattered.

Caution is therefore needed in assessing the role of custom and practice in one workplace, and even more so when trends are inferred from a variety of information. Some conclusions can, however, be drawn. BR is an interesting illustration. The general tightening of rules was evident. This could have led an investigation which was limited to managers and union representatives to conclude that custom and practice had been eliminated. In fact we found it surviving much as it had always done. In the past, the railways were a classic example of the sharp distinction between formal rules and informal understandings: a detailed rulebook specified formal demands, but everyone knew that the rules were contradictory or unrealistic, and informal practices grew up; from time to time the rules might be enforced; but this did not really impact on day-to-day behaviour. At the time of our study, the rules were being applied more firmly in some respects, but in such areas as time-keeping and absence during working hours old traditions continued. These traditions, moreover, were not just restrictive: they contributed to production directly, as when workers did overtime in exchange for being allowed to use time at work when they were not required to be working for their own purposes, and indirectly, by generating a degree of consent. Whether or not a form of work organization was feasible in which workers spent more of their working time in directly productive activities is an open question; but it is a question of how management arranged work schedules and not one of worker restrictions interfering with managerial rights.

The surprising resilience of customary regulation in BR certainly questions the view that the managerial offensive destroyed it. Yet the offensive was evident, and it made workers aware that they could be disciplined for actions that previously went unquestioned. Informality survived, but it did not do so as a self-contained process unaffected by the wider disciplinary regime. It was less and less part of shared understandings about the 'railway service', and more of residual activity increasingly at odds with the language of efficiency.

As discussed at length elsewhere, situations in which custom and practice rules operate relatively independently are rare (Edwards, 1988). Their main homes were the docks and parts of the car industry; even without any reduction in their presence in surviving workplaces, the sheer reduction in employment in such sectors must have reduced their prevalence across the economy. In our three organizations other than BR anything resembling custom and practice was rare. There were traces of it in two parts of Multiplex: the factory, where the workers making the product sometimes engaged in the classic Saturday morning overtime fiddle of being clocked on for the shift but of not needing to turn up, and the warehouse, where some workers practised a little early leaving. But these activities were highly particular to the specific groups concerned: they were not generalized in any way. And they were about the only form of fiddle available: they did not comprise part of a wider set of customary regulation. Accordingly, they did not represent a set of social rules that were alternatives to the official rules: they were marginal means of evading official requirements. In FinCo and the hospital custom was even less developed.

This is not to say that all forms of give and take were absent. At a day-to-day level supervisors anywhere have a degree of discretion in how tough they are. In FinCo, for example, if a day's work had been completed managers might be relatively lenient about coffee breaks. Marchington and Parker (1990: 162) note similar variation in a retail store. Yet this is precisely the point. The firms that we studied had not made a decisive break towards a new form of workplace relations in which managerial authority was rationalized or workers were granted the scope to practise self-discipline. Supervisors continued to have to cajole, persuade, and threaten. The corrective and punitive aspects of discipline were more to the fore. Detailed evidence on accommodative-participative aspects is too thin to make an overall judgement. But it seems likely that the space for them has been constrained by more firmly enforced formal rules.

Two main conclusions emerge. First, analytically, we have demonstrated the argument in Chapter 1 that modes of discipline such as punishment and correction do not produce free-standing models: they are aspects of multi-faceted structures. Second, empirically, the punitive and corrective aspects have become more prominent, the space for customary regulation has probably been reduced, and, to the limited extent that self-discipline has been instituted, this has not been of a collective kind but has been strongly geared to managerial aims. Managements were reconstituting some existing features of disciplinary control and not moving towards qualitatively different ones, a point which leads to the question of the wider re-organization of the shopfloor.

Changing Shopfloor Regimes

This question has been widely debated around a large number of controversial issues such as the extent to which 'flexibility' has been introduced, the impact of new technology, and 'post-Fordism'. We do not pretend to deal with such matters. But we can address one simple issue which lies at the heart of many of the debates: has the balance of power changed, and if so in what way?

Our results are consistent with other analyses finding change in the details of shopfloor control but no qualitative shift in the ways in which this control was exercised. Kelly's (1990) assessment of current research, cited in Chapter 1, argues that there has been little evidence of a break-through to a distinctively new system of shopfloor order based on trust or commitment. Similarly, Elger (1990) uses survey and case study evidence to argue that workers have been working harder and that the space for them to negotiate their own interpretations has been reduced. Marchington and Parker (1990: 225-8) summarize the results of their four case studies thus: in an engineering firm, workers were critical of managerial efforts to communicate with them and adversarial traditions remained; in a food packaging firm, the flow of information was felt by workers to have improved, but the effects had not been very great; and in a retail store and a chemicals manufacturer there was more welcome to efforts at communication, though in the former this was not always seen as very relevant. As noted in Chapter 1, these authors did not set out to measure shopfloor responses in detail, and they do not offer any wider interpretation of this evidence. But it seems likely that in three of the four cases there was little real impact of communication on workers' general views of management. Even in the fourth, communication is surely unlikely to have produced deep commitment. Certainly, we found that in some of our firms, notably FinCo, workers on balance felt that communication had improved, but this was plainly relatively unimportant when set against how hard they were expected to work and how closely they were monitored.

Our findings on effort levels have been discussed elsewhere (Edwards and Whitston, 1991), as have general assessments of workplace change (Edwards, 1992). We need only highlight a few points. The overall picture was one in which workers saying that they were working harder than in the past outnumbered those identifying little change in this respect (Table A.12). Yet the largest group comprised those who were uncertain whether effort levels had changed or not. Those identifying change were thus in the minority, which might imply that there was in fact no significant trend towards rising effort levels. This would, however, be an inappropriate conclusion. First, we found no one saying clearly that he or she was working less hard, so that the balance of opinion would still be towards growing effort levels. Second, managers, in Multiplex and FinCo in particular, were clear that demands on workers had risen. Third, the 'uncertain' group really were uncertain as to change, and forced to make a choice a good number of them might have opted for saying that they were working harder. The size of this group is not surprising. Workers may well be unaware of changes, particularly when these are introduced incrementally and when the absolute level of effort demanded is still seen as reasonable. We have seen in the case of tighter controls on absence, for example, that changes that were quite evident to managers did not lead to a hundred per cent 'yes' response among workers. Reactions are often inchoate, and to expect clear-cut statements of opinion would be unrealistic. Finally, we have shown that workers' perceptions correlated with objective trends, for example in the fact that BR drivers felt that they were not working harder and in the clear division of opinion between workers in Multiplex's factory and warehouse.

The point about diversity of opinion is, however, important in considering the effects on behaviour. A conventional case study approach, using only qualitative methods, might have concluded that effort levels were rising and implied that this intensification was cutting deep into workers' willingness to work. Two images of workers' response would then emerge: passive acceptance of change, and potential revolt. Our data point to a less stark situation: objective change was interpreted in a variety of ways, and there was rarely a majority having a clear, shared view of the change. Even where there was such a majority, it did not imply specific lines of action. BR drivers had a commonly-felt deep resentment of management. Yet they were unlikely to leave, because many still liked the work, some were too old to move, and all had specific skills that few other employers would value. Protest in the workplace was also constrained by the limited space for open effort bargaining. Shopfloor regimes may have been growing more demanding, but the effects will depend on many other factors.

It is worth stressing this point. Qualitative case studies often analyse objective changes in labour regimes but then imply that direct effects should be expected. It may for example be shown that workers are subject to more direct surveillance of their work, and the analysis may stop at that point, though with the implication that workers have either accepted the change without question or may, in some unspecified circumstances, begin to react against this new system. By combining qualitative and quantitative data we have tried to give a more balanced picture. Objective changes were certainly evident in all our organizations, but the effects in terms of workers' reactions were mixed. In the case of absence control, only a minority will be affected directly. With shopfloor changes, some workers may find that they impose no special strain on them, others may feel that they were inevitable, some others may grumble, while yet others will be new to the organization and may have little sense of change.

We found evidence that workers were aware of the changes, and that these were often resented, for example in the low levels of morale in the two public sector cases and in the FinCo workers' scepticism about the appraisal system. But there was little evidence of any more organized protest. There were, however, suggestions that it could emerge, most evidently in BR if customary bargains between workers and supervisors were further eroded or, less obviously, even in a case like Multiplex if resentment continued to build up over tighter work standards. In the latter case, it is conceivable that discontent would surface in an apparently unrelated area. Workers had no tradition of bargaining at the point of production, and probably lacked the will to engage in it, but annual pay negotiations were a time when the reward-effort bargain was brought to the front of their attention and a willingness to support strong demands on the company might be sustained by a deeper and inchoate sense of shopfloor frustration.

These are only possibilities: precisely because links between objective change and reactions in terms of behaviour are indirect and contingent, firm predictions are impossible. But one can be clearer about objective trends. We have painted what may be seen as a negative picture: of the balance being towards workers working harder and of little evidence of any change in attitude on the shopfloor. We have also suggested that there was a trend towards heavier demands on workers as a result of intensifying competition. The test of the accuracy of this interpretation is whether the trend continues. Plainly, it will do so only to the extent that the pressure of competition is not only present but is also perceived as significant by managers. The more that this condition is fulfilled, the more likely it is that demands for the efficient use of labour will rise, and hence that pressures will increase in areas such as absence control and the deployment of labour on the shopfloor. We have stressed that these are not the only developments on the shopfloor: it is not a simple matter of managerial autocracy but of a re-structuring of shopfloor order. We do not wish to deny that new forms of the technical division of labour can generate genuine efficiency improvements. The evidence of Japanese firms in Britain suggests that their use of highly trained managers and their meticulous attention to detail has enabled them to eliminate unproductive effort (Trevor, 1988). We have also argued, however, that a component of change has been tighter demands on workers, which, as noted elsewhere (Edwards, 1989), are probably present within Japanese transplants. Much analysis has focused on the benefits of new production systems. The tensions within them should also not be forgotten. We are not suggesting that a tendency towards growing demands on labour is the only or even the major trend. But it is one among others. The test for its presence is whether, if the relevant causal factors continue to operate, evidence continues to appear of the stricter control of attendance and the closer monitoring of effort within the workplace.

But how far can we generalize from four cases? There is no reason to think that BR and the hospital are unrepresentative of the public sector.

The picture of change that they offer may in fact be understated. As noted above, they did not stand out in terms of absence levels. It is possible that those parts of the public sector with higher levels would be even more marked by managerial efforts at control and a collapse of morale. Similarly, some experienced observers in the health service have been surprised at our finding that nurses did not report working harder and have commented that rising work effort is a feature of the service as a whole. Such trends may well have become more prominent since the completion of our fieldwork in 1988. Between 1988 and 1992 the number of managers rose, commercialism became more prominent in the light of self-governing trusts, and new training arrangements may also have reduced the stress on a professional ethos. We noted that, at the time of the study, differing managerial views meant that belief in a health care team had not been destroyed; indeed this is crucial in showing that commercialism had not yet created the divisions between management and worker that exist in much of the private sector. But developments since 1988 suggest that change may have continued and that the low morale that we observed may have worsened.

Multiplex probably reflects matters in at least a good part of the core of manufacturing firms which have not tried to break through to high-commitment systems. Given that change here was relatively modest and that strong paternalistic strands were still evident, our results, that there was no evidence of improved co-operation on the shopfloor, may have more general applicability: if the position here was one of recognition of growing demands and grudging acceptance of change, this may also be the case in other firms with a more conflictual past. In the case of FinCo, we noted in Chapter 6 Lockwood's (1989) comments that most studies have not reflected the situation of white-collar employees as a whole. This is certainly true of our study. But we can claim that our results may apply to workers in large offices where financial pressures have been growing. More speculatively, it is likely that large bureaucratized firms will be the first to implement systematic changes on the office floor, and hence that we may have identified a trend which will be generalized in the future.

A related point is that we have not explored cases where management claimed a breakthrough to high commitment and self-discipline. Yet several considerations suggest that this is not a major problem. First, such cases are rare. Second, studies of the long-term changes that they involve suggest that permanent shifts of attitude are difficult to achieve. Ahlstrand (1990) concluded that 25 years of productivity bargaining at Fawley had not significantly altered the plant's productivity record as compared with that of other plants in the same company, and the picture that he paints is one of continuing uncertainty and distrust. Marshall's (1987) study that we discussed above took place in a plant which had made a major shift, some eight years previously, towards harmonized terms and conditions and a uniform pay system for all workers; yet a failure to produce a new atmosphere of commitment was palpable.

Third, studies of contemporary efforts to institute change have returned highly sceptical conclusions. Scott (1988) studied three food manufacturing plants in England, two of which are relevant here. In one, a package of new working practices intended to create a consensual climate on the shopfloor had done little to alter patterns of bargaining or workers' deep-seated distrust of management. The second was owned by a firm with a long-established policy of operating without a union and of deploying advanced personnel techniques. The shopfloor atmosphere was more one of grudging acquiescence than of eager commitment, and the main bond tying workers to the firm was the material one of high wages and job security. Findlay (1990) considered one sector where 'new' employment practices might be expected to be particularly prevalent: the electronics industry in Scotland. She found scant evidence from a study of employers of such practices. Geary (1991) conducted analysis at the level of the shopfloor in three electronics plants in Ireland and likewise found that sophisticated human resource management was conspicuous by its absence. Newell (1990) studied greenfield sites and again found that workers' attitudes were not markedly different from those that would be expected elsewhere. Reviewing several recent studies, Kelly and Kelly (1991) conclude that there is no evidence that 'them and us' attitudes were significantly eroded during the 1980s.

Fourth, a depressingly familiar story in Britain is the introduction of new schemes to improve commitment, such as quality circles or communication systems, followed either by the demise of the schemes, as in the common tendency for quality circles to fade away, or by their routinization. As Cressey et al. (1985: 156) conclude from their study of participation exercises, these were too 'marginal and ineffectual' to play any substantial role in the regeneration of the enterprises in question. MacInnes (1985) has argued, more generally, that, despite the apparent upsurge of joint consultation during several periods, there is little evidence of any increase in the spread of the practice, a result which he explains by the tendency for new arrangements introduced in a blaze of publicity to fade away. It is true that Marchington (1989: 399) concludes his survey of joint consultation by questioning this view and underlining the success of the practice.

But his definition of success is modest: employers and unions 'will make use of any institution which helps them in the process of managing their people or best representing their members' interests no matter how messy or ill-defined that arrangement [be]'. We would agree that joint consultation can survive, but it is surely questionable how far it has gone beyond being a useful tool to actively re-shaping the pattern of shopfloor relations.

These case study findings parallel those from larger social surveys. Marshall et al. (1988) conducted a general survey of British adults. As against any expectation that people would abandon their old values and embrace individualism, they found that belief in the existence of a class system was as strong as ever, that people identified themselves as members of classes, and that there was a widespread feeling that income inequalities were too high and should be remedied through state intervention. Gallie (1989) similarly detected little shift in workers' commitment to collective values in general or to trade unions in particular. In short, the picture of little change in workers' views of, and trust in, management seems reasonably well-established.

Along with writers such as Elger (1990) we would also argue that there is little evidence to support the contention that workplace regimes are in the course of transition from a 'Fordist' to a 'post-Fordist' character. The lengthy and convoluted debate about post-Fordism is no concern here, but there are two simple points to be made. First, the characteristics of the alleged transition seem to be very ill-defined. Second, even if there has been some shift at the macro level, to expect this to be reflected in workplace practice would be naive. As the debate about the introduction of new technology has shown, the pace of introduction of new technology and the effects in terms of skill levels and the balance of power have depended on a wide range of factors. More generally, at any time in the history of capitalism a variety of modes of workplace control will be observable: labour control does not fall into neat patterns stemming from a structure of accumulation (Nolan and Edwards, 1984).

While unhappy with attempts to identify whole new systems of labour regulation, we are also reluctant to follow the fashionable reaction, namely, to argue that everything is contingent and that there is no pattern to events. All four of our, otherwise very different, workplaces faced similar pressures and had responded in broadly comparable ways. They had tightened their use of labour, for example in Multiplex and FinCo by producing more precise work standards and in BR by eliminating some labour and restricting the use of overtime to the levels that pre-determined budgets could bear. We have summarized above the consequences for absence control and disciplinary practice. The exact outcomes plainly varied, and we have stressed the different ways, even within one organization, in which shopfloor order was negotiated and sustained. But it would not be too much of an exaggeration to say that efforts to promote active commitment had had little effect, that the tendency was towards closer regulation and more demanding effort levels, and that a spirit of trust between managers and workers remained rare.

This is not to argue that workers have simply been subordinated to managerial demands: on the contrary, we have stressed how, in a case like BR, management had not established a new autocracy and remained dependent on traditional ways of generating workers' co-operation. Some aspects of change, such as communication and team-working, may also balance the more demanding aspects of shopfloor regimes. It is not a matter of movement along a continuum of control and autonomy but of a re-organization of the elements of shopfloor order. Underlying this process, there has been a rationalization of managerial control: it is not that there is more or less of it, but that the ways of seeking it have become more explicit and organized.

What, though, does a study of the late 1980s say more generally: it is plainly important to look at a period of significant economic and political change and to assess the pattern at shopfloor level, but are there any more lasting lessons? This particular study has two such lessons. First, it has looked at the place of attendance control within the management of labour as a whole. It has indicated the conditions which lead to managerial interest in the issue and how this interest connects symbolically with other elements of labour management. It has also looked at specific issues such as the extent of workplace norms governing attendance. Such general information is not time-specific. Second, the 1980s can be seen as a case of a wider phenomenon, namely, a period of attempted workplace change in the context of changing external circumstances. We have noted, for example, similarities in the case of BR with a similar period at the end of the nineteenth century. A major theme running through a range of studies of the 1980s concerns the ways in which external forces are mediated by existing institutions and assumptions. Thus even major outside developments did not totally overturn established ways of managing the shopfloor. In addition to the issues addressed above, work in areas such as the introduction of new technology has repeatedly identified the mediation of external pressures. Such work has been able to demolish several assumptions about the process. In short, it has produced lessons of general applicability.

One such lesson also has contemporary relevance. If the history of industrial relations teaches anything, it is that periods of managerial ascendancy are often followed by a renewed shopfloor challenge. To the extent that managements are merely tactically determined while failing to re-organize the shopfloor order, they are likely to experience difficulties subsequently. This was true of British firms in the 1890s, when bargaining power was not used to root out custom and practice from the shopfloor, whereas managements at similar turning points in other countries developed whole new modes of regulation (Sisson, 1987). The reasons have been located in the fragmentation of firms and the lack of a technically trained elite to press through a programme of rationalization. The continued presence of such factors may play a role in the future. Plainly, the future is unlikely to repeat the past. But the lack of a qualitatively new form of shopfloor order suggests that external pressures during the 1990s may create new strains and tensions on the shopfloor for which managers are less prepared than they think they are. If such pressures do continue, we would expect the management of attendance to be a significant feature of the changing shopfloor order.

Footnotes

1. To explain our procedures in more detail, the third dependent variable, a measure of days lost through absence, was used not because we anticipated much effect on it (for days lost will be heavily affected by long-term sickness) but because it was used by Drago and Wooden (1988) in a study discussed in Chapter 1. We wished to reproduce their model as closely as possible. They defined their dependent variable as the logarithm of the absence rate. This rate was calculated as RATE/(1 - RATE), where RATE is the number of days absent as a proportion of the number of days that could be worked. On the independent variables, we took our three questions about how the work group gets along (see the questionnaire, Question B3). Each was recorded on a three-point scale, so that we could compute a continuous variable from 1 to 9. Those with scores of 7 or more were termed the 'high cohesion' group, and were identified by a binary variable. The trust measure was taken from Question C3, with scores running from 1 (low trust) to 5 (high trust). This was multiplied by the cohesiveness score to produce a measure of the interaction between group solidarity and trust. The binary variable identified those in the high cohesion group who were also high on trust (having a score of 4 or 5).

Appendix A

Tables A.1 to A.12

TABLE A.1 Frequency of Thinking about Going Absent

Per Cent	Multiplex (N=89)	BR (N=82)	Hosp. (N=57)	FinCo (N=72)	Total (N=300)
Every day	4	1	2	5	6
Once a week	9	4	14	11	8
Occasionally	63	58	75	65	63
Never	23	37	9	18	23

TABLE A.2 Reasons for Thinking of not Going to Work

Per Cent Mentioning Each Reason	Multiplex (N=59)	BR (N=46)	Hosp. (N=51)	FinCo (N=54)	Total (N=210)
General boredom	64	17	29	39	41
Features of work on a particular day	8	26	27	18	21
Escape from supervisor	2	4	6	5	5
Escape from fellow workers	3	0	8	2	4
Travel problems	8	11	6	3	8
Family illness, domestic duties	32	55	27	39	40
Time with family, leisure interests	13	26	17	14	19
Other	19	6	27[a]	16	19

Note: a. Most of these replies related to tiredness or stress.

TABLE A.3 Importance of Family and Friends in Thinking about Going Absent

Per Cent	Multiplex (N=59)	BR (N=46)	Hosp. (N=51)	FinCo (N=54)	Total (N=210)
Very important	1	2	2	0	1
Fairly important	10	10	7	28	14
Not very important	3	8	18	5	8
Not at all important	86	79	72	67	77

TABLE A.4 Patterns of Absence

	Multiplex	BR	Hosp.	FinCo
Absence Frequency (per cent of workers with specified number of absence spells in a year)				
None	22	31	13	19
1	22	17	16	19
2	22	12	20	20
3	15	10	17	12
4	9	6	14	12
5	4	9	6	7
6–10	5	13	13	8
11 or more	(..)	3	3	3
Absence Duration (per cent of absence spells of given duration)				
1–2 days	39	66	51	67
3–5 days	42	17	21	24
6–19 days	(	12	19	7
20 days and over	(19	6	9	2
Severity Measures				
Mean number of days absent per worker per year	12.5	16.6	27.9	9.3
Mean length (days) of each spell of absence	6.0	5.9	8.9	3.4

TABLE A.5 General Views on Attendance

Per Cent	Multiplex	BR	Hosp.	FinCo	All
In general people should:					
Attend whenever possible	91	82	83	87	86
Be free to take time off as they wish	9	18	18	13	14
Whether had themselves:					
Thought about not going to work	71	57	91	79	76
Taken a day off when able to attend	21	30	37	13	26

TABLE A.6 Most Important Reason for Attending Work

	Multiplex (N=78)	BR (N=76)	Hosp. (N=48)	FinCo (N=65)	All
Duty to firm	12	13	15	17	14
Loss of money	22	41	8	3	19
Discipline	17	7	2	5	8
Duty to work mates	4	1	44	31	21
Enjoyment of job	7	13	6	6	8
Duty to oneself/ self-respect	23	16	10	23	18
Backlog of work	3	0	2	8	3
Family/social pressures	7	4	2	3	4
Other	5	5	10	5	6

TABLE A.7   Perceptions of Managerial Control of Attendance and Discipline

Per Cent		Multiplex	BR	Hosp.	FinCo	All
Aware of pressures on attendance:	Yes	67	60	63	31	56
	No	33	40	38	69	44
Change in management approach to attendance control:						
	Yes	66	84	41	22	61
	No	34	16	59	78	38
Rules are:						
Too rigid		12	26	18	18	18
About right		77	62	69	76	71
Too loose		12	5	9	6	8
Don't know/other		0	7	4	0	2
Rules are applied:						
Equally		54	59	59	44	54
Unequally		46	41	42	56	45
Personal experience of being disciplined:						
	Yes	37	40	19	16	29
	No	63	60	81	84	70

TABLE A.8   Measures of Group Norms on Absence

Per Cent	Multiplex	BR	Hosp.	FinCo	All
Whether discuss with others idea of taking time off					
Yes	39	14	40	25	29
No	61	86	60	75	71
Whether discuss the absence of other workers					
Yes	75	57	58	43	59
No	25	43	42	57	41

TABLE A.9 Reasons for Thinking of Leaving Present Employer

	Multiplex	BR	Hosp.	FinCo	All
Whether had thought of leaving (per cent)					
Yes	39	44	54	26	40
No	61	56	46	74	60
Reasons given by those thinking of leaving (per cent mentioning)					
Money/insecurity	36	70	16	21	38
Poor promotion chances	7	0	10	11	6
Nature of work	74	37	13	26	40
Bad management	0	11	6	0	5
Too far to travel	0	4	3	0	2
Unfriendly shop	0	0	(..)	0	(..)
Wants wider experience	6	0	3	5	3
Other	0	0	71	57	27

TABLE A.10 Attitudes to Management

	Multiplex	BR	Hosp.	FinCo	All
Managers are:					
Very friendly	21	9	20	27	19
Quite friendly	56	38	57	54	51
Quite distant	20	25	11	14	18
Very distant	1	12	11	4	7
Other	1	16	0	1	5
Trust:					
Complete	19	0	4	10	9
Most of time	26	25	25	35	28
Fair amount	31	33	27	30	30
Not much	18	36	22	19	23
None	2	5	22	6	8
Other	3	1	0	0	1
Trust has:					
Improved	23	21	11	22	19
Stayed same	62	26	46	56	46
Worsened	15	53	44	22	35
Functions performed by management:					
All three	18	10	2	10	10
Two	13	13	16	19	15
One	58	40	70	56	55
None	10	37	12	15	19
Which functions performed by management:[a]					
Knowledge and experience	48	31	30	46	40
Ensure people do work	40	60	25	40	41
Administration	71	64	79	67	70

Note: [a] per cent of sample mentioning each item: base is those mentioning at least one function.

TABLE A.11   Changes in Management Approach to Workers

Per Cent Mentioning	Multiplex (N=60)	BR (N=68)	Hosp. (N=34)	FinCo (N=25)	All
Work is harder	43	32	41	36	38
Work is not harder	13	21	0	20	14
Stricter	25	40	15	4	26
Less friendly	8	0	41	20	13
Friendlier	12	0	12	4	6
No more communication	20	62	27	16	26
More communication	35	28	24	32	30
Fairer	5	0	3	4	3

TABLE A.12   Length of Service and Attachment to the Organization

Per Cent	Multi-plex	BR	Hosp.	FinCo	All
Length of Service (per cent)					
Less than 1 year	3	6	0	23	8
1 – 2.99 years	7	6	16	38	16
3 – 4.99 years	25	9	22	13	17
5 – 9.99 years	24	16	30	11	20
10 years and over	41	63	32	16	40
Whether had worked anywhere else (per cent)					
Yes	75	84	79	83	80
No	25	16	21	17	20
Reasons for staying with present employer (per cent mentioning)					
Money	48	23	18	27	31
Security	39	26	18	7	24
Promotion chances	7	3	14	18	10
Interest in job	20	39	67	28	35
Good management	1	0	0	1	1
Near home/convenient	5	5	33	20	13
Good work-mates	22	10	33	27	22
Too old to move	18	27	0	3	14
Other	15	0	13	55[a]	16

Note: [a]Most of these replies concerned cheap home loan facilities.

Appendix B
Shopfloor Questionnaire

This appendix reproduces the questions that we put to our samples of shopfloor workers. In many cases we had pre-coded categories into which to record the replies, for example the question on reasons for thinking of leaving. We have omitted these coding schemes. We also followed up topics that seemed pertinent. For example, in section B if workers commented about work standards we asked how they were enforced, how the work group behaved and so on. In short, the questionnaire was used universally, but we did not restrict ourselves rigidly to it.

Before listing the questions, we provide some notes which explain the questions, indicate the use that we made of them, and discuss some detailed methodological points about the literatures that we address.

Rationale of the Questioning

Section A asked standard background questions about attachment to the firm. The questions have been widely used, and need no special comment.
Section B. As noted in Chapter 1, the literature on absence cultures categorizes the meanings of absence according to the climate of shopfloor relations. Nicholson and Johns (1985) argue that this is shaped by two dimensions: the degree of trust between workers and managers, and what they term salience. As shown elsewhere (Edwards and Whitston, 1989a: 9), these dimensions are forced to measure several things at once and their definition is not very clear. Moreover, 'salience', which refers to the

strength of work group ties, could be assessed in two ways: by asking workers directly, or by the researcher's reaching a judgement of the character of a workplace. For example, train drivers would generally be felt to be cohesive while hospital ancillary workers would be more individualized. The former has the limitation of assessing a collective characteristic on the basis of individual replies. Thus a railway worker may say that cohesion is low by his own standards, and a hospital worker that it is high by hers, even though 'objectively' the situation may be the reverse of what these replies suggest. We were not convinced of the logic of using it. But we wanted to show empirically the problems with the thesis of absence cultures, and we also felt that some material of value would emerge ù as in fact it did ù from raising the issue of work group cohesion, even if replies to the specific questions did not differentiate one workplace from another.

The section on the work group used the questions developed by Seashore (1954) to measure work group cohesiveness. These start, however, by asking workers whether they felt that they were 'really a part' of their groups. This begs the question of whether groups exist at all, and we therefore began by asking, 'do you think that the workers here work together as groups?' We also went on to ask about shared ideas about how hard people should work and about the degree of common identity across a workplace. We did not, in fact, expect the pattern of replies to be particularly revealing. Seashore used his questions to compare groups within one company, where technical conditions of work were similar. Using them across different organizations may not be very meaningful. The question about helping each other out with the work (Question B3c), for example, was felt by many BR workers to be irrelevant in that they worked on their own. Variations in the score of group cohesiveness between organizations may not be revealing, and we do not make much use of the results. The questions were useful in two respects, however: they offered an initial evaluation of the extent of work group solidarity, and they often stimulated spontaneous comments. One of our concerns was to assess the extent of norms of fair effort levels, and the question about shared ideas of how hard to work was one way of opening up this topic. In general, in fact, we used the questionnaire not as a rigid instrument but as a means of gaining qualitative information, and several workers spoke revealingly about their fellows and about the social organization of production.

Section C addressed the question of relations with management raised by the absence culture literature. More importantly, we used it to consider

252 Shopfloor Questionnaire

the substantive issue of the nature of workers' views. As we show in the case of the hospital, for example, the questions revealed a great deal about workers' views of their situation.

The first question was used by Gallie (1978) in his study of oil refinery workers, while the second is taken from Low-Beer's (1978) analysis of technicians in Italy. Low-Beer does not report the raw scores on this question, but it does throw light on the extent to which workers respect the technical competence of managers. The third question asked directly about trust. This could be taken to refer to how far an individual supervisor was trusted as an individual or to how much trust a worker placed in management as a whole. In cases of uncertainty, we stressed that the focus was the latter, and in general workers did not have any difficulty in grasping what the question was driving at.

Section D. The opening question has been used in several previous studies by Ingham (1970), Newby (1977), and Edwards and Scullion (1982). We followed it with a more specific question about pressures leading workers to want to take time off work. We gave some attention to the role of factors outside the workplace. This is a theme which a small strand of the absence literature has addressed (Morgan and Herman, 1976; Hackett, 1986). We also asked directly whether family influences had any effect on a worker's decision whether to attend work.

Section E. We included some questions about 'self-discipline': how far work groups established their own standards of discipline. We found that these questions tended to produce rather general answers, however, and we ceased to use them systematically, preferring to follow up specific points about each particular workplace. We did not, therefore, always ask Questions after E3, though we did try to discuss the general issue of workplace rules and their negotiability.

Section F. The vignette technique has been used in several contexts, for example to study perceptions of the fairness of the distribution of income (Alves and Rossi, 1978) and the ways in which people suffering from disability should be cared for (West, 1984; West et al., 1984). It has not, however, been used in absence research, and there are no doubt ways in which it could be refined. We would stress that we did not see the three questions as tapping fundamental beliefs about absence. But they do indicate something. We found that workers could easily understand the moral dilemmas posed, which suggests that the questions had some validity in addressing issues with which workers were familiar. The results of studies in other areas are also similar to our own, namely, that there is little variation according to such potential explanatory variables as age and gender. This gives some support to our use of the technique. We think that it offers a new dimension to the study of absence, which might well be pursued by those interested in the question of how far workers' behaviour indicates anything more than a minimal pragmatic adjustment to managerial demands.

The Questionnaire

A. *The Worker and the Job*

1.   When did you first come to work here?

2.   Have you ever left since then?
        IF YES: 2a.   When was that?
                        2b.   When did you come back?

3.   Have you ever worked anywhere else?
        IF NO, GO TO Q. 5.

4.   Roughly how many different *firms* would you say you had worked for before coming to work here?

5.   Have you ever thought of leaving this firm?
        IF YES: 5a.   Why? (RECORD UP TO 3 REASONS)
                        5b.   Have you done anything about it?
                                PROMPT IF NEEDED, SUCH AS LOOKING
                                FOR A JOB IN THE PAPER.

6.   What are the main things that keep you here? (RECORD UP
        TO 3 REASONS).
        IF MORE THAN ONE REASON: 6a. Which is the most important?

        IF FRIENDLY WORK MATES MENTIONED:
        6b.   How important is it to you that you have friendly work
                mates?

        IF FRIENDLY WORK MATES NOT MENTIONED:
        6c.   Would you say that working with a friendly group of people
                was important in keeping you here?
        IF YES: 6d. How important?

B. *The Worker and the Work Group*

1. Do you think that the workers here work together as groups?
(EXPLAIN, IF NECESSARY, THAT WE MEAN BY A GROUP A NUMBER OF WORKERS WHO HAVE A SENSE OF MATESHIP AND MUTUAL SUPPORT).

   IF NO: GO TO Q5
   IF YES: 1a. How strong is the sense of group membership?

2. Do you feel that you are really part of your work group?

3. How does your work group compare with other groups here on the following points?
a. The way people get along together;
b. The way people stick together;
c. The way people help each other out with the work.

4. And would you say that there are shared ideas about how hard you should work?
IF YES: 4a.   Would you say that these ideas were very strong and clear, fairly strong, only general and not very strong or not strong at all?

5. How would you feel if you were moved to another job in this workplace doing similar work to what you do now but away from the people who work near you? Would you feel very upset, fairly upset, not bothered, quite pleased, or very pleased?

6. Thinking about this site as a whole, would you say that there is a feeling of common identity among workers, or do the separate parts tend to go their own ways?
IF COMMON: 6a. How strong is this feeling? Is it very strong, fairly strong, or not very strong?
IF SEPARATE: 6b. How much division is there between the different parts?
Would you say there is a lot of division, a bit of division or only minor and occasional differences?

C. *Management*

1. Would you say that, in their relations with workers, managers above your immediate supervisor were very friendly, quite friendly, quite distant or very distant?

2. In situations such as yours, what are managers for? Which of the following statements apply?
   a. They are needed to put their knowledge and experience at the service of the group;
   b. They are needed to make sure that people do their work;
   c. They take care of the administrative aspects of work;
   d. They aren't really needed at all.

3. What do you think of the overall level of trust that exists between management and workers here? Would you say that there is complete trust, trust most of the time, a fair amount of trust, not much trust or no trust at all?

4. Over the last five years or so, do you think there has been any change in the amount of trust?
   IF YES: 4a. Has it increased or decreased?
          4b. Why has there been a change?

5. Overall, how do you think this firm compares with others as a place to work? Would you say that it was a lot better than most, a bit better, about average, worse than average or a lot worse than average?

6. Would you say that, over the last five years or so, management has altered its way of dealing with workers?
   IF YES: 5a. In what ways?

D. *Absence and Attendance*

I'd now like to turn to how you feel about coming to work and about the rules on attendance and behaviour that are in operation here.

1. Here are two statements about attendance at work. Which one comes closer to your own view?
    a. A person should not stay away from work in any event except when it is really necessary, as in the case of genuine sickness;
    b. People have the right to take a day off once in a while if they want to.

    1a. Why do you say this?

2. A worker has to decide each day whether to go into work. How often would you say that you *consciously* thought about not going to work when there was nothing actually preventing you from working, eg you were not ill? Would you say: every day, once a week, occasionally, or never?

    IF 'NEVER' GO TO Q. 3

    IF EVER THINKS ABOUT IT:
    2a. Which of the reasons on the card encouraged you to think about not going into work? HAND CARD A (RECORD UP TO 3)
    [Reasons listed on the card were: general boredom; disliked features of work on a particular day; escape from supervisor; escape from work mates; travel problems; expectations of family and friends; family illness and domestic duties; leisure interests and time with family; other].
    (NB DISTINGUISH CAREFULLY BETWEEN DOMESTIC DUTIES, I.E. THINGS THAT HAVE TO BE DONE, AND LEISURE INTERESTS.)

    IF MORE THAN ONE REASON: 2b. Which reason is most important?

    2c. How important to you are the views of your family and friends in thinking about not going into work, eg warnings that the roads are icy or requests that you do jobs at home?

3. And what about the factors encouraging you to go to work? What sort of things work against the temptation to stay away? Can you pick out the reasons on the card? HAND CARD B (RECORD UP TO 3).
[Reasons listed were: duty to the firm; loss of money; possibility of discipline; duty to workmates; fear of mockery for being an absentee; expectations of family and friends; enjoyment of job itself; backlog of work if you stay away; feeling you would be letting yourself down; other.

IF MORE THAN ONE: 3a. Which is most important?

4. Have you ever taken a day off work when you have been able to get in?
(IE EXCLUDES BAD WEATHER AS A 'YES').

    IF YES: 4a.   What sort of factors encouraged you to do so?
                    4b.   How often do you take days off?
                    4c.   Has your supervisor ever asked you about this or warned you in any way?
                          IF YES: 4d. What form did this take?

5. And what about times when you have been off sick. Some people say that workers use sick pay benefits to stay off longer than they really should. Have you ever extended a spell off work longer than was needed to get fit?

IF YES: 5a. What reasons prompted you to do this?

6. And what about the people you work with: would you say that you are aware of how much time they take off work?

IF NO: GO TO Q. 7
IF YES:
6a.   How closely aware are you?
6b.   Would you say that most people behaved much the same, or do people vary in how much time they take off?
6c.   How much absence is there?
          IF A LOT OR QUITE A BIT: 6d. How do you feel about this?

IF NOT MUCH OR VERY LITTLE: 6e. Why do you think this is?

7. Why do you think most workers attend work as often as they do? PROBE THOROUGHLY.

8. Do you ever discuss with the people you work with the idea of taking the odd day off work? Would you say you discussed it frequently, sometimes, rarely, or never?

   IF NOT NEVER: 8a. What sort of things do you discuss?

9. Do you ever discuss with your work mates the amount of time off that other workers take? Would you say you discussed it frequently, sometimes, rarely or never?
   IF NOT NEVER: 9a. What sort of things do you discuss?
   PROBE FOR GROUP DISAPPROVAL OF SKIVERS, EXPECTATIONS OF LEVELS OF ATTENDANCE, ETC.

10. Let's turn now to all times you are off work, including sickness as well as the odd day off. Are you aware of any pressures or expectations from management about how much time you should have off?
    IF YES: 10a. What do these involve?

11. What do you think about the way the sick pay scheme is operated here? Would you say that it's too easy for people to take time off when they are not really ill, that the system is generally fair or that the rules are applied too strictly?

12. Workers are sometimes accused of exploiting sick pay schemes by staying away when they are not really ill or extending a spell off unnecessarily. Do you think that this ever happens here?
    IF YES: 12a. How common in this?
                12b. What do you think about it?

13. Has there been any change in the past few years in the way in which management deals with absenteeism?

    IF YES: 12a. What sort of changes?

E. *Discipline*

1. All organizations need rules for how work is done, but the rules are sometimes difficult to apply in particular cases. Would you say that management here applies the rules too rigidly, in about the right way, or too loosely?
    IF TOO RIGIDLY OR LOOSELY: 1a. Why do you say this?

2. Would you say that the rules are applied the same to different groups of workers, or are some treated better?

    IF SOME TREATED BETTER: 2a. Which groups are these?
    2b. In what ways are they treated better?

3. Have you ever been subjected to discipline, either in the shape of a formal warning or an informal reprimand from your supervisor?
    IF YES: 3a. Has this happened very often?
    3b. What have the main issues on which you have been disciplined?
    3c. Do you think that management had a case?
    3d. Was your trade union representative involved in the case/any of the cases?
    IF YES: 3e. What do you think of the way he/she handled it?

4. Does management generally use discipline a great deal here, or is discipline applied only sometimes, rarely, or almost never?
    IF OTHER THAN NEVER:
    4a. What do you see as the main sorts of behaviour that attract discipline?
    4b. How justified do you think management is? Is management in the right all of the time, most of the time, some of the time, rarely or almost never?
    4c. Would you say that the general aim of management was to *punish* offenders or to show them how they had broken the rules and to encourage them to *correct* their behaviour?

5.   It is sometimes said that groups of workers can exercise discipline over each other by encouraging a sense of proper conduct. Do you think that this happens at all here?

IF NO GO TO Q. 6
IF YES:
5a.   Would you say this happens a great deal, quite commonly, or only to a limited extent?
5b.   Do these standards generally support managerial rules, have the same aims as management while going about things in a different way or do they tend to set up alternative ideas of proper conduct?
IF NOT 'SUPPORT MANAGEMENT':
5c.   What are the main differences from managerial rules?

6.   How secure do you feel that you will not be subjected to arbitrary discipline by management?
IF TOTALLY OR REASONABLY: 6a. What are the main reasons for this?
IF NOT VERY OR NOT AT ALL:
6b.   Why do you say this?
6c.   Is there anything workers can do about it?

7.   Some people say that management can promote a sense of self-discipline among workers by encouraging them to take responsibility. How far would you say that this is true here?
IF HAPPENS AT ALL:
7a.   What are the main ways of doing this?
7b.   How do you feel about it?

F. *Vignettes*

1.   Bill Thompson normally has very little time off work. One Saturday he goes down with 'flu and has to stay off work until the next Wednesday. He is better by Thursday but thinks that, since he lost his week-end and never normally loses any time, he might as well stay away for the rest of the week. Was he reasonable to do this?

1a.   Why do you say this?

2.   Janet Roberts is a single parent with a young son. She works full-time but finds it hard to make ends meet. When her son is ill, she needs to take a couple of days off work. If she asks for time off unpaid she will be short of money and her absence might be counted against her. But if she reports sick her absence might not be questioned and she will not lose money. What should she do? [NB SHE HAS NO HOLIDAYS LEFT AND CANNOT TAKE THAT OPTION]

   2a.   If she reported sick, would you say this was: understandable and not a very serious offence; something quite serious that needs a warning; or a very serious offence of dishonesty that needs severe punishment?

3.   Sally Harris has been finding work a strain and has been under a lot of pressure. She has had rows with her work mates and has been spoken to by her supervisor. She feels she can't take any more and thinks she would be happier at work if she took a day off. Should she do this?

   3a.   [IF 'YES' USE WORDING (i), IF 'NO' USE (ii)]
          (i)   So she feels worn out and stays away. Should she report sick, ask for unpaid leave, stay away and say nothing, or come in to work?
          (ii)   She feels worn out when she wakes up next day. Should she report sick, ask for unpaid leave, stay away and say nothing, or come in to work?

   3b.   Suppose she decides to stay away and say nothing. When she comes back, should she admit what has happened, or say she was ill?

   3c.   Why?

   3d.   Suppose she explains the whole situation. Should her supervisor stop her pay?

   3e.   Why?
          EXPLORE FOR APPROACH THE SUPERVISOR SHOULD TAKE: BE SYMPATHETIC, GIVE A FRIENDLY WARNING, GIVE A MORE STERN WARNING, ETC.

References

Ahlstrand, Bruce W. 1990. *The Quest for Productivity: a Case Study of Fawley after Flanders*. Cambridge: Cambridge University Press.

Alves, Wayne M., and Peter H. Rossi. 1978. 'Who Should Get What? Fairness Judgements of the Distribution of Earnings'. *American Journal of Sociology*, Vol. 84 (November), 541-64.

Armstrong, Peter. 1988. 'Labour and Monopoly Capital', in Richard Hyman and Wolfgang Streeck (ed.), *New Technology and Industrial Relations*. Oxford: Blackwell.

Armstrong, Peter, and J.F.B. Goodman. 1979. 'Managerial and Supervisory Custom and Practice'. *Industrial Relations Journal*, Vol. 10 (Autumn), 12-24.

Ashdown, R.T., and K.H. Baker. 1973. *In Working Order: a Study of Industrial Discipline*. Department of Employment Manpower Papers 6. London: HMSO.

Atkin, Robert S., and Paul S. Goodman. 1984. 'Methods of Defining and Measuring Absenteeism', in Goodman et al., 1984.

Bach, Stephen. 1989. 'Too High a Price to Pay? A Study of Competitive Tendering for Domestic Services in the NHS'. Warwick Papers in Industrial Relations, 25. Coventry: Industrial Relations Research Unit.

Bagwell, Philip S. 1963. *The Railwaymen: the History of the National Union of Railwaymen*. London: Allen and Unwin.

Baldamus, W. 1961. *Efficiency and Effort*. London: Tavistock.

Behrend, Hilde. 1984. *Problems of Labour and Inflation*. London: Croom Helm.

Bennett, A., and S. Smith-Gavine. 1987. 'The Percentage Utilisation of Labour Index (PUL)', in Derek Bosworth and David F. Heathfield (ed.), *Working Below Capacity*. London: Macmillan.

Beynon, Huw. 1973. *Working for Ford*. Harmondsworth: Penguin.

Beynon, Huw. 1988. 'Regulating Research: Politics and Decision Making in

Industrial Organizations', in Alan Bryman (ed.), *Doing Research in Organizations*. London: Routledge.

Blackburn, R.M., and Michael Mann. 1979. *The Working Class in the Labour Market*. London: Macmillan.

Blau, Peter M. 1963. *The Dynamics of Bureaucracy*. Rev. edn. Chicago: University of Chicago Press.

Block, Howard, and Richard Mittenthal. 1985. 'Arbitration and the Absent Employee', in Walter J. Gershenfeld (ed.), *Arbitration 1984: Recent Law, Panels, and Public Decisions*. Washington, DC: Bureau of National Affairs.

Bowles, Samuel, and Herbert Gintis. 1976. *Schooling in Capitalist America: Educational Reform and the Contradictions of Economic Life*. London: Routledge.

Burawoy, Michael. 1979. *Manufacturing Consent: Changes in the Labour Process under Monopoly Capitalism*. Chicago: University of Chicago Press.

Carpenter, Michael. 1977. 'The New Managerialism and Professionalism in Nursing', in Margaret Stacey et al. (ed.), *Health and The Division of Labour*. London: Croom Helm.

Carpenter, Michael, Ruth Elkan, Peter Leonard and Anne Munro. 1987. 'Professionalism and Unionism in Nursing and Social Work'. Mimeo, Department of Applied Social Studies, University of Warwick.

Chadwick-Jones, J.K. 1978. *Absenteeism in the Canadian Context*. Ottawa: Labour Canada.

Chadwick-Jones, J.K., Nigel Nicholson and Colin Brown. 1982. *Social Psychology of Absenteeism*. New York: Praeger.

Clark, Jill. 1975. *Time Out? A Study of Absenteeism among Nurses*. London: Royal College of Nursing.

Cohen, Robin. 1987. *The New Helots: Migrants in the International Division of Labour*. Aldershot: Gower.

Corrigan, Philip. 1977. 'Feudal Reics or Capitalist Monuments? Notes on the Sociology of Unfree Labour'. *Sociology*, Vol. 11 (September), 435-63.

Cousins, Christine. 1987. *Controlling Social Welfare: a Sociology of State Welfare Work and Organization*. Brighton: Wheatsheaf.

Cressey, Peter, John Eldridge and John MacInnes. 1985. *Just Managing: Authority and Democracy in Industry*. Milton Keynes: Open University Press.

Crompton, Rosemary, and Gareth Jones. 1984. *White-collar Proletariat: Deskilling and Gender in Clerical Work*. London: Macmillan.

Crozier, Michel. 1964. *The Bureaucratic Phenomenon*. London: Tavistock.

Cunnison, Sheila. 1966. *Wages and Work Allocation: a Study of Social Relations in a Garment Workshop*. London: Tavistock.

Dalton, Dan R., and James L. Perry. 1981. 'Absenteeism and the Collective Bargaining Agreement: an Empirical Test'. *Academy of Management Journal*, Vol. 24 (June), 425-31.

Daniel, W.W., and Neil Millward. 1983. *Workplace Industrial Relations in Britain*. London: Heinemann.

Dawson, Patrick, and Janette Webb. 1989. 'New Production Arrangements: the

Totally Flexible Cage?' *Work, Employment and Society*, Vol. 3 (June), 221-38.

Dickens, Linda, Moira Hart, Brian Weekes and Michael Jones. 1985. *Dismissed: a Study of Unfair Dismissal and the Industrial Tribunal System*. Oxford: Blackwell.

Dilts, David A., Clarence R. Deitsch and Robert J. Paul. 1985. *Getting Absent Workers Back on the Job: an Analytical Approach*. Westport, Ct: Quorum.

Disney, Richard. 1987. 'Statutory Sick Pay: an Evaluation'. Institute for Fiscal Studies Working Paper 87/1, January.

Ditton, Jason. 1979. 'Baking Time'. *Sociological Review*, Vol. 27 (February), 157-67.

Drago, Robert, and Mark Wooden. 1988. 'An Empirical Study of Absence Rates: Labour-leisure Choice, Work Discipline, and Workgroup Norms'. National Institute of Labour Studies, Flinders University of South Australia, Working Paper 101, December.

Edwards, P.K. 1986. *Conflict at Work: a Materialist Analysis of Workplace Relations*. Oxford: Blackwell.

Edwards, P.K. 1988. 'Patterns of Conflict and Accommodation', in Duncan Gallie (ed.), *Employment in Britain*. Oxford: Blackwell.

Edwards, P.K. 1989. 'The Three Face of Discipline', in Keith Sisson (ed.), *Personnel Management in Britain*. Oxford: Blackwell.

Edwards, P.K. 1992. 'Industrial Conflict: Themes and Issues in Recent Research'. *British Journal of Industrial Relations*, Vol. 30 (September), 361-404.

Edwards, P.K., and Hugh Scullion. 1982. *The Social Organization of Industrial Conflict: Control and Resistance in the Workplace*. Oxford: Blackwell.

Edwards, P.K., and Hugh Scullion. 1984. 'Absenteeism and the Control of Work'. *Sociological Review*, Vol. 32 (August), 547-72.

Edwards, P.K., and Colin Whitston. 1989a. 'Industrial Discipline, the Control of Attendance and the Subordination of Labour: Towards an Integrated Analysis'. *Work, Employment and Society*, Vol. 3 (March), 1-28.

Edwards, P.K., and Colin Whitston. 1989b. 'The Control of Absenteeism: an Interim Report'. Warwick Papers in Industrial Relations, 23, January (Industrial Relations Research Unit, University of Warwick).

Edwards, P.K., and Colin Whitston. 1991. 'Workers Are Working Harder: Effort and Shopfloor Relations in the 1980s'. *British Journal of Industrial Relations*, Vol. 29 (December), 593-602.

Edwards, P. K., and Coiln Whitston. 1992. 'Disciplinary Practice: A Case Study of the Railways, 1860-1988'. Unpublished paper, Industrial Relations Research Unit, University of Warwick, July.

Elger, Tony. 1990. 'Technical Innovation and Work Re-organization in British Manufacturing in the 1980s: Continuity, Intensification or Transformation?' *Work, Employment and Society*, Additional Special Issue, May, 67-102.

Ferner, Anthony. 1985. 'Political Constraints and Management Strategies: the Case of Working practices in British Rail'. *British Journal of Industrial Relations*, Vol. 23 (March), 47-70.

Ferner, Anthony. 1988. *Governments, Managers and Industrial Relations: Public Enterprises and Their Political Environment*. Oxford: Blackwell.

Ferner, Anthony. 1990. 'The Changing Influence of the Personnel Function: Privatization and Organizational Politics in Electricity Generation'. *Human Resource Management Journal*, Vol. 1 (Autumn), 12-30.

Finch, Janet. 1987. 'The Vignette Technique in Survey Research'. *Sociology*, Vol. 21 (February), 105-14.

Findlay, Patricia. 1990. 'What Management Strategy? Labour Utilisation and Regulation at Scotland's "Leading Edge"'. D.Phil. thesis, University of Oxford.

Fitzgibbons, Dale Edward. 1988. 'An Ethnographic Study of Employee Absences: the Impact of Uncertainty, Negotiation and the Employment Relationship'. Ph.D. thesis, University of Illinois at Urbana-Champaign.

Fowler, Alan. 1988. 'New Directions in Performance Pay'. *Personnel Management*, November, 30-34.

Fox, Alan. 1974. *Beyond Contract: Work, Power and Trust Relations*. London: Faber and Faber.

Friedman, Andrew L. 1977. *Industry and Labour: Class Struggle at Work and Monopoly Capitalism*. London: Macmillan.

Gallie, Duncan. 1978. *In Search of the New Working Class: Automation and Social Integration within the Capitalist Enterprise*. Cambridge: Cambridge University Press.

Gallie, Duncan. 1989. 'Trade Union Allegiance and Decline in British Urban Labour Markets'. Social Change and Economic Life Initiative Working Papers, 9, August (Nuffield College, Oxford).

Geary, John. 1991. 'Human Resource Management in Practice: Labour Management in Irish Electronics Plants'. D. Phil. thesis, University of Oxford.

Gersuny, Carl. 1976. '"A Devil in Petticoats" and Just Cause: Patterns of Punishment in Two New England Textiles Factories'. *Business History Review*, Vol. 50 (Summer), 131-52.

Goodman, Paul S., Robert S. Atkin and associates. 1984. *Absenteeism*. San Francisco: Jossey-Bass.

Gouldner, Alvin W. 1954. *Patterns of Industrial Bureaucracy*. Glencoe: Free Press.

Guest, David E. 1989. 'Human Resource Management: Its Implications for Industrial Relations and Trade Unions', in Storey, 1989.

Guest, David E. 1990. 'HRM and the American Dream'. *Journal of Management Studies*, Vol. 27 (July), 377-98.

Haccoun, Robert R., and Serge Dupont. 1988. 'Une analyse des comportements de travailleurs masculins et féminins selon deux formes d'absence au travail'. *Relations Industrielles/Industrial Relations*, Vol. 43 (Winter), 153-65.

Hackett, Rick D. 1986. 'New Directions in the Study of Employee Absenteeism: a Research Example'. McMaster University Faculty of Business, Research and Working Papers 263, October.

Halverson, G.C. 1952. 'Development of Labour Relations in the British Railways since 1860'. Ph. D. thesis, University of London.

Harris, Rosemary. 1987. *Power and Powerlessness in Industry: an Analysis of the Social Relations of Production*. London: Tavistock.

Henry, Stuart. 1982. 'Factory Law: the Changing Disciplinary Technology of Industrial Social Control'. *International Journal of the Sociology of Law*, Vol. 10 (November), 365-83.

Henry, Stuart. 1983. *Private Justice: Towards Integrated Theorising in the Sociology of Law*. London: Routledge.

Henry, Stuart. 1985. 'Private Justice and the Policing of Labour: the Dialectics of Industrial Discipline'. Old Dominion University Department of Sociology and Criminal Justice, Working Paper 7.

Henry, Stuart. 1987. 'Disciplinary Pluralism: Four Models of Private Justice in the Workplace'. *Sociological Review*, Vol. 35 (May), 279-319.

Hill, J.M.M., and E.L. Trist. 1953. 'A Consideration of Industrial Accidents as a Means of Withdrawal from the Work Situation'. *Human Relations*, Vol. 6 (November), 357-80.

Hobsbawm, E.J. 1964. *Labouring Men: Studies in the History of Labour*. London: Weidenfeld and Nicolson.

Huczynski, Andrej A., and Michael J. Fitzpatrick. 1989. *Managing Employee Absence for a Competitive Edge*. London: Pitman.

Hudson, Kenneth. 1970. *Working to Rule. Railway Workshop Rules: a Study of Industrial Discipline*. Bath: Adams and Dart.

IDS (Incomes Data Services). 1986. 'Absenteeism'. IDS Study 365, July.

Ingham, Geoffrey K. 1970. *Size of Industrial Organization and Worker Behaviour*. Cambridge: Cambridge University Press.

Institute of Personnel Management. 1979. *Disciplinary Procedures and Practice*. London: IPM.

IRLIB (Industrial Relations Legal Information Bulletin, pub. Industrial Relations Services) 361. 20 September 1988.

IRLIB 369. 24 January 1989.

IRLIB 386. 10 October 1989.

IRLIB 405. 17 July 1990.

IRS (Industrial Relations Services). 1985. 'Occupational Sick Pay 2: Administration'. *Industrial Relations Review and Report* 344, 21 May.

IRS. 1987. 'Taking the Pulse of Sickness Absence'. *IRRR* 405, 1 December.

IRS. 1990. 'Attending to Absence'. *IRRR* 461, 3 April.

IRS. 1991. 'Sickness Absence 3: Levels, Costs and Monitoring'. *IRRR*, 499, 1 November.

Jacoby, Sanford M. 1985. *Employing Bureaucracy: Managers, Unions and the Transformation of Work in American Industry, 1900-1945*. New York: Columbia University Press.

Jacoby, Sanford M. 1990. 'The New Institutionalism: What can it Learn from the Old?' *Industrial Relations*, Vol. 29 (Spring), 315-42.

Jenkins, Richard. 1986. *Racism and Recruitment: Managers, Organisations and Equal Opportunity in the Labour Market*. Cambridge: Cambridge University Press.

Jenkins, Richard. 1988. 'Discrimination and Equal Oportunity in Employment: Ethnicity and "Race" in the United Kingdom', in Duncan Gallie (ed.), *Employment in Britain*. Oxford: Blackwell.

Johns, Gary. 1984. 'Unresolved Issues in the Study and Management of Absence from Work', in Goodman et al., 1984.

Johns, Gary, and Nigel Nicholson. 1982. 'The Meanings of Absence', in B.M. Staw and L.L. Cummings (ed.), *Research in Organizational Behavior*, Vol. 4. Greenwich, Conn.: JAI.

Jones, A.W. 1941. *Life, Liberty and Property*. Philadelphia: Lippincott.

Keller, Robert T. 1983. 'Predicting Absenteeism from Prior Absenteeism, Attitudinal Factors and Non-attitudinal Factors'. *Journal of Applied Psychology*, Vol.68 (August), 536-40.

Kelly, John. 1990. 'British Trade Unionism 1979-89: Change, Continuity and Contradictions'. *Work, Employment and Society*, Additional Special Issue, May, 29-66.

Kelly, John, and Caroline Kelly. 1991. '"Them and Us": Social Psychology and the "New Industrial Relations"'. *British Journal of Industrial Relations*, Vol. 29 (March), 25-48.

Kelly, Michael P., and Robin Roslender. 1988. 'Proletarianisation, the Division of Labour and the Labour Process'. *International Journal of Sociology and Social Policy*, Vol. 8, no. 6, 48-64.

Kingsford, P.W. 1970. *Victorian Railwaymen: the Emergence and Growth of Railway Labour,1830-1870*. London: Frank Cass.

Kusterer, Ken. 1978. *Know-how on the Job*. Boulder, Col.: Westview.

Lane, Christel. 1987. 'Capitalism or Culture?' *Work, Employment and Society*, Vol. 1 (March), 57-84.

Lane, Christel. 1988. 'New Technology and Clerical Work', in Duncan Gallie (ed.), *Employment in Britain*. Oxford: Blackwell.

Legge, Karen. 1989. 'Human Resource Management: a Critical Analysis', in Storey, 1989.

Léonard, Christine, Marie-Reire Van Ameringer, Shimon L. Dolan and André Arsenault. 1987. 'Absentéisome et assiduité au travail: deux moyens d'adaptatien au stress?' *Relations Industrielles/Industrial Relations*, Vol. 42 (Autumn), 774-89.

Lockwood, David. 1989. *The Blackcoated Worker: a Study in Class Consciousness*. 2nd edn. Oxford: Clarendon.

Low-Beer, John R. 1978. *Protest and Participation: the New Working Class in Italy*. Cambridge: Cambridge University Press.

Lupton, Tom. 1963. *On the Shop Floor*. Oxford: Pergamon.

MacInnes, John. 1985. 'Conjuring up Consultation: the Role and Extent of Joint Consulation on Post-war Private Manufacturing Industry'. *British Journal of Industrial Relations*, Vol. 23 (March), 93-113.

McKenna, Frank. 1980. *The Railway Workers, 1840-1970*. London: Faber and Faber.

McLoughlin, Ian, and Jon Clark. 1988. *Technological Change at Work*. Milton Keynes: Open University Press.

Manwaring, Tony, and Stephen Wood. 1984. 'The Ghost in the Machine: Tacit Skills in the Labor Process'. *Socialist Review*, no. 74 (March), 57-86.

Marchingtom, Mick. 1989. 'Joint Consultation in Practice', in Keith Sisson (ed.), *Personnel Management in Britain*. Oxford: Blackwell.

Marchington, Mick, and Philip Parker. 1990. *Changing Patterns of Employee Relations*. Hemel Hempstead: Harvester Wheatsheaf.

Marcus, Philip M., and Catherine B. Smith. 1985. 'Absenteeism in an Organizational Context'. *Work and Occupations*, Vol. 12 (August), 251-68.

Marginson, Paul, P.K. Edwards, Roderick Martin, John Purcell and Keith Sisson. 1988. *Beyond the Workplace: the Management of Industrial Relations in the Multi-establishment Enterprise*. Oxford: Blackwell.

Mars, Gerald. 1982. *Cheats at Work: an Anthropology of Workplace Crime*. London: Counterpoint.

Marshall, Catherine. 1987. 'Who's in Control of Absence? A Case Study'. MA Thesis (Industrial Relations), University of Warwick.

Marshall, Gordon, Howard Newby, David Rose and Carolyn Vogler. 1988. *Social Class in Modern Britain*. London: Hutchinson.

Metcalf, David. 1989. 'Water Notes Dry Up: the Impact of the Donovan Reform Proposals and Thatcherism at Work on Labour Productivity in British Manufacturing Industry'. *British Journal of Industrial Relations*, Vol. 27 (March), 1-31.

MMC (Monopolies and Mergers Commission). 1980. *British Rail Board: London and South-east Commuter Services*. Cmnd 8046. London: HMSO.

MMC. 1987. *British Rail Board: Network Southeast*. Cm 204. London: HMSO.

MMC. 1989. *British Rail Board: Provincial Services*. Cm 584. London: HMSO.

Montgomery, David. 1979. *Workers' Control in America: Studies in the History of Work, Technology and Labor Struggles*. Cambridge: Cambridge University Press.

Montgomery, David. 1987. *The Fall of the House of Labor: the Workplace, the State and American Labor Activism, 1865-1925*. Cambridge: Cambridge University Press.

Morgan, Lillie Guinell, and Jeanne Brett Herman. 1976. 'Perceived Consequences of Absenteeism'. *Journal of Applied Psychology*, Vol. 61 (December), 738-42.

Newby, Howard. 1977. *The Deferential Worker: a Study of Farm Workers in East Anglia*. Harmondsworth: Penguin.

Newell, Helen. 1990. 'How Green are Greenfield Sites?' Paper to British Universities Industrial Relations Association Annual Conference, July.

Nicholson, Nigel. 1976. 'Management Sanctions and Absence Control'. *Human Relations*, Vol. 29 (February), 139-51.

Nicholson, Nigel. 1977. 'Absence Behaviour and Attendance Motivation: a Conceptual Synthesis'. *Journal of Management Studies*, Vol. 14 (October), 231-52.

Nicholson, Nigel, and Gary Johns. 1985. 'The Absence Culture and the Psychological Contract: Who's in Control of Absence?' *Academy of Management Review*, Vol. 10 (July), 397-407.

Nolan, Peter. 1989. 'Walking on Water? Manufacturing Performance and Industrial Relations under Thatcher'. *Industrial Relations Journal*, Vol. 20 (Summer), 81-92.

Nolan, Peter, and P.K. Edwards. 1984. 'Homogenise, Divide and Rule: an Essay on Segmented Work, Divided Workers'. *Cambridge Journal of Economics*, Vol. 8 (June), 197-215.

Noon, Michael Andrew. 1989. 'New Technology and Industrial Relations in Provincial Newspapers: Computerisation and Bargaining Power of Journalists'. Ph. D. thesis, University of London.

Osigweh, Chimizie A.B., and William R. Hutchison. 1989. 'Positive Discipline'. *Human Resource Management*, Vol. 28 (Fall), 367-83.

Osigweh, Chimizie A.B., and William R. Hutchison. 1990. 'To Punish or not to Punish? Managing Human Resources Through "Positive Discipline"'. *Employee Relations*, Vol. 12 (3), 27-32.

Park, Robert. C.R. 1962. 'A Study of Some of the Social Factors Influencing Labour Productivity in Coal Mines'. Ph.D. Thesis, University of Edinburgh.

Pendleton, Andrew. 1991a. 'The Barriers to Flexibility: Flexible Rostering on the Railways'. *Work, Employment and Society*, Vol. 5 (June), 241-57.

Pendleton, Andrew. 1991b. 'Integration and Dealignment in Public Enterprise Industrial Relations: a Study of British Rail'. *British Journal of Industrial Relations*, Vol. 29 (September), 411-26.

Platt, Steve. 1989. 'Signals to the Future'. *New Statesman and Society*, 3 March.

Pollard, Sidney. 1965. *The Genesis of Modern Management: a Study of the Industrial Revolution in Great Britain*. London: Arnold.

Pollert, Anna. 1981. *Girls, Wives, Factory Lives*. London: Macmillan.

Price, James L., and Charles W. Mueller. 1986. *Absenteeism and Turnover of Hospital Employees*. Greenwich, Conn.: JAI Press.

Price, Richard. 1986. *Labour in British Society: an Interpretive History*. London: Croom Helm.

Prins, R., and A. de Graaf. 1986. 'Comparison of Sickness Absence in Belgian, German and Dutch Firms'. *British Journal of Industrial Medicine*, Vol. 43 (June), 529-36.

Prude, Jonathan. 1983. 'The Social System of Early New England Textile Mills: a Case Study, 1812-40', in Michael H. Frisch and Daniel J. Walkowitz (ed.), *Working-Class America*. Urbana: University of Illinois Press.

Purcell, John, and Keith Sisson. 1983. 'Strategies and Practice in the Management of Industrial Relations', in George Sayers Bain (ed.), *Industrial Relations in Britain*. Oxford: Blackwell.

Railway Executive Committee. 1941-5. Files on absenteeism. Public Records Office: Files AN2/192 and 535.

Reid, Douglas A. 1976 'The Decline of Saint Monday, 1766-1876'. *Past and Present*, no. 71 (May), 76-101.

Rolfe, Heather. 1986. 'Skill, Deskilling and New Technology in the Non-manual Labour Process'. *New Technology, Work and Employment*, Vol. 1 (Spring), 37-49.

Rose, Howard, Ian McLoughlin, Robin King and Jon Clark. 1986. 'Opening the Black Box: the Relation between Technology and Work'. *New Technology, Work and Employment*, Vol. 1 (Spring), 18-26.

Rose, Michael. 1985. *Reworking the Work Ethic*. London: Batsford.

Roy, Donald F. 1954. 'Efficiency and "the Fix": Informal Intergroup Relations in a Piecework Macine Shop'. *American Journal of Sociology*, Vol. 60 (November), 255-66.

Royal Commission. 1911. *Report of the Royal Commission Appointed to Investigate and Report on the Working of the Railway Conciliation and Arbitration Scheme of 1907*. Cd 5922. London: HMSO.

Rubin, Gerry R. 1987. *War, Law and Labour: the Munitions Act, State Regulation, and the Unions, 1915-21*. Oxford: Clarendon.

Salaman, Graeme. 1974. *Community and Occupation: An Exploration of Work-Leisure Relationships*. Cambridge: Cambridge University Press.

Schilit, Warren Keith. 1987. 'An Examination of the Influence of Middle-level Managers in Formulating and Implementing Strategic Decisions'. *Journal of Management Studies*, Vol. 24 (May), 271-93.

Scott, Andrew. 1988. 'On the Shop Floor in thew 1980s: Generating the Politics of Workplace Compliance'. D.Phil. thesis, University of Oxford.

Seashore, Stanley E. 1954. *Group Cohesiveness in the Industrial Work Group*. Ann Arbor: Survey Research Center, University of Michigan.

Sisson, Keith. 1987. *The Management of Collective Bargaining*. Oxford: Blackwell.

Sisson, Keith, and Edward Blissett. 1989. 'Pay System Practices and Labour Flexibility in the UK'. Paper prepared for the International Labour Organization, Geneva, August.

Staw, Barry M. 1986. 'Organizational Psychology and the Pursuit of the Happy/Productive Worker'. *California Management Review*, Vol. 28 (Summer), 40-53.

Storey, John. 1986. 'The Phoney War? New Office Technology, Organization and Control', in David Knights and Hugh Willmott (ed.), *Managing the Labour Process*. Aldershot: Gower.

Storey, John. 1989 (ed.). *New Perspectives on Human Resource Management*. London: Routledge.

Storey, John. 1992. *Developments in the Management of Human Resources*. Oxford: Blackwell.

Strauss, George, and Leonard R. Sayles. 1980. *Personnel: the Human Problem of Management*. 4th edn. Englewood Cliffs: Prentice Hall.

Summerfield, Penny. 1984. *Women Workers in the Second World War: Production and Patriarchy in Conflict*. London: Croom Helm.

Tailby, Stephanie, and Colin Whitston. 1989 (ed.). *Manufacturing Change: Industrial Relations and Restructuring*. Oxford: Blackwell.

Taylor, Daniel E. 1979. 'Absent Workers and Lost Hours, May 1978'. US Dept of Labor Special Labor Force Report 229. Washington: USGPO.

Thompson, E.P. 1967. 'Time, Work-Discipline and Industrial Capitalism'. *Past and Present*, no. 38, December, 56-97.

Torrington, Derek, and John Chapman. 1979. *Personnel Management*. Englewood Cliffs: Prentice-Hall.

Townley, Barbara. 1989. 'Employee Communication Programmes', in Keith Sisson (ed.), *Personnel Management in Britain*. Oxford: Blackwell.

Trevor, Malcolm. 1988. *Toshiba's New British Company: Competitiveness through Innovation in Industry*. London: Policy Studies Institute.

Turnbull, Peter J. 1986. 'The "Japanisation" of Production and Industrial Relations at Lucas Electrical'. *Industrial Relations Journal*, Vol. 17 (Autumn), 193-206.

Turnbull, Peter J. 1989. 'Industrial Restructuring and Labour Relations in the Automotive Components Industry: "Just-in-Time" or "Just-too-Late"?' in Tailby and Whitston, 1989.

West, Patrick. 1984. 'The Family, the Welfare State and Community Care: Political Rhetoric and Public Attitudes'. *Journal of Social Policy*, Vol. 13 (November), 417-46.

West, Patrick, Raymond Illsley and Howard Kelman. 1984. 'Public Preferences for the Care of Dependency Groups'. *Social Science and Medicine*, Vol. 18 (July), 287-95.

Wickens, Peter. 1987. *The Road to Nissan: Flexibility, Quality, Teamwork*. London: Macmillan.

Wooden, Mark. 1988. 'The Management of Labour Absence: an Inventory of Strategies and Measures'. National Institute of Labour Studies, Flinders University of South Australia, Working Paper 97, March.

Young, Kelvin. 1986. 'The Management of Craft Work: a Case Study of an Oil Refinery'. *British Journal of Industrial Relations*, Vol. 24 (November), 363-80.

Index